POPULISM, DEMOCRACY AND COMMUNITY DEVELOPMENT

Rethinking Community Development series

Series Editors: **Mae Shaw, Rosie R. Meade** and **Sarah Banks**

Rethinking Community Development is an international book series that offers a critical re-evaluation of community development in theory and in practice.

Also available in the series:

Environmental Justice, Popular Struggle and Community Development

Edited by **Anne Harley** and **Eurig Scandrett**

Ethics, Equity and Community Development

Edited by **Sarah Banks** and **Peter Westoby**

Funding, Power and Community Development

Edited by **Niamh McCrea** and **Fergal Finnegan**

Find out more at:

policy.bristoluniversitypress.co.uk/rethinking-community-development

Rethinking Community Development series

Series Editors: **Mae Shaw, Rosie R. Meade** and **Sarah Banks**

Also available in the series:

Class, Inequality and Community Development

Edited by **Mae Shaw** and **Marjorie Mayo**

Politics, Power and Community Development

Edited by **Rosie R. Meade, Mae Shaw** and **Sarah Banks**

Find out more at:

policy.bristoluniversitypress.co.uk/rethinking-community-development

POPULISM, DEMOCRACY AND COMMUNITY DEVELOPMENT

Edited by
Sue Kenny, Jim Ife and Peter Westoby

Rethinking
Community
Development

First published in Great Britain in 2021 by

Policy Press, an imprint of
Bristol University Press
University of Bristol
1-9 Old Park Hill
Bristol
BS2 8BB
UK
t: +44 (0)117 954 5940
e: bup-info@bristol.ac.uk

Details of international sales and distribution partners are available at
policy.bristoluniversitypress.co.uk

British Library Cataloguing in Publication Data
A catalogue record for this book is available from the British Library

ISBN 978-1-4473-5383-6 hardcover
ISBN 978-1-4473-5384-3 paperback
ISBN 978-1-4473-5387-4 ePub
ISBN 978-1-4473-5386-7 ePdf

Cover design by Liam Roberts
Front cover image: Ian Martin

Bristol University Press and Policy Press use environmentally
responsible print partners.

Printed in Great Britain by CMP, Poole

Contents

Rethinking Community Development

Communities are a continuing focus of public policy and citizen action worldwide. The purposes and functions of work with communities of place, interest and identity vary between and within contexts and change over time. Nevertheless, community development – as both an occupation and a democratic practice concerned with the demands and aspirations of people in communities – has been extraordinarily enduring.

This book series aims to provide a critical re-evaluation of community development in theory and practice, in the light of new challenges posed by the complex interplay of emancipatory, democratic, self-help and managerial imperatives in different parts of the world. Through a series of edited and authored volumes, *Rethinking Community Development* will draw together international, cross-generational and cross-disciplinary perspectives, using contextual specificity as a lens through which to explore the localised consequences of global processes. Each text in the series will:

- *promote critical thinking* through examining the contradictory position of community development, including the tensions between policy imperatives and the interests and demands of communities;
- *include a range of international examples* in order to explore the localised consequences of global processes;
- *include contributions from established and up-and-coming new voices* from a range of geographical contexts;
- *offer topical and timely perspectives*, drawing on historical and theoretical resources in a generative and enlivening way;
- *inform and engage a new generation of practitioners*, bringing new and established voices together to stimulate diverse and innovative perspectives on community development.

If you have a broad or particular interest in community development that could be expanded into an authored or edited collection for this book series, contact:

Mae Shaw,	Rosie Meade,	Sarah Banks,
mae.shaw@ed.ac.uk	r.meade@ucc.ie	s.j.banks@durham.ac.uk

Acknowledgements

Dedicated to those across the globe who are practising community development in creative and radical ways, notwithstanding often hostile environments.

Our profound thanks to all the contributors to this book who have thought deeply about the provocations of populism. We also wish to thank our families, our students, our friends and our colleagues, who have supported and enriched our lives, and whose wisdom is reflected in our understanding of the challenges facing the world today.

As Australians, we acknowledge the traditional custodians of the lands and pay our respects to the Elders and Leaders, past, present and emerging, and to First Nations communities everywhere.

Notes on contributors

Suvi Aho (MPolSci) works as District Service Manager for the City of Vaasa in Finland, coordinating the programme for participation and local democracy. Between 2010 and spring 2018 she led several participatory projects in Helsinki, while working with wellbeing innovations in higher education as a Research and Development Specialist at the Metropolia University of Applied Sciences.

Jacques Boulet has studied, worked and lived on five continents. Originally from Belgium, he obtained his social work degree in 1965 and worked for three years as a volunteer in community development in the Congo. He lectured in Germany throughout the 1970s, then studied and taught at the University of Michigan, graduating with a PhD in Social Work and Sociology (1980–85). From 1985 to 1996 he lectured at Melbourne and RMIT Universities (Melbourne, Australia) and started the Borderlands Cooperative in 1997, being involved in consulting work in a broad range of research projects in social and community affairs. He was Founding Head of School of the OASES Graduate School for Sustainability and Social Change and lecturer/researcher at several universities. He has been an Adjunct Professor in International Development at Deakin University for several years.

Chan Yu-cheung is a PhD candidate in the Department of Social Work, Hong Kong Baptist University. He is a registered social worker and the chairperson of Community Development Alliance (CDA), which is an organisation aimed at furthering community development practice and social change. Its members consist mainly of local community workers, activists and academics. His research interests include community development, community capacity building, social economy, social movements and civil society.

Ismet Fanany is a sociolinguist with a PhD from Cornell University. He is currently Professor of Language and Society in the School of Humanities and Social Sciences at Deakin University in Melbourne. His interests relate to the experience of ageing and social change in modern Indonesia, in particular the interaction between local and national culture with an emphasis on language and language issues, as well as the impact of religion on the social environment. In addition to a range of scholarly works on topics such as modern Indonesian society in the global context, disaster reconstruction, ageing in Indonesia, and the development of the Indonesian language, he is the author of many short stories and two novels.

Rebecca Fanany has a PhD in Public Health from the University of Tasmania. She is currently in the School of Health, Medical and Applied Sciences at Central Queensland University in Melbourne, Australia. Her research centres on the impact of language and culture on health and illness, with a focus on cultural consonance and the conceptualisation of health. She has many years of experience in Asia and Indonesia, where she has several long-term research relationships and collaborations and has worked with WHO and UNESCAP in the region. She is the author of several books and numerous articles and publications. In particular, she is interested in the relationship between health and social change with a focus on language issues, social inclusion, resilience, and adaptation. In addition, she has more than 30 years of experience as a professional translator of Indonesian and Malay.

Fung Kwok-kin is Associate Professor in the Department of Social Work, Hong Kong Baptist University. He is the Programme Director of Master of Social Work. He has been researching and publishing extensively on the areas of gender and poverty, community development, social welfare and housing policies and urban studies. He has been Director (East Asia) of the International Association for Community Development (IACD) since 2013. He is also active in the local and international housing and community development movements. He is now leading a UGC-funded research project on bottom-up approaches that adopt participatory action research.

Juha Hämäläinen is Professor of Social Work and Social Pedagogy at the University of Eastern Finland. His research interests include social ethics; social sustainability; history and theory of social pedagogy; child, youth and family research, particularly in respect of child welfare, social exclusion of young people, parenting and policy making.

Hung Suet-lin is Associate Head and Associate Professor of the Department of Social Work, Hong Kong Baptist University. She is also the Director of the Social Work Practice and Mental Health Centre of the University. At present, her teaching and research work is in areas of women and family, gender-based violence, teenage pregnancy, narrative therapy/practice, group and community work. She has conducted research studies and published extensively on gender, narrative practice, social work and community development.

Jim Ife is Professor of Social Work at Western Sydney University. He has worked in social work and human rights education since the 1970s, and is the author of several books including *Community Development in an Uncertain World: Vision, Analysis and Practice* (2nd edition, 2016, Cambridge University Press), which in its various editions has been a major text in community development programmes. His research has focused on human rights and community development. He is a former Head of the Centre for Human Rights Education at Curtin University, and was Professor of Social Work and Social Policy at Curtin University and the University of Western Australia. He has been active in a number of community organisations, and is a former President of Amnesty International Australia.

Sue Kenny is Emeritus Professor in the Faculty of Arts and Education, Deakin University, Melbourne. Her previous position at Deakin University was Director, Centre for Citizenship, Development and Human Rights. She has 40 years of research, teaching, consultancy and activist work in Australasia, Europe, the United Kingdom, Asia and post-communist societies. She has extensive publications, including journal articles, chapters and books. Her publications include co-authored books, *Developing Communities for the Future* (5th edition, 2017, Cengage Learning); *Rhetorics of Welfare: Uncertainty, Choice and Voluntary Associations* (2000, Macmillan); *Challenging the Third Sector: Global Prospects for Active Citizenship* (2015, Policy Press); and co-edited books, *The Routledge Handbook of Community Development* (2018, Routledge); *Challenging Capacity Building* (2010, Earthscan); and *Post-Disaster Reconstruction: Lessons from Aceh* (2010, Policy Press).

Lau Siu-mei is Lecturer in the Department of Social Work, Hong Kong Baptist University. She is a registered social worker and a board member of the Sham Shui Po Community Association. Her research interests include young people, social policy, critical discourse analysis, housing studies, gender and community development.

Marcelo Lopes de Souza is Professor of Environmental Geography and Political Ecology in the Department of Geography of the Federal University of Rio de Janeiro (UFRJ), Brazil. He has acted as an academic visitor or visiting professor at several universities in Europe and Latin America, and published 17 books (13 monographs and 4 edited volumes) and more than 120 papers and book chapters in several languages, covering subjects such as urban environmental activism and environmental justice.

Marjorie Mayo is Emeritus Professor of Community Development at Goldsmiths, University of London, where her research has included a focus upon community action and development, community–university engagement, learning for active citizenship and access to justice in disadvantaged communities. Recent publications include *Changing Communities: Stories of Migration, Displacement and Solidarities* (2017, Policy Press); and jointly edited collections on *Class, Inequality and Community Development* (2016, Policy Press) and *Community Research for Community Development* (2013, Palgrave Macmillan). Previous publications include *Access to Justice for Disadvantaged Communities* (with G. Koessl, M. Scott and I. Slater, 2014, Policy Press).

Keith Popple is Emeritus Professor and previously Head of Social Work at London South Bank University, UK. Formerly editor of the *Community Development Journal* and currently a member of the journal's Editorial Board, he has written and lectured widely in the area of community, community development and social policy and is author of *Analysing Community Work: Theory and Practice* (2nd edition, 2015, McGraw-Hill Education). He is a Visiting Professor at Bournemouth University, Newman University and Honorary Fellow in the School of Applied Social Science at the University of Brighton. He is the Academic Adviser to the Department of Social Work, Hong Kong Baptist University.

Andie Reynolds is Lecturer in the Department of Social Work, Education and Community Wellbeing at Northumbria University. Her professional background is in youth work, community development, teaching, social enterprise and international development. Her main research areas lie in global community development practices, young people's political participation and the paradoxes inherent in volunteering.

Arto Salonen works as Associate Professor in University of Eastern Finland, Department of Social Sciences. The title of his doctoral dissertation was *Sustainable Development and Its Promotion in a Welfare Society in a Global Age*. His current research is in behavioural change, societal change, sustainable development and transformative social pedagogy.

Randy Stoecker is Professor in the Department of Community and Environmental Sociology at the University of Wisconsin, with an affiliate appointment at the University of Wisconsin-Extension Center for Community and Economic Development. He has a PhD in Sociology from the University of Minnesota, and an MS in Counseling from the University of Wisconsin-Whitewater. He conducts trainings, writes, and speaks on community organising and development, community-based participatory research/evaluation, higher education community engagement strategies and community information technology. He has led numerous participatory action research projects, community technology projects, and empowerment evaluation processes with community development corporations, community-based leadership education programmes, community organising groups and other non-profits.

Peter Szynka is a freelance social scientist in Germany. He obtained his diploma in social science at the University of Duisburg and his doctorate in philosophy at the University of Bremen. Throughout his life he has worked for welfare organisations of the Lutheran Church (Diakonie). He focuses on poverty and homelessness, social planning, community organising and the (international) history of social work. He has published numerous articles connecting social work to sociology and philosophy.

Peter Westoby has 30 years of experience as a community development practitioner, and 15 years' experience in scholarly work in the field. He has authored over 50 professional journal articles and also written or edited over 14 books. He has worked extensively in South Africa, Uganda, Vanuatu, Nepal, Australia, Papua-New Guinea and the Philippines. He is Adjunct Associate Professor of Social Science at the Queensland University of Technology, Australia; Visiting Professor at the Centre for Development Support, University of Free State, South Africa; and Director of Community Praxis Co-operative.

Benny Witkovsky is a PhD student in the Department of Sociology at the University of Wisconsin – Madison. His current research examines the connection between local political conflict and the rise of populism in Wisconsin and beyond.

Wong King-lai is Lecturer in the Department of Social Work, Hong Kong Baptist University. He is a registered social worker. His research interests include community development, policy transfer, urban regeneration, macro social work and social innovation.

ONE

Introductory overview

Sue Kenny, Jim Ife and Peter Westoby

This book is part of the *Rethinking Community Development* series. As such, it offers diverse critical perspectives, both international and cross-disciplinary, on the challenge of how to make sense of contemporary forms of populism and also how community development responds to these. Like the first two books in this series, *Politics, Power and Community Development* (Meade et al, 2016) and *Class, Inequality and Community Development* (Shaw and Mayo, 2016), our contribution has a primary focus on the structural, social and political contexts within which community development functions. Understanding these contexts helps us to make sense of what is often known as a time of populist politics, albeit we focus more on right-wing forms of populism. Such politics is in turn linked to what can be construed as a contemporary crisis of liberal democracy (Grayling, 2017) and neoliberalism, or perhaps even hyper-capitalism itself (Beradi, 2009). *Populism, Democracy and Community Development* examines the pressures and shifts linked with populism, yet many chapters also probe the complexity of community development itself, reaching for possible responses from this professional and citizen project.

Our challenges in editing this book

There have been three key challenges in editing this book. The first, linked to the challenge of populism and the contemporary crisis of liberal democracy, is simply the fluidity of the issues we are exploring. Quite literally, as editors, we were reading news analyses and articles arriving daily in our inboxes, as well as the burgeoning body of literature on populism being produced within the academy. Since the three of us gathered at a 2017 Melbourne Forum to first discuss the phenomena and concerns that this book focuses on, until late 2019, we had to grapple with Trump's erratic policies; the saga of Brexit; Bolsonaro's attacks on civil society, the poor and the environment in Brazil; Erdogan's embrace of populist Islam in Turkey; and a populist right-wing polity in Australia, to give a few examples. There had been a sense that every paragraph, once written, could easily be out of date.

But when we submitted the typescript for review in November 2019 we were unaware of the profound contextual changes that would be facing us by March 2020. The swiftness of the COVID-19 pandemic took us all by surprise. In April 2020, as we are in the process of submitting the final typescript, the pandemic is still spreading. No one can say when a vaccine will be widely available. Social scientists dare not venture a definitive analysis of what the long-term effects will be. Nevertheless, we can pick up some early trends that could play into, or against, the hands of right-wing populists. It seems clear that the health crisis of COVID-19 and the efforts to deal with it are giving rise to an economic crisis that will be deeper than the global financial crisis of 2007–09. How governments, both populist and non-populist, navigate the inevitable collapse of businesses, vast increases in unemployment and wide-scale poverty will influence the appeal and take-up of populism. The literature on populism highlights how economic crises are key drivers of support for populism. We are already seeing how those who lack economic and political power are being particularly affected by the pandemic, as disadvantaged and vulnerable groups lose jobs and livelihoods and as they are pushed into social isolation.

There is a new narrative challenging the populist construction of the society. Alongside the fear and panic generated by COVID-19, the binary divide between elites and the people has been reshaped. COVID-19 has resulted in the repositioning of some experts, namely medical and health policy experts, so that they are no longer in the category of enemy elites, but are rehabilitated as friends of the people, or even part of the people. Nevertheless, the populist tendency to conceptualise society through the lens of a binary of the virtuous people and others remains. At this stage (April 2020) it is not clear whether the status of the whole category of experts will be restored or only certain sections of experts. Whatever direction this shifting of categories takes, in part it does challenge the anti-expert rhetoric of populism. Interestingly, the category of virtuous people currently includes those who follow the rules and laws set by government, for example compulsory self-isolation and social distancing. Condemnation of transgressors is expressed within a framework of individual moral righteousness. While there are sound reasons for self-isolation and social distancing, in some places moral righteousness has given rise to a fledgling culture of informing on those who flout health rules and norms. An informer culture and a milieu of distrust of fellow citizens provide fertile ground for a turn to strong populist leaders.

While refugees and foreigners remain outsiders, the category of those requiring welfare, especially the newly unemployed, now forms part of the category of 'deserving people', even in right-wing populism. At the same time, suspicion of strangers, and the social divisiveness that this brings, has strengthened. As state borders have been tightened and the narrative of securitisation has become more intense, there has been a surge in nationalism and a deepening of exclusionary politics globally.

We are clearly witnessing a return of the state, in both the rhetoric and actions constituting the responses to COVID-19. Governments globally are promising to support those affected by COVID-19. Government policies offering economic support for the newly unemployed and small businesses have been particularly welcomed. While there has been some concern about governments being too 'slow to act' (in providing face masks and test kits, for example) and of governments failing to assist those who are most vulnerable, such as homeless people and refugees, criticism of government responses in many countries, with the exceptions of the USA and the UK, seems to be muted.

As in other times of crisis, there have been public calls for strong leadership, even if this were to involve by-passing democratic processes. In the urgency of the situation there has been a lack of scrutiny of government decisions and civil liberties have been curtailed. State powers have been expanded, allowing the policing of social isolation and social distancing requirements. Punishments for infringements include hefty fines and even prison sentences. New forms of surveillance, such as monitoring the movement of individuals (which so far are seemingly accepted by most citizens), have been introduced to ensure compliance with new government regulations and laws. None of these developments augers well for human rights.

What does all this mean for populism, democracy and community development? There are no straightforward answers to this question and, of course, the answers will vary depending on country and region. In April 2020 there are certainly examples of right-wing populists attempting to take advantage of the COVID-19 crisis. In Hungary, measures ostensibly aimed at controlling the spread of the coronavirus have made objective reporting of the pandemic very difficult, further undercutting freedom of speech and handing additional powers to Prime Minister Viktor Orbán (Pogany, 2020; Walker, 2020). In Brazil, President Bolsonaro sacked his health minister for criticising the president's handling of the coronavirus crisis (Phillips, 2020).

Alongside the culture of compliance and the strengthening of state power, there is evidence of many spontaneous acts of solidarity in which volunteer groups have stepped up in situations where the state has failed, including such actions as dropping in food parcels and sending notes of concern. These examples of civility are consistent with community development. They indicate that citizens do not need strong (populist) leaders to encourage mutuality and to nurture solidarities. Such independent action can provide a bulwark against populism. On the other hand, as indicated previously, 'good acts' are dressed in the cloak of moral righteousness. The virtue signalling expressed by those identifying as the (good) people reinforces the binary divide of the good 'us' and defective, immoral, 'them' and the surge in assertions of individual moral righteousness feeds into exclusionary politics, which is at odds with community development. Exclusionary politics, nationalism, securitisation and state surveillance are convenient tools for right-wing populism.

What happens politically, socially and economically as a result of COVID-19 matters for the future of a planet already challenged by the enormity of climate change. As Runciman (2020) points out:

> The ultimate judgments are about how to use coercive power ... And the contest in the exercise of that power between democratic adaptability and autocratic ruthlessness will shape all of our futures.

Globally, the current political trajectory appears to be an authoritarian one, which opens up more space for right-wing populism. This trajectory does not bode well for either democracy or community development. Yet whether populist leaders are able to colonise this space is uncertain, as evidenced by the difficulties facing Bolsonaro in Brazil, Trump in the USA, Salvini in Italy and Modi in India. As for ways of countering the new impetus for populism and authoritarianism, we are just beginning to explore these and we hope that this book can contribute to the exploration.

The second challenge is the contested nature of the three themes in the book: populism, democracy and community development. Consistent with the community development commitment to encourage different ways of framing issues and 'seeing things', we did not try to impose on the authors any particular approach to the three main concepts. Chapters have differing areas of focus and readers will find a variety of understandings of the key themes. Surely, the editors of the book themselves do not always hold a common position in regard to defining issues and ways of responding to populism.

The third challenge is that while there are many scholars involved in understanding populism, there is a scarcity of scholar/practitioners who have researched the linkages between populism, democracy and community development and therefore no corpus of literature to draw upon and debate. We hope that this book might contribute to the development of such a literature.

Mapping the issues

To understand how populism has affected community development it is necessary to locate contemporary populism in historical context. While authors in this book focus on different historical factors, many comment on the harsh effects of neoliberalism. Chapters concerned with populism in the UK, for example, discuss how the backdrop of neoliberalism has been associated with the political shift to the right (Popple in Chapter Ten; Reynolds in Chapter Thirteen). Neoliberal agendas were evident in the austerity measures taken in the wake of the Global Financial Crisis of 2008/9. These measures, including reduced spending on welfare and public services, threatened often precarious living standards and exacerbated existing anxieties. In Hong Kong (Chapter Twelve), neoliberalism has underpinned what Fung and colleagues call a market productivist welfare regime, which focuses on the productive function of social policy rather than the rights based nature of social protection. This productivist welfare regime subordinates social welfare/protection to economic growth, and, as it does, it affects the lives of young people and those living below the poverty line, including elderly people, single mothers and disadvantaged communities. As in the UK, the backdrop of deteriorating living conditions has generated fear and uncertainty about the future. And given their inability, or lack of interest in responding to the disquiet, as well as charges of corruption, there has been increasing distrust in established leaders, including politicians, intellectuals and policy makers – those who have come to be understood as elites

In western societies, then, the main objects of blame for people's misfortunes are the elites, who are deemed to always be working against the interests of 'the people'. For Mudde the core populist belief is that society is 'ultimately separated into two homogeneous and antagonistic groups, "the pure people" versus "the corrupt elite"' (Mudde, 2004: 543). Populists have been able to harness this distrust of elites by applying the binary of 'us' (the good people) and 'them' (the bad elites) and use this as the basis for a new kind of wedge politics.

The importance of this binary construction of society is discussed in a number of chapters in the book. Importantly, while the dominant boundaries set up in populist movements are organised around a putative distinction between people and elites, the content of the category of 'them' can be set differently, particularly between right- and left-wing populism. In right-wing populism the category of 'them' also covers outgroups that are deemed to be protected or supported by elites, including, at various times, welfare recipients, refugees, Roma, minority ethnic group, and LGBTQIA (Lesbian, Gay, Bisexual, Transsexual, Queer, Intersex and Asexual) communities. These outgroups are identified as enemies, in so far as they are seen to threaten the integrity of the 'people's way of life'. They are subjects of the derision and contempt that feed xenophobia and hatred. In contrast to right-wing populism, for the left, outgroups are embraced, that is, they are included in the category of 'us', the people. While a binary construction of society is applicable to populism in general, 'us' 'the people' is formed differently again in the contemporary democracy movement in Hong Kong, where it is mainland Chinese, both poor and wealthy, who are identified as the adversaries of Hong Kong citizens.

In the literature on populism there is disagreement as to whether all forms of populism are problematic politically, or it is only (or mainly) right-wing populism that undermines the values of social justice and participatory equality. Fung and colleagues (Chapter Twelve) direct us to the schema presented by March (2017: 300). For March, when right-wing populism is the threat, 'the host ideology is more important than populism', and in the case of both left and right forms of populism being equally problematic, then 'populism trumps (underlying) ideology'. The chapters in this book vary in regard to which of these positions they embrace. Whatever approach is taken, it is important to acknowledge that left-wing populism has a more inclusive notion of the people (see, for example, Westoby, Chapter Four; Popple, Chapter Ten; and Fung et al, Chapter Twelve in this book).

Stoecker and Witkovsky (Chapter Eight) provide a complementary framework to the traditional right/left distinctions used to analyse populism. They differentiate types of populism on the basis of whether they are inclusionary or exclusionary. Their historical analysis of community development in the US traces the populist trajectory from inclusionary to exclusionary populism. This is linked to the community development trajectory that involves a transition from a politicised community development model, which emphasises participatory and redistributive community power building, to a corporatist neoliberal model, which legitimates, encourages and mobilises local resentment.

The destruction of the power-based model of community development has meant the loss of a countervailing force that could undermine the power of exclusionary populism. Stoecker and Witkovsky explain that the two forms of community development and the two forms of populism exist in tension with each other. What is clear in the different constructions of 'them' and 'us' is the ways in which the frontiers of exclusion/inclusion can cut across established ways of segmenting society through class and status criteria.

In Indonesia, the context in which populism has grown has been somewhat different from that occurring in western countries. The boundaries of 'them' and 'us' are often drawn around religious criteria. It has not been neoliberalism, as such, or the austerity policies that have facilitated the new populist binary of 'us' and 'them', or even new experiences of distrust in elites and government (governments have always been treated with significant cynicism in Indonesia) that have provided decisive conditions for the ascendancy of populism. Yet in the context of rapid social and political change since the fall of President Suharto's authoritarian government in 1998 many Indonesians have felt themselves adrift. At the same time, the democratisation of Indonesia since 1998 opened the way for strengthening identity politics based on religion. In their study of Islamic organisations in Indonesia, Ismet and Rebecca Fanany (Chapter Fourteen) trace the growth of the Aksi 212, a right-wing populist movement based on a particular construction of 'us' as those supporting the views of the movement, who are deemed to be the true and moral Muslims, and 'them', comprising non-Muslims and those (putatively non-pious) Muslims who do not support the movement. The 'them' includes the elite, and particularly the liberal elite, and the non-pious poor.

Unlike in Indonesia, the culture of democracy in Finland is well established. At the same time, as in Indonesia, democracy, with its acceptance of competing ideas, has provided an opening for populists. Aho and colleagues (Chapter Eleven) discuss the paradox that the commitment to democracy, openness to different ideas and the high levels of social trust in Finnish society embed a tolerance of the populist aspiration to undermine people's confidence in institutions, particularly political institutions.

The idea that democratic politics and left-wing political parties can be largely unwitting midwives to right-wing populism has been clearly evident in Brazil. In Chapter Nine, Lopes de Souza explains the trajectories of political regimes in Brazil: from the authoritarianism that dominated the Latin American political landscape in the 1960s and 1970s; to liberal governments in the 1980s and 1990s; then to leftist neo-populism; this being replaced in 2018 by the right-wing populism of Bolsonaro. As leftist neo-populism co-opted and demobilised civil society, authoritarian politics resurfaced. At the same time, the neo-extractive model of economic development that was embedded in Brazilian politics by leftist neo-populism has been embraced by Bolsonaro. Thus, struggles for environmental justice have been undermined by both left- and right-wing populism. Community development has been caught up in all these political machinations, its radical potential diminished by various processes of incorporation. However, against the ideological co-option of community development as a practice, the idea of community and the notion of the commons, with their connections to communitarian organisation, continue to be strongly supported.

What is evident in chapters in this book are the complexities in understanding how populism operates and how forms of populism relate to community development, communities and democracy. Both Ife (Chapter Three) and Kenny (Chapter Two) explain some of the many challenging twists and turns in the relationships. Ife focuses on the contradictory ways in which right-wing populism and community development connect with modernity. At the same time, there are some ironic similarities between community development and populism. For example, both community development and populism are disillusioned with established politics; they use the lexicon of the 'voice of the people', and make worthy pronouncements about maximising participation. Both are suspicious of globalisation, neoliberalism and the impacts of global capital. And both validate the authenticity of disadvantaged groups, while at the same time encouraging a mistrust of elites, preferring 'bottom-up' initiatives. However, the ways in which these concerns are put into practice vary significantly, as discussed by both Ife and Kenny. For Kenny, taking a theoretical approach similar to Stoecker and Witkovsky, one way of thinking about intersections and disjunctions between community development and populism is to place the varying configurations in a societal tension field comprising both synergies and contradictions.

The ability to seize upon disquiet and emotions is important for the success of all forms of populism. This point is taken up Mayo (Chapter Five), Westoby (Chapter Four) and Szynka (Chapter Seven). The message from these authors is that when thinking about community development responses to populism it is important to include ways of working with emotions and passions, recognising that people's vulnerabilities to populism are based on grievances that are felt. Mayo points out that populists typically appeal to people's emotions and feelings of identity. She comments on the ways in which current conditions give rise to anxiety, feelings of weakness and powerlessness, and how people come to believe that others are being treated more favourably. In turn, the weakness and powerlessness can become a mixture of bitterness, complaint, envy and shame. As Mayo notes, it is possible to fire up these feelings into moral panics, which become effective tools in the hands of populists.

For Westoby, much like Mayo, right-wing populism is an animating force fuelled by anxiety that easily becomes anger, and as such one of the key challenges is how the language of anger and outrage can be harnessed for the 'common good', and not the malignant appetite of any corrupted populist leader. Szynka discusses how the community development organiser Alinsky described his technique for dealing with frustration and aggression. Alinsky differentiated between two ways of using the metaphors of 'rubbing raw the resentments' and 'fanning the sores of discontent'. The first, which is used by populists today, is to manipulate, mislead and 'stir up' people. The second, which is Alinsky's approach, is to bring issues to the surface for confrontation and ventilation, rather than let them fester and generate hate (Alinsky, 1960). That is, it is important to talk about problems, to try to understand them and cooperatively search for a way to solve them. Reflecting on the re-emergence of populism in Germany today, Szynka comments on how what he calls the new prophets of deceit operate through populist politics and carry out the 'fine art of propaganda again', using the new forms of mass communication and the new opportunities opened up by social media. Like Mayo, Szynka discusses how such feelings can be manipulated.

Social media have been a central part of the successes of populism. The current forms of populism have been adept at using social media for their own purposes. They can be used to present positive ways of dealing with social issues, but mainly they have been conduits for resentment and hate and have been brought in to service the promotion of populist leaders. For example, the power of social media has been used skilfully in the Indonesian populist movement Aksi 212 (see Chapter Fourteen). The language of Aksi 212, mainly articulating who they are against, has found fertile ground in Indonesia, where there has been widespread take-up of digital communication. The chapter by Boulet in this book (Chapter Six) explores the role of new information technologies, focusing on social media. He comments on how social media have penetrated all aspects of our lives, with profound implications for the future. While Boulet sees parallels between Arendt's notion of 'totalitarianism' (Arendt, 1976) and present-day populism(s), the current forms of social media are in some ways more intrusive and efficient than at the time in which Arendt was writing. We can point to how the surveillance methods through social media that are now in place have set up structures for new forms of authoritarianism and totalitarianism (Zuboff, 2019).

Responses

How can those committed to community development endeavours respond to populism? As a preface to this section, the editors would like to point out that when thinking about any community development response to populism, it is important to understand that feelings of alienation and resentment, and concerns about uncertainty and material insecurity, have a rational basis. From this perspective, populism should be viewed as a symptom of underlying factors that have characterised much of the global state of affairs since the last decades of the twentieth century. Taking the viewpoint that populism is a symptom, any response to populism must be cognisant of the underlying conditions in which populism has arisen. And at one level, the populist explanations of these experiences and the promises made by their leaders make sense.

There is considerable agreement between the authors in this book regarding the need for a historical perspective that considers the conditions that facilitate populist ideas and practices. There is also a view in many of the chapters that strengthening communities and refocusing community development should be a central part of any action to combat the problematic aspects of populism. Popple (Chapter Ten), noting that populism is a symptom of the wide issues of deteriorating living standards and distrust of government, argues for changes on a national scale. Community development practitioners could mobilise around broad issues of material deprivation and racism, including the injection of massive resources into local institutions such as local pubs, post offices and networks that keep communities together. At the same time, Popple is pessimistic about the future for community development in the UK. It continues to be poorly funded and there is a lack of support for education and training of community development workers. He calls for efforts to raise awareness of the value and effectiveness of community development in the struggle for a more democratic, equal, prosperous and consensual UK.

In a very different context, Fanany and Fanany (Chapter Fourteen) are also concerned about the future of community development in Indonesia when assailed by the rise of undemocratic right-wing populists who present themselves as leaders and saviours of those at the grassroots. The dilemmas facing community development practitioners in Indonesia are, of course, found elsewhere when community development practitioners are challenged by those who present as leaders or saviours but eschew any effort to engage democratically.

Ife (Chapter Three) refers to the literature that identifies communities as pivotal to a future based on sustainability and social justice. Rather than simply reacting to populism within the limitations of modernity and liberal democracy, we need new paradigms of practice based on the values of community development (for which he provides examples), while at the same time we need to connect with progressive politics and movements.

Having argued that conservative neo-populism is just an uglier form of earlier populisms, and having pointed out that community development in Brazil had been co-opted, Lopes de Souza (Chapter Nine) calls for utilising the self-organising efforts of civil society for the purposes of a truly emancipatory approach to community development. Similarly, Stoecker and Witkovsky (Chapter Eight) explain how community development has been co-opted in the US. Yet unlike Lopes de Souza, they do not consider all forms of populism to be a threat. As noted earlier in this chapter, they distinguish between inclusionary populism and exclusionary populism. It is exclusionary populism that poses the threat. An inclusionary populism, which builds power at the local level and constructs an alternative economy that draws on existing progressive models, offers a way forward. Stoecker and Witkovsky ponder whether developing a power base by rebuilding local associations might be an appropriate direction for community development. However, a turn to what they call hyper-localness has a number of risks, including a backward-looking orientation which ignores the importance of social change; a tendency towards exclusionary politics (like exclusionary populism); and pressures for sameness rather than diversity. Following Geoghegan and Powell (2009), Stoecker and Witkovsky comment that there are three choices for community development: a neoliberal version; a corporatist version; and an activist version. Community development in the US is currently caught in the first two choices. While they propose the third choice, Stoecker and Witkovsky identify a number of issues confronting community activists today.

A well-informed citizenry, one that understands the scope of complexities, and the nuances and contradictions of everyday life, is a necessary part of any effective response to right-wing and exclusionary populism. Drawing on experiences in Finland, Aho and colleagues (Chapter Eleven) argue for a strengthening of active citizenship as a way of overcoming simplistic and deceptive populist propositions. In Finland, they contend, populism has brought to the surface the failures of community engagement and participatory civic processes. They emphasise the importance of deliberative democracy. What is needed is citizens who believe in their own capabilities to influence and a new approach based on how citizens themselves want to be engaged. Following the new Finnish Local Government Act, which came into force in 2017, multiple methods for community engagement have been established, including participatory budgeting, food circuits, local recycling groups and the sharing of local services that by-pass market and state transactions. However, at the time of finalising their chapter (October 2019) the outcomes of these new participatory programmes and their ability to counter the influence of right-wing populism in Finland is unclear.

While there might be considerable agreement regarding the conditions for populism and the significance of community development in responding to populism, there are also some points of disagreement. First, for some commentators, who distinguish clearly between left and right populism, the way forward is to embrace or at least link up with left-wing populism. Reynolds (Chapter Thirteen) takes such an approach. Drawing on the work of Mouffe (2018), for whom the contemporary populist moment is one that opens up opportunities for adversarial politics organised around left-wing themes, Reynolds' position is that community development should unite with left-wing populist strategies to generate and practise counter-hegemonic discourses.

The second type of disagreement concerns whether there is a place for dialogue between community development and populists. As noted previously, while there might be some overlap between the two, there are profound differences. There is some ambivalence in regard to this matter. For Kenny, encouraging discussion between people holding different views and/or coming from different cultures is an important part of community development, although it is not without its difficulties. A clear position is taken by Ife, who argues that the superficial commonalities do not constitute useful grounds for dialogue. The fundamentalist nature of populism, the simplistic analyses and promises of populists, the differences in views of what constitutes participation, and the racism, sexism, heteronormativity and other forms of prejudice mean that the values and practices of populism have no place within the values of community development.

What is clear so far in this discussion is that regardless of whether strategies for dealing with populism based on deliberative democracy are labelled as such, they fall into the community development tradition of popular education. A number of the chapters focus specifically on popular education (see Chapters Three, Four and Five). Community education and consciousness-raising have a strong tradition in community development, perhaps best exemplified by Freire's work (1972). As Mayo points out, popular educators can promote the politics of hope rather than exacerbating the politics of hate. She notes that in the age of populism, such education-focused community development becomes more important than ever, although it needs to be reformulated for the contemporary world.

Westoby (Chapter Four) argues for a truly popular (as opposed to populist) agenda that will support people to become better informed as a basis for their activism. For Westoby, beginning with the centrality of the community development roles of listening; dialogue; connecting people; building organic movements; accounting for emotions; and facilitating social and ethical decision making provides a useful framework for dealing with populism. But like several other authors in the book, Westoby argues for a radical path for community development, which includes establishing a countervailing organisational force; building alliances; linking local issues to broader regional, national or international movements; popular education; and a revival of deliberative democracy. Importantly, Westoby also champions the development of what he calls the 'social state' to address the issues that give rise to populism.

Drawing on his critical analysis of the power of digital media, and particularly social media, Boulet (Chapter Six) proposes using technology in new ways. He suggests building what he calls a 'hybrid social–digital economy', harnessing digital technologies while being inserted in a localised 'social economy'. Like other authors in this book he calls for redeveloping communities, experimenting with new organisational and relational forms and formats.

The deterioration of democracy

There is another deeper issue that lies at the heart of our struggle against right-wing populism. Earlier in this chapter we mentioned the importance of understanding populism as a symptom. In this final part of the chapter we visit the view that populism is a symptom of the deterioration of the project of democracy. As indicated, one of the important aspects of the current context of populism in western countries is the erosion of liberal democracy. Populism has moved into spaces formerly occupied by liberal democracy. One of the perpetual concerns about the Trump administration in the US has been the way it has not only flouted the conventions of liberal democracy, but has been able to 'get away with it', with few consequences. The level of corruption, and the devaluing of constitutional conventions, the rule of law, the separation of powers, fair electoral boundaries, voter registration, and what has previously passed as 'good government', has left opponents and commentators astounded, and unsure of how to act. In the UK the impact of Brexit has been in some ways similar, and it seems as if the old rules and conventions that people once took for granted no longer apply. Some mainstream media outlets and social media sites have encouraged and reinforced these trends, often in the interests of the powerful and of media owners.

Such cavalier treatment of constitutions and conventions is typically seen as more common in non-western jurisdictions, where coups, blatant corruption and military interventions have apparently been more frequent, but rather than the smug colonialism that assumes the West will be able to 'teach' others about 'good governance', it now seems that the West is joining the rest of the world. Indeed, western 'democracies' have never been totally free of corruption, 'soft coups' and manipulation by the powerful, and it can be argued that liberal democracy has been effectively a fiction to cover up such behaviour with a veneer of constitutional respectability. Increasingly, however, that corruption has been revealed for all to see, yet such governments continue to be elected and supported. Appeals to the traditions, conventions and 'common sense' of liberal democracy appear to have been unable to stem the tide of populism.

This is significant because community development, at least in the Global North, has largely operated within the framework of liberal democracy. It has encouraged and empowered communities to seek public funding, lobby political representatives, engage with electoral politics, advocate for new or improved 'services', encourage voting, advocate for social justice and human rights, pursue legal redress, support progressive policy change, collect signatures for petitions, research and document social problems, and so on. This is partly the result of the organisational contexts within which most community workers are employed, where managerialism has effectively limited their capacity for more radical or creative practice. Community development has thus found itself co-opted by the dominant paradigm. But even when community development seeks to speak truth to power, it has often done so through traditional liberal democratic means, assuming that a combination of well-researched argument and strong citizen advocacy is sufficient to bring about progressive change. One of the characteristics of right-wing populism is that it has succeeded in challenging and further undermining many of the liberal democratic institutions to the extent that they can no longer be taken for granted.

At a time when liberal democratic institutions, which community development has taken for granted, are eroding and proving to be not as resilient as we had assumed, it is timely for community development workers, educators, researchers and scholars to rethink our assumptions about democracy. Indeed, community development risks irrelevance unless it can effectively address the challenges and the opportunities of rethinking democracy in a post-Freire and a post-Alinsky world, where globalisation, social media and ecological imperatives have redefined the territory and set new parameters for the experience of 'community'. This is the context, well beyond the imagination of conventional liberal democracy, within which the phenomenon of right-wing populism has emerged, and within which it must now be addressed.

What, then, are the alternative forms of 'democracy' that may be a basis for community development? As discussed, the chapters in this book argue for strengthening democracy. But what if the very idea of democracy is now so compromised that it has lost much of its meaning and its substance? Traditionally, community development has emphasised participatory democracy, and has worked towards maximising 'citizen participation' in decision making and in community service delivery, largely within the constraints of the liberal state. This view of democratisation through community development is evident in this book. Even so, the idea of participatory democracy has also been appropriated by the populist right, with a strong narrative of 'power to the people' located within a broader narrative of the mistrust of elites. It will be imperative for community development practitioners to think much more carefully about participation, and to examine forms of participation that do not fall into the traps of false engagement that are set up by populism. We need to consider and critique more fully the ideas and processes of democracy. We need participation that requires people to 'do the hard yards' and recognises that democratic participation is not just a duty free right but that it carries with it the responsibility to be well-informed about important issues. It is important that projects for participation and deliberative democracy are, as far as possible, truly owned by communities, and operate in spaces where communities themselves set up the scope, agendas and processes, rather than operate in what Coelho and Cornwall (2007) call invited spaces.

It would seem that whatever way we understand populism, populist politics will be with us for some time. And what is clear to us, as editors of this book, is that there is an urgent need for those committed to community development endeavours to confront the challenges presented by the political dominance of right-wing populism. We can try to keep going on a 'business as usual' basis, but this sets us on a dangerous path, one that continues to support the political systems, social inequalities and vested interests that have led to a situation in which not only societies, but also our planet, are facing an untenable future. Ironically, populists are able to understand the sense of disaster. And yet notwithstanding the hyperbole of getting rid of elites, or 'draining the swamp', for the good of society, populists actually maintain many of the existing institutions because they are of use to them. In many ways it suits them to continue with 'business as usual' while they shape what is left of representative democracy according to their needs.

In the big picture of radically rethinking and reactivating democracy in a way that does not ease the way for right-wing populism, community development has a modest role to play. Nevertheless it does have a role. This role must be based on our experiences, research and critical analyses that can help us reconfigure the ways in which community development relates to the world. Challenging right-wing populism and reconstructing populism are daunting, but necessary tasks, and, in a final addition to this book, they are all the more urgent in the threatening world of the COVID-19 pandemic.

References

Alinsky, S.D. (1960) 'The urban immigrant', in T. Mac Avoy (ed), *Roman Catholicism and the American Way of Life*, Notre Dame, IN: University of Notre Dame Press, pp 142–55.

Arendt, H. (1976) [1951] *The Origins of Totalitarianism*, New York: Schocken.

Beradi, B. (2009) *The Soul at Work: From Alienation to Autonomy.* Los Angeles, CA: Semiotext.

Coelho, V. and Cornwall, A. (2007) 'Spaces for change? The politics of participation in new democratic arenas', in A Cornwall and V. Coelho (eds), *Spaces for Change*, London: Zed Books, pp 1–9.

Freire, P. (1972) *Pedagogy of the Oppressed*, Harmondsworth: Penguin.

Geoghegan, M., and Powell, F. (2009) 'Community development and the contested politics of the late modern agora: of, alongside or against neoliberalism?', *Community Development Journal*, 44(4): 430–47.

Grayling, A.C. (2017) *Democracy in Crisis*, London: Oneworld.

March, L. (2017) 'Left and right populism compared: the British case', *British Journal of Politics and International Relations*, 19(2): 282–303.

Meade, R., Shaw, M. and Banks, S. (2016) 'Politics, power and community development: an introductory essay', in R. Meade, M. Shaw and S. Banks (eds), *Politics, Power and Community Development*, Bristol: Policy Press, pp 1–27.

Mouffe, C. (2018) *For a Left Populism*, London: Verso.

Mudde, C. (2004) 'The populist zeitgeist', *Government and Opposition*, 39(4): 541–63.

Phillips, T. (2020) 'Bolsonaro fires popular health minister after dispute over coronavirus response', *The Guardian*, 16 April, [online]www.theguardian.com/world/2020/apr/16/bolsonaro-brazil-president-luiz-mandetta-health-minister

Pogany, S. (2020) 'The coronavirus and the "quarantining" of Hungarian democracy', Social Europe, 1 April, [online] www.socialeurope.eu/the-coronavirus-and-the-quarantining-of-hungarian-democracy

Runciman, D. (2020) 'Coronavirus has not suspended politics – it has revealed the nature of power', *The Guardian*, 27 March, [online] www.theguardian.com/commentisfree/2020/mar/27/coronavirus-politics-lockdown-hobbes

Shaw, M. and Mayo, M. (eds) (2016) *Class, Inequality and Community Development*, Bristol: Policy Press.

Walker, S. (2020) 'Hungarian journalists fear coronavirus law may be used to jail them', *The Guardian*, 3 April, [online] www.theguardian.com/world/2020/apr/03/hungarian-journalists-fear-coronavirus law-may-be-used-to-jail-them

Zuboff, S. (2019) *The Age of Surveillance Capitalism: The Fight for a Human Future at the New Frontier of Power*, London: Profile Books.

PART 1

Framing the challenges

TWO

The challenges of populism

Sue Kenny

Introduction

Community development can be described as a process in which communities take collective action to gain control over their resources and futures. It aspires to establish processes and structures which are 'democratic, participatory, empowering and inclusive' (Meade et al, 2016: 3). The ways in which community development practitioners work to empower communities are framed by social, economic and political contexts. This chapter discusses the contextual landscape of populism. It offers some introductory thoughts on the problematic intersections between community development, democracy and populism. Setting out ways of thinking about these intersections has been a daunting task. Each phenomenon is multifaceted. Moreover, currently there is no corpus of research that deals with the ways in which populist political culture affects community development processes, or the extent to which populism has been embraced or rejected at the level of specific communities. Yet it is possible to identify major themes in both populism and community development and to draw out points of overlap and divergence. After analysing convergences and disjunctions the chapter discusses the ways in which the beliefs and practices of populism challenge community development. The chapter concludes with a brief discussion of community development responses to populism.

Populism as political culture

Populism is now a global phenomenon. Populist leaders, parties and movements have significant control or influence on political regimes, governments and public policies in countries as diverse as the Philippines, Germany, the US, Brazil, India and Hungary. While there is a huge literature on populism, conceptual descriptors of populism vary. A simple starting point is to conceptualise populism as a form of politics based around specific beliefs. The term 'populism' is used to describe a political logic (Laclau, 2005; Judis, 2016; Mudde and Kaltwasser, 2017); a political style (Moffitt, 2016); and a political strategy (Muller, 2016; Eatwell and Goodwin, 2018). But it is also understood as an ideological world view (Wodak, 2015) and a (thin-centred) ideology (Mudde and Kaltwasser, 2017). The generally accepted position in the literature is that populism per se is not linked to any particular ideological stance (Laclau, 2005; Mudde and Kaltwasser, 2017). For example, political leaders such as the late Hugo Chavez and Donald Trump have both been described as populist, yet they represent different ideological persuasions.

The approach taken in this chapter is to acknowledge these various conceptualisations of populism but to analyse populism through the framework of political culture, which is manifested in the rhetoric and actions of populist movements and leaders. This approach has some overlap with that of Wodak (2015).[1] A political culture refers to a set of shared views, imaginaries, beliefs and normative judgements about the political world. It provides a mindset that focuses attention on certain events, institutions and behaviour (Elkins and Simeon, 1979: 128). Importantly for community development, a political culture sets out ways of perceiving events in daily life. It organises experiences and guides action (Snow et al, 1986: 464) and thus provides a frame of reference through which communities think about and practise community empowerment.

At the same time, understanding the complexities of populism requires appreciating the reflexive nature of populist political culture. That is, the construction of populist political culture is not only a top-down process. It draws on elements already existing in a society, amplifying these and adding new elements. An investigation of the range of empirical elements that comprise populist political culture is a complex task. However, for analytical purposes it is possible to identify five overlapping themes, comprising an ideal type construct, which can throw light on the nature of populism as a form of political culture. These themes are, first, a social ontology that constructs society around two main groups, the people and the elite (and their associates); second, the rhetoric of commitment to the sovereignty of the people; third, the claim that populist politics are democratic; fourth, validation of the anxieties of ordinary people; and, finally, populist leaders' assertions that they can speak for the people and solve their problems. These themes are expressed with various degrees of commitment and the ways in which they are manifested can differ. It is for this reason that Muller (2016: loc 586) comments that we can speak of degrees of populism. A similar analytical approach can be used to understand community development. That is, while there are inconsistencies and different traditions in community development, it is possible to discern themes in normative stance, theories and practices. This chapter discusses claims made around these themes. And, of course, the claims of community development practitioners are 'situated somewhere between rhetoric and reality, actuality and aspiration' (Meade et al, 2016: 2).

Intersections and disjunctions

Analyses of populism tend to begin with the way in which populist politics are assembled around a particular construction of society that identifies two main groups, 'the people' and the elite (Mudde, 2004). In what is known as a Manichean approach, this segmentation is often seen through a lens that conceives of the world through the binary of good and bad. The populist standpoint is that good resides in the people, who are virtuous and morally pure. Members of the elite are often labelled 'enemies of the people'.[2] The category of elite includes those who control businesses, law and government, and those who are deemed to be experts, intellectuals and journalists. Paradoxically, in this politics of identity the idea of 'the people' is presented by populists as representing the whole, while at the same time it excludes parts of society. This means, as Muller (2016: loc 319) notes, that 'Only some of the people are really the people'. Examples of the view that society comprises 'virtuous people' and 'bad' or corrupt experts are found in both right-wing and left-wing populism. From the right, Nigel Farage, who has been a staunch proponent of Brexit, claimed that the win for the leave campaign was the 'will of the people' and a 'victory for real people' (Withnall, 2016). In August 2019, Darren Selkus, a member of Farage's Brexit Party, suggested that those with anti-Brexit views should be thrown into the Tower of London as traitors (Gregory, 2019). In these cases, the boundary between good and bad is drawn on the basis of pro- and anti-Brexit stances. In a speech in Ankara in 2011 the populist leader Erdogan stated that 'the tyranny of the elites is over' (Url, 2019). From the left, the Greek populist party Syriza organised its political discourse around the antagonistic schema, between 'us', the people, and 'them', the corrupt political parties of the 'old' establishment, that is, the economic oligarchy, who support the neoliberal obsessions of the European Union (Markou, 2017).

The dominant form of populism in the current period is right-wing populism. In right-wing populism there is another element of segmentation, containing disparate people, such as those in minority ethnic groups, LGBTQIA communities, welfare recipients and refugees. It is in regard to how the frontiers of 'us' and 'them' demonise subaltern groups that right-wing populism can be most clearly differentiated from left-wing populism. While left-wing populists align with the category of subaltern groups or Others, in right-wing populism 'Others' are deemed to be protected and supported by the elite and thus are included in the category of enemies.

Like populism in general, community development practice is critical of groups wielding significant power in their own interests. And like left-wing populism, community development practice is committed to the empowerment of subaltern groups. Nonetheless, in general, community development practice does not work through a simple binary conception of society organised around unitary concepts of 'the people' and elites. It is based on a more nuanced understanding of power relationships. While community development practice involves strategic actions to empower ordinary people to take collective control of their own lives (often in constrained circumstances), these endeavours are not focused on a quest to identify 'enemies'.[3] In a similar way to left-wing populism, community development approaches are at odds with right-wing populism when it stigmatises and demonises certain groups of disadvantaged people.

The second populist theme is the idea of the sovereignty of the people, which begins from the assumption that the people are the source of power. This means that political decisions should be an expression of the beliefs and desires held in common (by the people). Populists argue that elites have usurped the people's sovereignty and by supporting a populist leader, the people are able to reclaim their power. For example, speaking at his inauguration, Donald Trump stated that he was 'transferring power from Washington DC and giving it back ... to the people' (Fabian, 2017). In populist thought moral virtue resides in the people and populist leaders enact the 'will of the people'. A corollary is that populism ensures the unity and purity of the nation. Populists in Poland, for example, have adopted the idea of 'moral revolution' not only as a way of stamping out corruption, but also to endorse the ideal of a (religiously) uniform Polish nation (Wysoka, 2009). Like populism, community development theory and practice are based on the principle that the people should be the source of power. Interestingly, both community development and populism tend to reify their constituencies, comprising people in communities and nations, and as the objects of empowerment these constituencies are suffused with moral worthiness. But while they might have rhetorical use, the heuristic value of both concepts, 'the people' and 'the community', is problematic. As Crick (2013: 42), points out, the mantra of the 'sovereignty of the people' means little more than 'an affirmation that governments should be in the interests of everyone'. It is an empty doctrine.

Third, linked with assertions regarding the sovereignty of the people are claims concerning the democratic attributes of populism. These claims rest on a number of arguments: populist politics nurtures political interest; it successfully mobilises large sections of society, and in so doing, it reinvigorates democratic politics. Populist leaders are elected democratically by the people; they have largely unmediated relationships with the people; and thus legitimately represent the 'will of the people'. Community development is also based on democratic principles. Community development practitioners are concerned with making political processes comprehensible and ensuring the accessibility of, and engagement with political processes. Like populist leaders, community development practitioners claim to respond to people's real concerns. Even so there are significant differences in the ways in which populists and community development practitioners conceptualise and practise democracy. While the rhetoric of people's sovereignty and 'rule by the people' is used extensively in populism, the democratic credentials of populist politics fall far short of the notion of democracy as 'collective self-rule under conditions that provide relatively equal chances for citizens to influence collective judgements and decisions' (Warren, 2001: 60). In populism, notions of 'collective self-rule' and 'rule by the people' are encased in electoral politics. 'The people' have little or no on-going input into 'collective judgements and decisions'.

Notwithstanding processes such as managerialism and the hollowing out of democratic practices, both outside and within community development, there is an enduring tradition of on going political contestation in community development, based on commitment to participation and deliberation which challenge what Shaw (2011: 130) describes as the de-politicisation of democracy and de-democratisation of politics. The focus of community development is not elections. Community development offers spaces in which citizens can learn and enact democratic processes. At its best, it provides effective 'schools for democracy' (Dodge and Ospina, 2016).

Fourth, populist leaders and movements recognise and validate the grievances and anxieties of those who feel 'left out' in the contemporary world. While there is a great deal of debate about the causes of the ascendancy of populism, the position taken in this chapter is that populism is in many ways a rational response to the injustices and insecurities that are experienced by ordinary people globally. Not only has the neoliberal form of capitalism made already insecure livelihoods even more vulnerable, but established politics is largely 'at odds with the hopes, fears and concerns of ordinary citizens (Judis, 2016). Indeed, in long-standing democratic countries distrust of politicians and institutions has reached the point where many citizens believe that they no longer have any voice in the direction of their society (Eatwell and Goodwin, 2018). Populist parties and movements understand the importance of citizens' anxieties and alienation from mainstream politics. Populist leaders are able to engender such disquiet with feelings of resentment and moral righteousness. In western societies, the moral righteousness of the disaffected and disadvantaged has traditionally been wrapped in the solidarity of established political parties and working class neighbourhoods. Over recent decades these traditional loci of solidarity have been significantly eroded. In the process of what Eatwell and Goodwin (2018: xxiii) call de-alignment, political systems are 'far more fragmented and unpredictable than in any point in the history of mass democracy'. This de-alignment means that populist appeal cuts across traditional class loyalties. As well as appealing to many of those in clearly disadvantaged groups, populist ideas are also embraced by those who are (not yet) at 'the bottom of society', a group that Bauman calls 'the precariat', comprising those who live in dread of losing their status, power, possessions and privileges (Bauman, 2016: loc 231).

In many ways there is a clear symbiosis between community development and populism in regard to the authentication of the anxieties and grievances of the people. For example, community development practice is located in the interstices of the power of capital and the state and the struggles of disadvantaged groups. It is underpinned by a commitment to affirm grievances and redress injustices. Nevertheless, there are some subtle differences regarding ways of responding to the grievances of the people. There is no structural or class analysis underlying the populist understanding of grievances. The populist notions of 'authentication', 'validation' and 'legitimation' are located in the context of asymmetrical relations that assume that one group has the authority and power to validate and legitimate another group. In right-wing populism in particular, while leaders express sympathy for the distress of those who feel 'left behind', they often amplify the disquiet and package it up in the politics of fear (Wodak, 2015). While notions of practitioners 'doing things for communities' does exist in community development, it is important for practitioners to be sensitive to the power relations between communities and community development practitioners. No such sensitivity concerning asymmetrical power exists in the relations between populist leaders and their claimed constituency, 'the people'.

In community development practice it can be tempting to dwell on grievances and draw on resentments as a political strategy to gain concessions and resources for communities, yet the dangers of such strategies are profound. Dwelling on grievances involves a deficit approach to community development in which assets are forgotten and community members are cast as victims (Kretzmann and McKnight, 1996). The deficit approach underplays the agency of citizens and the assets that exist in any society or community. Critically, the populist strategy of amplifying grievances and legitimating resentments sets the backdrop for scapegoating of minority groups, and these are the very groups that community development practitioners work alongside around issues of social justice and human rights.

Finally, with the recognition and validation of the anxieties of ordinary people comes the assertion that populist leaders can speak for the people and solve their problems (Wodak, 2015; Judis, 2016; Muller, 2016). These claims are expressed in many different contexts, including in places where both left- and right-wing politicians are in power. Yet what stands out is the declaration that populist leaders uniquely understand and represent the people and *they alone* can solve their problems. There seems to be a contradiction between commitment to the idea that power resides in the people (the people's sovereignty) and the actions of populist leaders in speaking for them and 'solving their problems'. This apparent contradiction is resolved conceptually by the amalgamation of the people and populists. It is at this point that populism slides into the metaphysical claim that populist leaders *embody* the people. The viewpoint of Chavez, when he was the President of Venezuela, was that he *was* the people (*Sydney Morning Herald*, 2010).

The ability to hear and speak for the people has particular salience in the context of the ways in which populist politicians are able to communicate with the public via the internet, and particularly through social media. It is now possible for leaders to present simple ideas and messages in largely unmediated form, bypassing traditional platforms and institutions such as the daily press and television, which have previously shaped what citizens see and hear. Donald Trump's use of Twitter to present his opinions is perhaps the best known example of such a direct connection. Other populist leaders adept in the use of social media are Beppe Grillo of the Five Star Movement in Italy and Narendra Modi in India.

In so far as major goals of community development are to ensure that citizens have their own voices and can express their needs and visions within their own terms of reference, there are obvious differences in the ways that populism and community development conceptualise the practices of representation. Nevertheless, this does not mean that community development practitioners are always able to facilitate the communities' own voices, rather than 'speak for' them. Certainly, there is a fine line between facilitation, which involves 'giving voice', and the leadership style that involves 'knowing what is best' and 'speaking for'. Such politics of representation are immensely challenging for community development practitioners. There are situations in communities where the advocacy roles of community development practitioners slide into leadership roles. For example, in negotiating for funds from governments and other funding bodies for a community project, community development practitioners are often required to 'speak for' a community.

Populist solutions to the many issues facing citizens today are invariably simplistic. However the issues are complex and the resolutions are never straightforward. As Bauman (2000) and Beck (1992) have elaborated at length, certainty is unattainable in this unsettled world. Rather than offering certainty and proposing simple explanations and uncomplicated solutions to problems, community development literature is cognisant of the complex, dynamic, messy and often contradictory nature the world in which we live.

The challenges

One way of thinking about the complex configurations of relationships between community development and populism is to place them in a societal tension field, where synergies and contradictions coexist. Operating in such a field, community development practitioners are presented with a conundrum concerning how they should react to populist political culture. Given the paradoxical relationships and the multidimensional nature of the issues, it might be tempting to withdraw into the security of academic ambivalence, and to argue that the effects of populism on community development are just too complex to respond to. However, practising community development entails more than critical analyses and ambivalent responses. It also requires taking a standpoint. The standpoint taken in this chapter is that notwithstanding some convergences between community development and populism, overall populism is a threat to community development.

There are now many criticisms of populism, from a variety of perspectives. But for the purposes of this chapter the focus is on the ways in which populism undermines civil society. Civil society can be defined as a self-constituted sphere of social interaction, separate from the state and the market, which is organised around the freedom to associate (Powell, 2007: 7; Kenny et al, 2017). In this sphere, citizens come together in the spirit of mutual respect. They share ideas, raise and discuss issues, critique structures and processes, debate standpoints and possible alternative futures; and organise 'collective action, negotiation and struggle' (Edwards, 2009: loc 132). Civil society sets the backdrop for movements to reinvigorate 'the commons' in which public space and public good are paramount and where principles of collective decision making and ownership can be nurtured. The institutions that comprise civil society are non-government organisations (NGOs) and a range of not-for-profit organisations, including local community organisations; social movements; trade unions; the independent media; and educational institutions. Although many of these institutions have been co-opted to the needs of those in power, they might still offer the best chance we have of practising deep participatory democracy.

Understanding populist assaults on civil society is important for community development, because civil society provides the habitat in which the various forms of community development operate. To understand the ways in which populism threatens civil society, we can begin with the contrast between civil society and populism in regard to pluralism. Civil society celebrates pluralism based on the rights of freedom of thought and action. From a civil society standpoint, human life is enriched by pluralism, including a diversity of viewpoints, ideas, identities and cultures. As part of civil society, community development is organised around a commitment to social and cultural diversity and discussion of different ideas. At the same time, community development acknowledges our shared humanity by promoting social and cultural interconnections and the recognition of mutuality. Populism, especially right-wing populism, is constructed on another view of society altogether. As discussed previously, it is premised on the arguments that people can be classified on the basis of a single identifier and society is divided into homogenous, antagonistic groups. This view involves what Sen (2006) calls a solitarist approach to human identity, which is based on the 'odd presumption that the people of the world can be uniquely categorized according to some singular and overarching system of partitioning' (Sen, 2006: xii). As the solitaristic imaginary works its way into populist political culture, it becomes normalised, providing a frame of reference through which to interact with the social world. This frame of reference facilitates the stigmatisation of Others and the demonisation of elites. It can legitimate uncivil relationships, including behaviours based on deliberate disrespect[4] and what Moffitt (2016) calls bad manners.

Loss of civility in a society is a considerable threat to civil society. When the solitaristic view of the world is applied to the concept of sovereignty, it nurtures nationalism and xenophobia. It sets up zones of conflict which enable the wedge politics that have become the hallmark of populism. Civil society flourishes in pluralist democracies, which not only reject the solitaristic view of the world but also nurture active citizenship through structures and processes for genuine democratic participation in decision making at local and national levels, and perhaps in the future at the global level.

A robust civil society is based on the view that information regarding government activities is freely available and it is possible to call government to account, through the oppositional activities of NGOs, exposure by the media and a judicial system that is able to uphold the rule of law. These institutions are commonly understood as the 'checks and balances' of democracy. They exist in liberal democracies, although in liberal democracies the ability to hold government to account is circumscribed by the cartels of power, particularly where the state is beholden to large corporations. Indeed, one of the factors contributing to the rise of populism has been the ways in which liberal democracies have reinforced the power of these cartels.

Ironically, in populist regimes the checks and balances are similarly eroded, but through the rhetoric that they are not necessary, because the populist leader 'knows what is best for the people'. As indicated previously, the democratic credentials of populist regimes are usually organised around a narrow construction of representative democracy, in which 'the people' can vote in elections, but beyond voting at this level they have little or no say in developing policies that affect them or how a country is run.[5] It is for these reasons that populist regimes can be thought of as ersatz democracies. Given the neglect of the principle of transparency in populist regimes, it is difficult, if not impossible, to successfully call populist governments to account for their actions. For example, recent research undertaken by the *Global Populism Database Composite Study*[6] of 40 countries has revealed the destructive effects of populist governments on press freedom, civil liberties and constraints on executive power (Lewis et al, 2019). The rule of law in the Philippines and Brazil has been eroded to such an extent that extra-judicial killings of suspected drug dealers and criminals have been encouraged by their leaders, Duterte (Cumming-Bruce, 2019) and Bolsanaro (Londono and Andreoni, 2019).

NGOs, which provide organisational settings in which much community development takes place, are often at the forefront of the struggle to maintain a civil society in populist regimes. Paradoxically, they are both attacked by populists and are used to support populist leaders. In Hungary, under the government of the populist party Fidesz, there have been sustained attacks on NGOs since 2013, as part of a campaign to eliminate voices of opposition (Hungarian Civil Liberties Union, 2018). In Brazil, conservative NGOs have been important allies of right-wing populists. They have demonstrated considerable skill in use of social media, with simple, emotional and negative messages (von Bulow, 2018). From a civil society perspective not only do NGOs provide autonomous mediating institutions, as part of activities to keep monopoly power in check, but also spaces for nurturing and articulating diverse views. In a recent blog, John Clarke (2019) contrasts what he calls 'dialogism', which involves talking together, embracing different voices and opening up disparate perspectives on the world, including other ways of thinking and feeling, with monologism, which is 'the singular authoritative voice telling us what to think'. Populism is embedded in monologism, while civil society cultivates informed, active citizens, who are continually wrestling with new questions and puzzles. With monologism comes the erosion of the principles of freedom of thought and action, the undermining of free media, intellectuals and oppositional NGOs, the very institutions of civil society.

Threats to civil society based on the erosion of pluralism, accountability and freedom of thought and action are where considerable dangers to community development lie. When accountability is sabotaged (Glasius, 2018), opposing views are silenced and people are told 'what to think', we have the beginnings of authoritarianism. And when pluralism and dialogism are replaced by a totalising ideology, this opens the way to totalitarianism, which is 'bent on the destruction of humanity', as Arendt (1976: xxvii) pointed out nearly 70 years ago.

Conclusion

In many ways understanding populism and its threats is the easy part for those committed to community development. How to respond is much more difficult, confounding and full of dilemmas. At the end of 2019 it is unclear as to how the 21st century rise of populism will eventually play out. We will need to be doing a lot of thinking and talking about how best to respond to populist views. Reponses require critical self-reflection, including reflecting on the complicity of some community development programmes in accepting neoliberal and managerial agendas.

At the present conjuncture we can identify four interrelated courses of action. First, we can work at the level of discourse, and while acknowledging that there are some points of overlap between community development and populism, we can challenge populist agendas and reframe the way in which experiences and issues are understood. Second, we can endeavour to break down barriers by encouraging discussion (dialogism) between people holding different views and/or coming from different cultures (for example, in situations where migrants and refugees are blamed for job losses). Third, drawing on the power of progressive forces within social media we can organise direct social and political action. Finally, we can connect with wider movements that are mobilising to change the very structures and policies that have contributed to the current social and political conjunctures.

Reframing the discourse requires acknowledging the real anguish of large sections of the population, while at the same time working to shift populist statements of the factors that give rise to the distress. This might involve, for example, explaining how the policy decisions of right-wing governments and the logic of neoliberalism have affected the structure of the labour market, rather than blaming migrants for taking jobs. Of course, attempts to reframe issues must be undertaken sensitively. If not they will be seen to be no different from the patronising attitudes that elites are being accused of. Facilitating exchanges and collaboration between groups with different viewpoints, at the local, national and global level, can break down barriers, and in so doing it can challenge populist assumptions about those who are deemed to be different (Allport, 1954). What is clear, though, is that with the state of the world as it is today we cannot afford to go back to 'business as usual'. The profound failures of democracy cannot be dealt with through a return to liberal democracy as we have known it in the West, as pointed out in the introductory chapter of this book. The existential climate crisis and the deep inequalities cannot be attended to by denial, the rhetoric of 'trust me', or the simple resolutions proffered by populist leaders. If ever there was a time for purposeful change, this is it.

None of the community development responses identified can be taken lightly. For example, reframing understandings and facilitating intercultural exchanges are formidable tasks in the context of discussions with people who hold racist, xenophobic and homophobic views. Moreover, it might be all well and good to be able to reframe people's understandings of the factors contributing to their disadvantaged situation, but understanding itself does not change the structures and policies that have given rise to inequality, disadvantage and distress. Moreover, any critique of populism must be accompanied by an analysis of the very conditions that facilitated its occurrence. Herein lies another issue for community development in responding to populism. The vast myriad of causes of people's disenchantment with the world are largely beyond the control of communities and community development practitioners. Much of the disenchantment, anger and resentment fuelling populism is caused by the unsettling effects of contemporary modernity on society, whether it be the brutal consequences of neoliberal policies or living without certainty. Nonetheless, there are now examples of ways in which communities have fought back against populism, such as through the creative strategies of Operation Libero in Switzerland (Henley, 2019) and the democratic participation and collective ownership initiatives in energy cooperatives in Italy, Spain and Scotland (Kreiger et al, 2017). While we might disagree with some aspects of such projects, we can certainly learn from them. And while community development practitioners are minor players in national and global power politics, they still have a role as part of wider movements challenging the existing populist forces of manipulation and domination. We cannot just sit back in despair and passively watch the continuing ascendancy of populist politics.

Notes

[1] However, it is not exactly the same. Wodak (2015: 2) is concerned with the processes of populist control and influences, in particular the 'dynamics of everyday performances', while at the same time describing right-wing populism as a 'political ideology' (Wodak, 2015: 7). The concept of ideology is not at the forefront of the political culture approach used in this chapter.

[2] For example, in 2016 the pro-Brexit London Daily Mail branded three judges 'enemies of the people' because they had ruled that the UK Government would require the consent of Parliament to trigger Article 50 to begin the UK's exit from the European Union (Phipps, 2016).

[3] There are several exceptions here. For example, Saul Alinsky (1971), an American community organiser working in the mid-20th century, used a binary construct consisting of what he called 'Haves' and 'Have-Nots'. The Marxist tradition in community development emphasises the binary class structure and class struggle. Narratives of struggles against enemies are found in both community organising and Marxist discourse.

[4] Personal attacks on those deemed enemies are commonly used by Donald Trump and Nigel Farage and his associates. An example of disrespect occurred when the Brexit party members of the EU Parliament turned their backs on the chair and the musicians playing the EU anthem 'Ode to Joy' at the opening of the EU Parliament on 2 July 2019 (Rankin, 2019).

5   There are exceptions. For example, Venezuela under Chavez and Bolivia under Morales created participatory institutions to increase citizen's political participation (de la Torre, 2013).

6   This project involves an annual survey of global attitudes in 23 of the world's biggest countries, covering almost 5 billion people. The 2019 survey canvassed 25,325 people online across much of Europe, the Americas, Africa and Asia in February and March. Questions about populist attitudes and convictions were inserted in order to derive a 'populist cohort', and discover what this group of people think about major world issues from immigration to vaccination, social media and globalisation. Those who held strongly populist views comprised 22% of global survey respondents (Lewis et al, 2019).

References

Alinsky (1971) *Rules for Radicals*, New York: Random House.

Allport, G.W. (1954) *The Nature of Prejudice*, Reading, MA: Addison-Wesley.

Arendt, H. (1976) [1951] *The Origins of Totalitarianism*, New York: Schocken.

Bauman, Z. (2016) *Strangers at Our Door*, Cambridge: Polity Press. Kindle edition.

Bauman, Z. (2000) *Liquid Modernity*, Cambridge: Polity Press.

Beck, U. (1992) *Risk Society*, London: Sage.

Clarke, J. (2019) 'Thinking together: encounters with Bakhtin's ghost', 4 August, [online] www.transformingsociety.co.uk/2019/07/15/thinking-together-encounters-with-bakhtins-ghost/

Crick, B. (2013) *In Defence of Politics*, London: Bloomsbury.

Cumming-Bruce, N. (2019) 'U.N. Rights Council to investigate killings in Philippine drug war', *New York Times*, 8 March, [online] www.nytimes.com/2019/07/11/world/asia/philippines-duterte-killings-un.html

De la Torre (2013) 'In the name of the people: democratization, popular organizations, and populism in Venezuela, Bolivia, and Ecuador', *European Review of Latin American and Caribbean Studies* [*Revista Europea deEstudios Latinoamericanos y del Caribe*], 95 (October): 27–48.

De Tocqueville, A. (2000) *Democracy in America*, London: Penguin Books.

Dodge, J. and Ospina, S. (2016) 'Nonprofits as "schools of democracy": a comparative case study of two environmental organizations', *Nonprofit and Voluntary Sector Quarterly*, 45(3): 478–99.

Eatwell, R. and Goodwin, M. (2018) *National Populism: The Revolt against Liberal Democracy*, London: Pelican.

Edwards, M. (2009) *Civil Society* (2nd edn), Cambridge, Polity Press. Kindle edition.

Elkins, D.J. and Simeon, R.E.B. (1979) 'A cause in search of its effect, or what does political culture explain?', *Comparative Politics*, 11(2): 127–45.

Fabian, J. (2017) 'Trump: We're giving power back to the people', *The Hill*, 20 January, [online] https://thehill.com/homenews/administration/315275-trump-were-giving-power-back-to-the-people

Glasius, M. (2018) 'What authoritarianism is … and is not: a practice perspective', *International Affairs*, 94(3): 515–33.

Gregory, A. (2019) 'Brexit Party candidate suggests Remainers should be thrown into the Tower of London', *Independent*, 20 August, [online] www.indy100.com/article/brexit-party-tower-of-london-remainers-traitors-darren-selkus-9071056

Henley, J. (2019) 'Change the narrative: how a Swiss group is beating rightwing populists', *The Guardian*, 7 April, [online] www.theguardian.com/world/2019/apr/07/we-had-to-fight-operation-libero-the-swiss-youth-group-taking-on-populism

Hungarian Civil Liberties Union (2018) 'Hungary steps up its attack on civil society', *Hungarian Civil Liberties Union*, 15 February, [online] www.liberties.eu/en/news/new-governmental-attack-against-civil-society-in-hungary/14374

Judis, J. (2016) *The Populist Explosion. How the Great Recession Transformed American and European Politics*, New York: Columbia Global Reports.

Kenny, S., Taylor, M., Onyx, J. and Mayo, M. (2017) *Challenging the Third Sector: Global Prospects for Active Citizenship*, Bristol: Policy Press.

Kreiger, K., Kropp, M. and Roland Kulke, R. (2017) 'Fighting populism with energy politics – energy cooperatives in Europe', *Global Policy*, 5 May, [online] www.globalpolicyjournal.com/blog/05/05/2017/fighting-populism-energy-politics-%E2%80%93-energy-cooperatives-europe

Kretzmann, J. and McKnight, J.P. (1996) 'Assets based community development', *National Civics Review*, 85(4): 23–9.

Laclau, E. (2005) *On Populist Reason*, London: Verso.

Lewis, P., Clarke, S. and Barr, C. (2019) 'Global Populism Database Composite study', *The Guardian*, 8 March, [online] www.theguardian.com/world/2019/mar/07/revealed-populist-leaders-linked-to-reduced-inequality

Londono, E. and Andreoni, M. (2019) 'Brazil's police "kill five people daily" in brutal crackdown on crime in Rio', *Independent*, 27 May, [online] www.independent.co.uk/news/world/americas/brazil-police-killings-violence-crime-gangs-bolsonaro-witzel-a8931651.html

Markou, G. (2017) 'The left–wing populist revolt in Europe: SYRIZA in power', *Identities: Journal for Politics, Gender and Culture*, 14(1): 148–54.

Moffitt, B. (2016) *The Global Rise of Populism. Performance, Political Style, and Representation*, Palo Alto, CA: Stanford University Press.

Meade, R., Shaw, M. and Banks, S. (2016) 'Politics, power and community development: an introductory essay', in R. Meade, M. Shaw and S. Banks (eds), *Politics, Power and Community Development*, Bristol: Policy Press, pp 1–27.

Mudde, C.(2004) 'The populist zeitgeist', *Government and Opposition*, 39(4): 541–63.

Mudde, C. and Kaltwasser, C. (2017) *Populism: A Very Short Introduction*, Oxford: Oxford University Press.

Muller, J.W. (2016) *What Is Populism?*, Philadelphia: University of Pennsylvania Press. Kindle edition.

Phipps, C. (2016) 'British newspapers react to judges' Brexit ruling: "Enemies of the people"', *The Guardian*, 2 July, [online] www.theguardian.com/politics/2016/nov/04/enemies-of-the-people-british-newspapers-react-judges-brexit-ruling

Powell, F. (2007) *The Politics of Civil Society: Neoliberalism or Social Left*, Bristol: Policy Press.

Rankin, J. (2019) 'Brexit party MEPs turn backs on Ode to Joy at European parliament', *The Guardian*, 2 July, [online] www.theguardian.com/politics/2019/jul/02/brexit-party-meps-turn-their-backs-european-anthem-ode-to-joy

Sen, A. (2006) *Identity and Violence: The Illusion of Destiny*, New York: W.W. Norton.

Shaw, M. (2011) 'Stuck in the middle? Community development, community engagement and the dangerous business of learning for democracy', *Community Development Journal*, 46(S2): ii128–46.

Snow, D.E., Burke, R., Worden, S.K. and Benford, R.D. (1986) 'Frame alignment processes, micromobilization, and movement participation' *American Sociological Review*, 51(4): 464–81.

Sydney Morning Herald (2010) '"I am the people", Chavez tells followers ahead of polls', *Sydney Morning Herald*, 24 January, [online] www.smh.com.au/world/i-am-the-people-chavez-tells-followers-ahead-of-polls-20100124-mryf.html

Url, T. (2019) 'The populist rise of Turkey's Erdoğan', *Aval*, 11 March, [online] https://ahvalnews.com/recep-tayyip-erdogan/populist-rise-turkeys-erdogan

Von Bülow, M. (2018) 'The empowerment of conservative civil society in Brazil', Carnegie Endowment for International Peace, 4 October, [online] https://carnegieeurope.eu/2018/10/04/empowerment-of-conservative-civil-society-in-brazil-pub-77371

Warren, M.E. (2001) *Democracy and Association*, Princeton, NJ: Princeton University Press.

Withnall, A. (2016) 'EU referendum: Nigel Farage's 4am victory speech – the text in full', *Independent*, 24 June, [online] www.independent.co.uk/news/uk/politics/eu-referendum-nigel-farage-4am-victory-speech-the-text-in-full-a7099156.html

Wodak, R. (2015) *The Politics of Fear: What Right-Wing Populist Discourses Mean*, London: Sage.

Wysocka, O. (2009) 'Populism in Poland: in/visible exclusion', in I*n/visibility: Perspectives on Inclusion and Exclusion*, IWM Junior Visiting Fellows' Conferences, Vol 26, Vienna: Institute for Human Sciences.

THREE

Right-wing populism and community development: beyond modernity and liberal democracy

Jim Ife

An important understanding of right-wing populism was developed by Berlet and Lyons (2016). Their analysis, specifically grounded in the US experience, suggests that the everyday followers of right-wing populism identify as 'producerist': they see themselves as doing 'real', 'productive' work, in the 'real world'. Typically, they are either small business owners or people employed in some kind of productive work. They have a mistrust of perceived 'elites', which include politicians, big business, professionals, intellectuals, academics, corporate leaders, Jews, mainstream media and government employees. These elites are seen as out of touch with the 'real world' inhabited by the producerists. They are therefore regarded as parasites, drawing wealth and power from the people, and their very existence is a reason why the right-wing producerists believe they are not doing as well as they should. This leads to a mistrust of expertise, of political leadership, of mainstream media and of conventional authority (Canovan, 1999; Taggart, 2000; Betz, 2013; Jansen, 2013; Wodak et al, 2015). Producerists can readily see all that is corrupt and unjust about liberal democratic institutions, and they have good reason to be critical of those in authority, who they see as having sold out the producerists for their own interests. This mistrust of elites has a strong appeal, with faint echoes both of socialist revolution and of anarchism, sometimes fuelled by anti-Semitism, and is readily adopted by new converts to populist causes. It has effectively contributed to politicians, bureaucrats, experts and academic researchers losing some of the authority they traditionally enjoyed, largely unquestioned, in public discourse.

The producerists also identify another group of threatening 'parasites', namely the welfare cheats, immigrants, people of colour, the unemployed, refugees, addicts, and others seen as sponging off the system and threatening the livelihood and well-being of the 'real people' (Wodak, 2015; Winberg, 2017; Vigil and Vigil, 2019). This is the group Marxists have understood as the *lumpenproletariat*, the group at the 'bottom' of society with no revolutionary potential (Khanna, 2013). It is the group that is readily vilified through racist narratives, hence the appeal to many populists of white supremacy or Islamophobia.

There is thus a producerist construction of the 'real world', inhabited by 'real people' who do 'real things', have 'real jobs' and lead 'real lives' (Rapley, 1998). The 'parasites' both above and below are excluded from this 'real world' and threaten its viability. The producerists – to whom right-wing populism appeals – thus feel threatened from both above and below (Sakki and Pettersson, 2015). This threat leads some to extreme responses, such as joining alt-right, racist or anti-immigration groups, while others will simply express their discontent through the ballot box or through social media.

Such a perspective on right-wing populism indicates the difficulties facing community development in this space. Community development is on the one hand open to populist mistrust in terms of expertise – it is after all taught in universities, has some of the status of a profession, and draws legitimacy from traditional liberal democratic institutions. On the other hand, community development is often identified with those excluded from the society, and works with immigrant groups, unemployed groups, welfare recipients, and so on; these are the people scorned and victimised by many right-wing populists. Indeed, the 'producerists' are often those who have also been forgotten by community development. Community development has identified itself as working with the most marginalised in society, as a result of its 'welfare' orientation and mandate to address social problems, and has also identified itself with more politically progressive movements for social change, such as anti-racism, feminism, Indigenous land rights, pro-LGBTIQ (Lesbian, Gay, Bisexual Transsexual, Intersex, Queer) rights, refugee rights, environmentalism, and so on (Ife, 2016). In both of these it positions itself as supporting the 'parasites' so mistrusted by right-wing populism.

Such a positioning of community development suggests that community development is as much an anathema to right-wing populists as right-wing populism is to community development workers, and that the two are fundamentally opposed. But we can also see that the relationship is more complex than this, and it is not a simple oppositional binary. The remainder of this chapter will consider the relationship between them first in relation to the crisis in modernity, and then more specifically in relation to one aspect of that crisis, namely the erosion of the legitimacy and the institutions of liberal democracy. This will lead to some suggestions of how community development might move to address some of these issues and retain both its relevance and its integrity in a world where right-wing populism will be a continuing presence.

Right-wing populism and modernity

Enlightenment modernity has had a profound influence on western, and increasingly non-western, thought. It has focused on science, rationality, progress, secularism, and universalising narratives, seeking to classify, order and thus 'manage' the world (Edelstein, 2010). Right-wing populism can be seen as a reaction against modernity, and a yearning for pre-modern times. It often embraces fundamentalist religion (especially, though not exclusively, Christianity) as part of its reaction against the 'elites' who epitomise secularism, rationality and science (Hind, 2007; Edelstein, 2010; Pelinka, 2015: 15; Marzouki et al, 2016). The universalist knowledge of Enlightenment modernity is replaced by local knowledge and experience (the 'real world'), by religious teaching and by accepted 'home truths'. Modernity, with its universalising narratives, is seen as threatening to these comfortable and reassuring world views (often based on unexamined racism, sexism, heteronormativity and colonialism, of course), and as a result populism retreats from the perceived dangers and challenges of modernity, in a profoundly conservative reaction, seeking desperately to hold on to received knowledges and narratives of the familiar. Climate change denial, common among many right-wing populists, can be readily explained in this way (Akkerman, 2003; Lockwood, 2018).

Yet right-wing populism, as well as a retreat *from* modernity, can also be seen as a retreat *into* modernity (see Sim, 2004). Right-wing populism, like other forms of fundamentalism, is at heart a search for certainty (Nicholson, 1999; Stove, 2003). The retreat from modernity described previously is a retreat into the certainties of pre-modernity, where truth could be received rather than having to be argued and discovered. The uncertainties of post-modernity are even more frightening though, and the post-modern world can be seen as fragmented and uncertain; modernity, after all, seeks certainty and predictability, and so there are aspects of it that are appealing to right-wing populism.

This ambivalence towards modernity is an important contradiction of right-wing populism. Populists will accept some aspects of modernity but not others, depending on whether or not they reinforce or upset the populist world view. And different populist groups may vary in the extent to which they embrace or resist modernity. But identifying the contradiction is important in terms of developing strategies that may challenge right-wing populism, from a community development perspective.

Community development and modernity

It is important to note that, like right-wing populism, community development also has an ambivalent relationship to modernity. Its development as a designated area of practice and expertise, at least in western cultural contexts, has taken place within modernity's world view. It has sought rationality, it has a research base, it is taught in universities, and much of its knowledge base was established, uncritically, within the epistemological assumptions of Enlightenment modernity (Ife, 2016). The very word 'development' in the name can imply an ideal of linear progress, and in many ways community development remains a project of modernity.

On the other hand, modernity has been a problem for community development. The rational, ordered, predictable world of modernity is far removed from the reality of community development practice: communities are typically chaotic, contradictory, messy and unpredictable. Community development workers work with this chaos and messiness, and indeed it is the ability of community workers to work in this environment that marks them out as especially skilled. Community development, therefore, also stands against modernity and its universalising project. For many community workers, post-modernism has helped to make sense of community work, as it accepts diversity, multiple narratives, contradiction and unpredictability. Those community workers who deliberately resist an outcome focus driving their work, and who instead concentrate on the integrity of process, on the assumption that a good process will achieve a good outcome, are in fact questioning the world view of modernity, with its focus on certainty, predictability and clear objectives.

Thus, like right-wing populism, community development has something of an ambivalent relationship with modernity. On the one hand it operates within the parameters of modernity, but at the same time it questions them, and more progressive community workers seek to work outside those limitations (Geoghegan and Powell, 2009).

Possible dialogue?

If both right-wing populism and community development share ambivalent relationships to modernity, does this provide a space for potential dialogue, for community workers to seek to understand the reality of right-wing populism, and for populists to learn something from the community experience of community development? After all, there are some commonalities in the rhetoric. Both community development and right-wing populism accept and emphasise the importance of the local, and of lived experience. Both like to talk about the central importance of something called 'community'. Both support the 'voice of the people' and make worthy pronouncements about maximising participation. Both are suspicious of globalisation, neoliberalism and the impacts of global capital. And both encourage a mistrust of elites, and prefer 'bottom-up' initiatives.

I would suggest, however, that these similarities are more apparent than real, and that they do not constitute useful grounds for dialogue. First, right-wing populism has a much more superficial understanding of participation; indeed, it is more of a 'karaoke' form of participation, singing along, following the lines while the tune is played by someone else (Kunnen, 2005). Community development workers understand participation in a much more sophisticated way, using a power analysis that is absent from populist rhetoric. While both community development and right-wing populism articulate an opposition to neoliberalism and global capital, they do so from different perspectives, and the alternatives they propose are different, based on very different values. Right-wing populism has accepted the individualism of the dominant order, and supports individualist notions of 'freedom' (Panizza, 2005: 30; Pelinka, 2015; Heywood, 2017: 64), without the more collectivist and holistic understandings commonly used by community workers. This has enabled right-wing populist leaders to argue that their ideal world is the only possible alternative to the dominant order (Taggart, 2000: 21; Kelsey, 2015; Mounk, 2018); this simplistic message had been tacitly accepted by many followers of populist movements and makes dialogue around alternatives very difficult. Similarly, the right-wing populist critique of globalisation allows no space for more nuanced positions about internationalism or cosmopolitanism (Pelinka, 2015; Heywood, 2017: 92). And the racism, sexism, heteronormativity and other forms of prejudice, so entrenched in the right-wing populist view of the 'parasites', has no place within the values of community development.

These are all reasons why the apparent common ground between community development and right-wing populism is more apparent than real, and why dialogue would be extremely difficult. But even more important is the fundamentalist nature of right-wing populism. Populists readily become fundamentalists (Di Tella, 1997; Mounk, 2018): they insist on seeing the world through only one set of lenses, they seek simple straightforward solutions without question, they believe strongly in the 'truth' of their position, they know they are right, they often accept the word of the charismatic leader, and they see their role as not to engage in dialogue, but to convince others of the one true way. These are characteristic of fundamentalists of all kinds, and they make dialogue all but impossible (Sim, 2004). For genuine dialogue to occur, both parties have to commit to respecting and exploring the views of the other, and however much community workers might wish to enter a respectful dialogue in this way, right-wing populists will not. Indeed, the recent history of right-wing politics is one of refusal to compromise or to dialogue. The experience of former Australian Prime Minister Malcolm Turnbull is instructive in this regard (Ife, 2018). He became leader of a conservative political party, in which his own relatively moderate and socially progressive views were opposed by many of his more right-wing colleagues. In an attempt at consensus leadership, he was prepared to compromise, but found that they were not willing to reciprocate, seeing his concessions as a sign of weakness and holding fast to their right-wing demands. Malcolm Turnbull found he was giving up a lot, receiving little or nothing in return, and continually facing more extreme demands from the right of his party. Eventually his position became untenable, and he was seen by many as selling out on his principles for the sake of political power. This is the likely fate of those who would seek to dialogue and compromise with the political right in the name of inclusion and consensus. Right-wing leaders, and also their followers, simply are not interested in accepting the preconditions for genuine dialogue.

The erosion of liberal democracy

While the aforementioned analysis of modernity indicated some superficial commonalities between community development and right-wing populism, a focus more specifically on liberal democracy shows up a sharper differentiation and underlines their incompatibility. This section will argue that right-wing populism is a response to the erosion of liberal democracy, while community development has largely remained within the liberal democratic discourse. If community development is to remain relevant in the coming decades, it will need to come to terms with its liberal democratic assumptions and reformulate both its ideas and its practices. If so, it will be likely to cope more effectively with the challenges of right-wing populism.

Much of the mainstream opposition to right-wing populism has concentrated on strengthening and using liberal democratic principles to counter this trend, assuming that liberal democratic institutions, if supported and reinforced, can create a more equitable and sustainable society (Galston, 2018). This has resulted in campaigns to elect anti-populist candidates, use of legal processes to try to halt right-wing agendas, referring to historical precedent, research projects and publications, public events sponsored by universities and other research/policy institutions, peaceful demonstrations, comments in the media – whether newspapers, radio, television or online – and so on. These amount to appeals to reason, assuming that in the 'marketplace of ideas' right-wing populism can readily be shown to be both inadequate and dangerous (Pelinka, 2015: 17). Yet this has had only limited success, as seen in its most extreme form in the inability of liberal institutions in the USA to counter the momentum of Donald Trump. This reliance on the mechanisms and institutions of liberal democracy to counter right-wing populism is a flawed project, given the ways in which the principles of liberal democracy have been corrupted, and are continuing to be corrupted, by the forces of neoliberalism and by powerful vested interests (Taggart, 2000: 21).

At this point I will briefly outline some of the principles of the liberal democratic project, often accepted uncritically as the 'natural' way to do things, but which are currently being eroded and compromised by the forces of neoliberalism and which no longer have the legitimacy and authority that they could claim in the twentieth century. These do not all apply to every national context, but taken together they represent a serious crisis in liberal democracy.

- *Elections* are at the core of the liberal democratic project and are used by governments to claim legitimacy for their actions. Yet elections are commonly compromised by manipulated electoral boundaries, vote rigging, fraud, and by false or misleading information (magnified by conservative media groups and social media).
- *An educated and engaged citizenry* is a requirement for representative democracy, yet 'education' is increasingly seen as preparation for a job rather than for citizenship, and the level of political disengagement in many jurisdictions means that well-informed views are frequently swamped by ignorance and prejudice.
- *Benign governments of goodwill* is another liberal democratic assumption that is now in question. Governments do not always act with the welfare of their citizens as their first priority, as is seen

with austerity policies and the steady erosion of welfare states in many western democracies.

- *The separation of powers* is a foundational principle of liberal democracy, yet the boundaries between the government, the executive and the judiciary have been steadily weakened in many jurisdictions, for example through the politicisation of the civil service, political attacks on the judiciary and so on. And indeed all are further corrupted by the pervasiveness of private sector interests.
- *The separation of church and state* has been seen as critical for liberal democracy since the time of Jefferson. Yet this is increasingly eroded through the pervasive influence of conservative and fundamentalist forms of Christianity (and, in non-western cultures, of other religions) in matters of government.
- *National sovereignty* is another core principle of the liberal democratic tradition; we assume that the government we elect will be free to act in the national interest. But the economic power of transnational capital, and of the economic, political and military power of a few powerful nations, has effectively undermined national sovereignty, leaving it as a myth propagated by political leaders clinging to the illusion of power.
- *Public accountability* is another assumption of liberal democracy, now more apparent than real. It has been eroded by increasing privatisation which hides key decisions under the guise of commercial confidentiality, increasing resort to 'national security' as an excuse for secrecy, and the legal and public harassment of whistle-blowers.
- *A free and responsible press* is often heralded as a key component of liberal democracy, yet concentration of media ownership, the vested interests of media corporations, and government harassment of independent media have rendered press freedom a myth rather than a reality.
- *Research and evidence-based policy* is a long-held ideal, and the basis of much research both in universities and elsewhere. Yet research and evidence are consistently trumped by ideology in most areas of government. One need only examine climate change policy or policy on drug abuse to see how readily research and rational analysis are side-lined when they don't suit a political agenda. University research is seemingly still based on this premise, though the corporatisation of universities and increasing reliance on business partnerships and corporate research funding has meant that they can no longer be regarded as neutral players.

- *Public debate*, necessary if liberal democracy is to be participatory as well as representative, is effectively mediated by powerful interests, specifically media owners, editors, producers and journalists, who not only set the agenda but also define the limits of what is 'reasonable'. Social media has provided an alternative forum, but here the very lack of mediation produces an environment of trolls, vicious personal attacks, insults and defamation; providing a lesson in how ill-prepared many people are to engage in respectful debate with others.

- *Human rights* are seen as central to the liberal democratic project. If citizens have universal and inalienable rights, those rights can be exercised, and human dignity can be guaranteed. However, there has been significant evasion of state responsibilities for the protection and realisation of those rights. Human rights may be a nice idea, but the reality is that they are regularly and flagrantly breached, in virtually all jurisdictions. They are hardly a robust basis for liberal democracy.

In summary, the liberal democratic tradition is in crisis, and its legitimacy has been seriously eroded. Right-wing populism has been a reaction to this. The mistrust of 'elites' that is a key part of the populist narrative is justified; those elites are no longer delivering their promised benefits and safety nets, but rather are seen as working against the interests of the citizenry. This has led to protest votes against people like Hillary Clinton and others who represent the liberal democratic status quo (Taggart, 2000: 94; Mounk, 2018). While some of the populist attacks on the 'elites' are undoubtedly exaggerations, there is also a legitimacy to the populist complaint. The institutions of liberal democracy, represented by the perceived 'elites', have been found wanting, and some form of revolt is justified. The rise of right-wing populism, therefore, is hardly surprising. For this reason, it is futile, and indeed counterproductive, to address right-wing populism by an appeal to the liberal democratic institutions that are still accepted as the political norm. Populists will be largely deaf to calls for reasoned debate, research-based policy, public accountability, public education, and so on. These are seen as having failed, and so do not provide a solution to the grievances that many followers of populist causes harbour (Mounk, 2018).

A major obstacle to moving forward in adequately addressing populism is thus the persistence of a belief in liberal democratic institutions. Politicians, journalists, opinion leaders, commentators, academics and many social movement leaders continue to believe in those institutions and to pretend that they are still working reasonably well and can be the mechanism for addressing the challenges facing society. They put a good deal of energy into electoral campaigns, public advocacy, policy research and rational analysis. This is in spite of the evident policy paralysis on significant challenges such as climate change and Brexit, and the irrelevance of much policy analysis and research when policies are actually designed and implemented. Liberal democracy has become so much the assumed background, and has been part of the socialisation of the 'political' class and the 'academic' class, that its increasing inadequacies are often overlooked, and solutions to problems, including the 'problem' of populism itself, are framed in liberal democratic terms (Canovan, 2004): the appeal to reason, the need for research, rational debate, reliance on the goodwill of policy makers, and so on.

Community development, it can be argued, is also trapped within the paradigm of liberal democracy. It has assumed the primacy of civil society, operating within a framework of rational debate, research and representative democracy, working to help communities become better resourced within that system (Mowbray, 2011; Shaw, 2012; Ife, 2016). Typically, community workers will help communities lobby politicians, seek resources from benevolent governments, organise petitions, advocate, use the mainstream media, and use the legal system to achieve their rights. Like other representatives of the 'elites' so mistrusted by populists, community development workers continue to accept the institutions, practices and narratives of liberal democracy as the context of their work. Despite longstanding academic critiques of liberal democracy, from both the left and the right, it has remained largely unquestioned by most, though not all, community workers (Ledwith, 2005; Shaw, 2011). Even more 'radical' approaches to community work have often accepted liberal democracy as defining what is normal and acceptable, and the term 'radical' is applied more to methods and tactics than to the philosophical basis for community development. Alinsky perhaps represents the most extreme example (Ledwith, 2005: 89): he was a self-defined radical, yet his assumptions about how society works remained firmly within the liberal democratic tradition.

We must therefore ask how long community development will remain with those who are pretending, with increasing desperation, that liberal democracy is still working well. Right-wing populism has been able to identify many of the weaknesses and inadequacies of liberal democracy, recognising that it is no longer meeting the needs of many people and communities, and perhaps community development now needs to take these critiques seriously, and find ways that it can stop being part of the problem and instead become part of a solution, though not the solution advocated by right-wing populism as the only real alternative.

Possibilities for creative community development

Community development thus needs to break free from the constraints of liberal democracy, and establish itself within different paradigms for practice, if it is to remain relevant in a world facing multiple serious crises, where many traditional institutions are falling apart, and where it faces the challenge of right-wing populism. It is important to accept, at least in part, the populist critique of the weakness of liberal democracy, but not to accept the populist prescription as the only viable alternative. Rather than seeking to address right-wing populism directly, and risk accepting the premises of either right-wing populism itself, or of liberal democracy as the traditional framework of opposition, community development – workers, academics and researchers – can instead articulate a creative alternative, more consistent with a value base of human rights, social justice and sustainability (Ledwith, 2005; Mowbray, 2011; Ife, 2016). Such an alternative vision moves beyond liberal democracy, but is in sharp contrast to that of right-wing populism. Rather than reacting to right-wing populism, therefore, community development can be active in helping to formulate alternative ways forward (Ledwith, 2005; Shaw, 2008; Ife, 2016). Community development, however, is not alone in this task. The articulation of such an alternative vision has become a major project involving progressive thinkers not just in progressive politics, but in fields as diverse as economics, agriculture, biology, ecology, climate science, engineering, cognitive science and theology.

An interesting feature of this writing is that many authors advocate 'community' as the most promising direction for a future based on sustainability and social justice (Ledwith, 2005; Mowbray, 2011). Resilient, sustainable communities are identified as the key to the future, and grassroots community action is regarded as necessary in moving beyond the failings of liberal democracy. This positions community development at front and centre of movements for progressive change.

This, then, suggests a more positive and less reactive response to right-wing populism by community development workers, academics, researchers and teachers. It sees community development as playing a key role within social movements that are working towards more holistic, sustainable, equitable and ecocentric world views. In so doing, community development is able to draw on a range of knowledge, principles and skills, which it can contribute to these movements. There is not space in this chapter to explore these in detail, but this is familiar territory for community development, and does not require much elaboration here. They can briefly be described as follows.

- The reinvention of democracy, from the old and corrupted representative model to a more genuinely participatory approach.
- Working with disasters – an area where community development already makes a substantial contribution, to counter the effects of disaster capitalism (Klein, 2007) and to use the opportunity to strengthen community.
- Working towards a new internationalism or cosmopolitanism, to replace globalisation and its purely economic emphasis in the interests of global capital, recognising the importance of genuinely local/global practice.
- Critiquing purely economic models of 'development' in favour of ideas of human flourishing.
- Recognising that 'community' can and should include the non-human world and the rights of Mother Earth.
- Recognising the importance of Indigenous knowledge systems and understandings of community as essential in the transition away from the anthropocentric growth and exploitation of modernity.
- Affirming the significance of relational reality (Gergen, 2000; Spretnak, 2011) and relationships, rather than the autonomous individual of the Cartesian world view.
- Celebrating and valuing difference and diversity as necessary for human and non-human flourishing.
- Challenging racism, misogyny, heteronormativity, ageism, ableism and other forms of discrimination, at individual, community and structural levels.
- Incorporating the creative arts as essential for human flourishing and human community.
- Recognising that we are happier, healthier and more human when we are giving and sharing, rather than when we are getting and taking, and using this as a basis for community.
- Asserting the importance of the public: public space, public ownership, public good, and so on, rather than private profit.

None of these is new for community development, although some may represent a minority position among community workers. Community development has established expertise across all these areas, and it is this expertise that many social movement activists are seeking. This, it is argued here, is a far stronger and more robust response to right-wing populism than simply trying to react and respond within the limitations of modernity and liberal democracy.

References

Akkerman, T. (2003) 'Populism and democracy: challenge or pathology?', *Acta Politica*, 38(2): 147–59.

Berlet, C. and Lyons, M. (2016) *Right-Wing Populism in America: Too Close for Comfort*, New York: Guilford Press, www.rightwingpopulism.us

Betz, H-G. (2013) 'A distant mirror: nineteenth-century populism, nativism, and contemporary right-wing radical politics', *Democracy and Security*, 9(3): 200–220.

Canovan, M. (1999) 'Trust the people! Populism and the two faces of democracy', *Political Studies*, 47(1): 2–16.

Canovan, M. (2004) 'Populism for political theorists?', *Journal of Political Ideologies*, 9(3): 241–52.

Di Tella, T.S. (1997) 'Populism into the twenty-first century', *Government and Opposition*, 32(2): 187–200.

Edelstein, D. (2010) *The Enlightenment: A Genealogy*, Chicago, IL: University of Chicago Press.

Galston, W. (2018) *Anti-Pluralism: The Populist Threat to Liberal Democracy*, New Haven, CT: Yale University Press.

Geoghegan, M. and Powell, F. (2009) 'Community development and the contested politics of the late modern "agora": of, alongside or against neoliberalism?', *Community Development Journal*, 44(4): 430–47.

Gergen, K. (2000) *Relational Being*, New York: Oxford University Press.

Heywood, A. (2017) *Political Ideologies: An Introduction* (6th edn), London: Palgrave.

Hind, D. (2007) *The Threat to Reason: How the Enlightenment Was Hijacked, and how We Can Reclaim It*, London: Verso.

Ife, J. (2016) *Community Development in an Uncertain World: Vision, Analysis and Practice* (2nd edn), Port Melbourne, VIC: Cambridge University Press.

Ife, J. (2018) 'Right-wing populism and social work: contrasting ambivalences about modernity', *Journal of Human Rights and Social Work*, 3(3): 121–7.

Jansen, R. (2013) 'Populist mobilisation: a new theoretical approach to populism', *Sociological Theory*, 29(2): 79–96.

Kelsey, D. (2015) 'Hero mythology and right-wing populism: a discourse-mythological case study of Nigel Farage in the Mail Online', *Journalism Studies*, 17(8): 971–88.

Khanna, R. (2013) 'The lumpenproletariat, the subaltern, the mental asylum', *South Atlantic Quarterly*, 112(1): 129–43.

Klein, N. (2007) *The Shock Doctrine: The Rise of Disaster Capitalism*, London: Allen Lane.

Kunnen, N. (2005) 'Participation in community practice: karaoke or fugue?', PhD thesis, Curtin University, Perth, WA.

Ledwith, M. (2005) *Community Development: A Critical Approach*, Bristol: Policy Press.

Lockwood, M. (2018) 'Right-wing populism and the climate change agenda: exploring the linkages', *Environmental Politics*, 27(4): 712–32.

Marzouki, N., McDonnell, D. and Roy, O. (eds) (2016) *Saving the People: How Populists Hijack Religion*, London: Hurst.

Mounk, Y. (2018) *The People vs Democracy: Why Our Freedom Is in Danger and how to Save It*, Cambridge, MA: Harvard University Press.

Mowbray, M. (2011) 'What became of *The Local State*? Neoliberalism, community development and local government', *Community Development Journal*, 46(S1): i132–i153.

Nicholson, L. (1999) *The Play of Reason: From the Modern to the Postmodern*, Buckingham: Open University Press.

Panizza, F. (ed) (2005) *Populism and the Mirror of Democracy*, London: Verso.

Pelinka, A. (2015) 'Right-wing populism: concept and typology', in R. Wodak, M. KhosraviNik and B. Mral (eds), *Right-Wing Populism in Europe: Politics and Discourse*, London: Bloomsbury Academic, pp 3–22.

Rapley, M. (1998) ' "Just an ordinary Australian": self-categorisation and the discursive construction of facticity in "new racist" political rhetoric', *British Journal of Social Psychology*, 37: 325–44.

Sakki, I. and Pettersson, K. (2015) 'Discursive constructions of otherness in populist radical right political blogs', *European Journal of Social Psychology*, 46(2): 156–70.

Shaw, M. (2008) 'Community development and the politics of community', *Community Development Journal*, 43(1): 24–36.

Shaw, M. (2011) 'Stuck in the middle? Community development, community engagement and the dangerous business of learning for democracy', *Community Development Journal*, 46(S2): ii128–ii146.

Shaw, M. (2012) 'Community work today: contested rationalities, competing practices', in J.P. Rothe, L.J. Carroll and D. Ozegovic (eds), *Deliberations in Community Development: Balancing on the Edge*, New York: Nova Science.

Sim, S. (2004) *Fundamentalist World: The New Dark Age of Dogma*, Crow's Nest, NSW: Allen & Unwin.

Spretnak, C. (2011) *Relational Reality: New Discoveries of Interrelatedness That Are Shaping the Modern World*, Topsham, ME: Green Horizon Books.

Stove, D. (2003) *On Enlightenment*, New Brunswick, NJ: Transaction Publishers.

Taggart, P. (2000) *Populism*, Buckingham: Open University Press.

Vigil, J.D. and Vigil, N.L. (2019) 'Continuity of American xenophobia under Trump and plausible alternatives', in W.S. DeKeseredy and E. Currie (eds), *Progressive Justice in an Age of Repression: Strategies for Challenging the Rise of the Right*, New York: Routledge.

Winberg, O. (2017) 'Insult politics: Donald Trump, right-wing populism, and incendiary language', *European Journal of American Studies*, 12(2), [online] https://doi.org/10.4000/ejas.12132

Wodak, R. (2015) *The Politics of Fear: What Right-Wing Populist Discourses Mean*, London: SAGE.

Wodak, R., KhosraviNik, M. and Mral, B. (eds) (2015) *Right-Wing Populism in Europe: Politics and Discourse*, London: Bloomsbury Academic.

FOUR

A radical community development response to right-wing populism

Peter Westoby

Introduction

This has been one of the hardest chapters I have ever tried to write in my scholarly life. Many times I have lost my way. At times, I truly pondered if community development praxis has any effective response to the large forces underpinning, and the actual phenomenon of, contemporary right-wing populism. There are large national and international forces that have been at work, shaping changes for 30-plus years, and that now manifest in clearly visible right-wing populist forms. And such sociopolitical–economic forces are now amplified by the challenge of climate change. How can such forces be stopped, or nudged in a different direction, and how can the *humble approach* of community development contribute to any kind of shift at all?

In writing this chapter I have also had to reassess many assumptions or myths about right-wing populism. Data and other scholarly work convinced me that I had made many false assumptions – for instance, that people who vote for national right-wing populists, such as for Brexit, are in a 'protest vote' (against the 'system', rather than for something). The data suggests otherwise, that most people who voted for national populists knew exactly what they voted for – for example, for reducing immigration, for 'walls', for welfare reform that such voters perceived to be favouring newly arrived refugees and so forth (Eatwell and Goodwin, 2018: 29ff). However, not all my assumptions were wrong – for example, most of the 'whites' who voted for Trump in the USA and for Brexit in the UK were less educated (that is, they did have high school education, but not university graduate education), so there are links between education levels and voting for right-wing national populists (Schultz, 2017: 9).

The point of saying this in the introduction to this chapter is that in my rethinking community development's response to contemporary right-wing populism, I am endeavouring to be 'data-driven', rather than ideologically driven, which implies interrogating myths, easy tropes and unsound ideas. But data-driven does not imply value neutrality either.

In doing this, I have pondered, mused, wandered and gone down many cul-de-sacs, but have eventually tried to craft a pragmatic yet radical response for community development praxis. As said, this does not suggest a value-free or value-neutral approach, but it does posit that while I argue for a particularly Freirean or critical community development tradition (Ledwith, 2015), I also want community development practitioners to be effective. At the same time I acknowledge community development praxis has both a methodology – within a Freirean tradition (Freire, 1972) this is a methodology of 'circle work' in which people come together in localities to make sense of their world in dialogue – and also an analysis. It is important that the analysis be as accurate as possible so that the methodology can be more effective.

Within this frame of 'method' and 'analysis' the methodology implies that the community development practitioner and the people come together (the methodology is a relational method of supporting people to come together in circle work) to 'do analysis' (see Westoby and Dowling, 2013; Kelly and Westoby, 2018). Their choices of what to do, of strategising for change, emerges from their analysis. And again, this analysis needs to be accurate.

Which brings us to a tension within community development theory. The tension emerges from two agendas. The first agenda is indicative of the need for people to be free to make their own analysis, that is, 'analysis from below', based on their experiences. If a community development practitioner is supporting people in a place to come together to make sense of their reality, then the practitioner is supporting those people to 'do their analysis'. It is, to use a Freirean meme, 'to start with the people'. But the second agenda is the analysis of the practitioner, which emerges not just from local experience, but from immersion in many other contexts (for example, professional training, being a member of a national network, or attending conferences and learning some new ideas, or gaining new information). Within this chapter it is argued that such a practitioner analysis needs to be informed by scholarly work. This enables the practitioner to insert into the circle work of the people some 'new ideas, or new information', as popular education describes it. This in no way implies that the 'people', as construed here, are not also searching for information, or attending their own networks and so forth. It is simply implied that, as an academic or scholar of community development, I can influence the practitioner more than I can 'the people' – you, the reader of this chapter, are more likely to be a professional (or on your way to becoming one). As such, I can insist that the practitioner, with an ethos of 'democratic professionalism' (Banks, 2019: 21) – with all the implications of on-going professional training, learning, reading and power sharing, be up-to-date on their thinking. I cannot insist on the same thing for citizens. Which of course is a challenge in itself, because, as A.C. Grayling points out, democracy relies on education, an informed citizenship (Grayling, 2017).

However, we are getting ahead of ourselves. What community development's response might be will be revisited towards the second half of this chapter. First, we will consider the literature's analysis of right-wing populism.

Some myths and propositions

Consider the following propositions:

- Eventually old white men will die off and be replaced by tolerant millennials.
- National populism is fuelled by the unemployed and those on low incomes.
- All the turbulence is a result of the 2008 financial crisis.

As examples, these propositions can be debunked by data. For example, according to Eatwell and Goodwin (2018: 4), 'during the US primaries, the median household income of a Trump voter was $72,000, compared to $61,000 for supporters of Hillary Clinton'. Other economic data confirms that unemployment is not so much the issue comparable to education levels (which are influential) (Eatwell and Goodwin, 2018. 25–9). The third proposition above, what is referred to as the 'crisis narrative', is also problematic. While such crisis did help national populists in their agendas, the data suggests something much more complex. Again, many countries that did experience economic crisis around 2008 did not see successful nationalist-populist uprisings (Eatwell and Goodwin, 2018: 7). Also, many upsurges occurred where the crisis did not lead to high unemployment (for example, Austria, the Netherlands and Switzerland). In contrast, this chapter takes the view that the trends that sit below this now visible upsurge of populism have been on track for a long time, well before the 2008 financial crisis. Finally, take the first proposition above, of angry old men. It is certainly a convenient one, for it would imply that no actual *ideas* of national populists need to be engaged. In this framing, demographics will take care of the problem. Again, however, the proposition fails to be true under scrutiny. For example, within the US, no less than 41% of millennials turned out for Trump (yes, they generally lacked college degrees), but the point is that many millennials are as concerned about immigration as their ageing parents or grandparents (Eatwell and Goodwin, 2018: xxvii).

Overall, typically myths about right-wing populism are linked to a 'one cause' argument – whether it be the economic cause, or the educational (that is, it is because of the economic crisis or due to low education levels). This is to fall into the trap of simplifying what is actually a complex, multifaceted phenomenon. This chapter acknowledges such complexity and probes for an accurate analysis that can support community development practitioners in their efforts with local communities.

What I mean by right-wing populism – characteristics

Previous writing have referred to these populist impulses as 'nativist', 'sham' and 'malignant populism' (Westoby, 2018). Others have called it 'authoritarian populism' referring to Hall's seminal work in the 1970s and 1980s, trying to make sense of the movements behind the rise of Thatcherism (Hall and Jacques, 1983). Importantly, as per Hall's historical approach, populism, like community development, is not a thing and is therefore not a concept to be imposed on history, but is a contextual concept understood within historical processes (Finchelstein, 2017: 128).

My approach is that populism is not necessarily a bad thing in itself, often with potential radical and egalitarian energies. Referring to the aforementioned work of Hall, Wendy Wolford (2014) suggests that:

> 'Authoritarian populism' describes a broad politics, resonant with appeals to 'common sense' and 'the people', and replete with imagery of imagined golden ages of prosperity and plenty.

Importantly, because populism is not a bad thing in itself, there needs to be a historical understanding and right now *right-wing populism* is dominant. A synthesis of the literature suggests that the key tenets of right-wing populism include:

- An animating force *fuelled by anger* – both directed at elites who have betrayed the people; and, importantly, *against out-groups* who threaten them. This is the 'nativist' element, drawing on forms of nationalism and patriotism. For Zizek the current formation is an 'anti-immigrant populism ... it speaks in antagonisms, of Us against Them' (Zizek, 2017: 241).

- Removing any doubt in a complicated world – transforming complexity and ambiguity in political controversies into a search for enemies (usually more vulnerable groups such as asylum seekers, refugees and migrants, but also the unemployed) (Schultz, 2017). This is potentially the 'sham' element, as the populist discourse is sometimes profoundly deceitful.
- A political style which matches intolerance of those various out-groups with a style of attention-seeking/confronting argument – whereby offensiveness implies authenticity (Tiffen, 2017: 13–14).
- Mobilising religion as part of the nationalist impulse, distinctively not as ethics, but as a marker of group identity.

To name the problem as 'right-wing' populism is not to suggest that the left cannot be mobilised by authoritarian populism – as has been seen most recently in Venezuela. And again, it is important to differentiate a left-wing populist *regime*, as per Venezuela which is authoritarian, with a left-wing populist *movement* such as occurred in Spain (Indignados, Podemos) and Greece (Syriza), and is representative of the kinds of energies harnessed by Bernie Sanders and Jeremy Corbyn. Several commentators make the case for this contemporary left-wing populism (Mouffe, 2018). In contrast, Zizek argues that a left-wing populism would be a mistake (Zizek, 2017: 248). But right now it is more often 'the right' that are mobilising in the way indicative of the aforementioned tenets.

As per the energies harnessed by Corbyn, Sanders and in Greece and Spain, in using the concept of populism, it is important to be very careful because populism is not a bad thing in and of itself. As US political writer Hightower argues, populism 'has been the chief political impulse in America's body politick – determinedly democratic, vigilantly resistant to the oppressive power of corporations and Wall Street, committed to grassroots percolate-up economics' (Frazer, 2017: 70). As noted in a 2018 Oxford University debate, 'Populism always has the genetic predisposition to be dangerous and devastating. But it does not always start that way. It starts as the proverbial canary in the coal mine that warns of toxicity, constriction of oxygen and the possibility of imminent danger' (Rasool, 2018).

Importantly for this chapter, populism similarly indicates the presence or emergence of grievance, discontent, alienation and humiliation.

This will be returned to in the following section, because this everyday discontent of people is also historically the energy that community development builds from, moving private concerns/private pain into public and collective action (Westoby and Dowling, 2013).

The reasons for right-wing populism now

For political scientist Chantel Mouffe, the key issue in this historical moment is collapse of the neoliberal hegemony that has been so dominant since the 1980s. Argued historically (and it is not possible to do justice to the nuances of the argument in this short chapter), her case is that pre-Thatcher modern politics held a tension between 'liberal forms of democracy' (rule of law, separation of powers) and the 'democratic tradition' (alive since the French Revolution, signified by the 'will of the people' and, significantly, aspirations for justice and equality). However, Thatcher and the globalising neoliberal project managed to delegitimise the latter tradition, creating a new hegemonic formation of liberal democracy infused with neoliberal economic commitments to free market, protection of private property and consumerism. This hegemonic formation, maintained for well over 30 years, is now collapsing, creating a crisis for democracy.

In turn, Mouffe sees the need to create a left-wing populism as a decisive intervention into this crisis, an opportunity not to be missed, and one that must be mobilised in an adversarial politics. As Zizek sums up, Mouffe wants a left-wing populism that,

> while retaining the basic populist coordinates (the logic of Us against Them, of the 'people' against a corrupted elite), fills them with a Leftist content: 'They' are not poor refugees or immigrants but financial capital, technocratic state bureaucracy, etc. This populism moves beyond the old working-class anti-capitalism: it tries to bring together a multiplicity of struggles, from ecology to feminism, from the right to employment to free education and healthcare. (Zizek, 2017: 246)

However, Zizek mounts a comprehensive critique of Mouffe, arguing that she ignores the big question of why the left abandoned the logic of 'Us against Them' some time ago. His argument is that this abandonment was due to deep structural changes within globalising capitalism that left (or right) popular mobilisation cannot undo. Zizek's counter-argument to Mouffe is that the populist moment has arisen because there is now an 'ongoing disintegration of the predominant mode of "manufacturing consent" which opens up the space for public vulgarity: liberal and populist' (Zizek, 2017: 248). He unequivocally argues that we should reject both the Trump (right) and Sanders (left) equivalents, suggesting that neither can deal with the real contemporary crisis of democracy. This 'manufactured consent', now collapsing, leads to 'false solutions', such as Brexit, or Trump's 'Make America Great Again', which is actually obscuring the big questions, such as 'how to fight "agreements" like the TTIP (Transatlantic Trade and Investment Partnership), which present a real threat to ecological catastrophe and economic imbalances, which breed new poverty and migration' (Zizek, 2017: 252).

Building on this, various analyses suggest that this is an historical time of profound anxiety and fear due to the many structural violences at play, whether people can 'see' them or not – such as Zizek's analysis of globalisation, or the thread of ecological catastrophe, or the violence of financialisation of the economy (Marazzi, 2011). Many important contributions could be added, such as Beck's seminal work on 'risk society' (Beck, 1992), which now comes home to roost, so to speak. For example, to endlessly 'privatise risk' – removing the historical social contract between state and citizen, leads to people being fearful for their futures. Added to this, with such anxiety and fear, often manifest as rage and vulgarity, people are 'sorting' themselves into groups, hunkering or bunkering down into group-think, or homogenous communities (the 'Us' versus 'Them' antagonism). This is not 'community' as 'people-in-dialogue' – or Martin Buber's idea of community (Buber, 1947) – and Nancy's 'community as difference' (Nancy, 1991), but it is collectivity, or group-think, the antithesis of community as understood by community development practitioners.

Drilling down into the present and attempting to name some of the key contemporary anxieties or fears, Eatwell and Goodwin's (2018) *National Populism: The Revolt against Liberal Democracy* provides a useful four-fold framework. In all my reading they have provided the most compelling arguments and data and shaped it into a useful framework of four Ds: distrust, destruction, deprivation and de-alignment.

Distrust signifies the long-term trend of a rising tide of distrust about politicians specifically, and the political and economic elites generally. At the heart of this distrust is a sense that people are no longer heard, no longer have a stake, no longer have a real say in what government does.

Destruction signifies the real fear that a 'group', their national group, their identity and way of life will fall behind, and eventually be destroyed. This is particularly true for 'white' groups, as explained in detail in Kauffman's (2018) controversial *Whiteshift*, and as per Ghassan Hage's analysis of the Australian context in *White Nation* (2000) and 'paranoid nationalism' (Hage, 2003). For example, in Australia, 20 years-plus of a 'politics of fear' and a growing distrust of politicians, elites and traditional political parties, has led many Australians to become deeply concerned with issues of security, linked to both concerns around immigration generally, the Muslim threat specifically, and also how immigration impacts on the economy (Hage, 2003). In much the same way, there is a good argument to suggest that the European phenomenon of right-wing populist sentiments has also been consolidated due to the crisis of Syrian refugees (ironically caused by what is understood to be the first climate change-related war). Hage, in acknowledging this fear-based politic, instead focuses on the 'distribution of hope', arguing that, 'The defensive society, such as the one we have in Australia today, suffers from a scarcity of hope and creates citizens who see threats everywhere. It generates worrying citizens and a paranoid nationalism' (Hage, 2003: 3).

Deprivation is the perceived sense that a wider group, such as 'white' Britons and Australians are being left behind relative to others in society.

De-alignment refers to the breakdown between traditional political parties and people, with the bonds no longer strong or tight.

Recognising the reality of these trends, fears, senses and breakdowns is not to legitimise the populist impulses that arise from them, but it is to acknowledge they exist.

Clearly, at least some of the fears and anxieties are founded on rational thinking, even if people's understanding of real solutions are not rational, in the sense of clear analysis of the root causes of their grievances. There are many aspects about the future that come towards people that are hard to make sense of, and so simplistic answers offered by populist politicians provide a sense of fraught yet brief security.

Thinking about a response – a theory of social change

With this analysis as the backdrop, let us now consider a theory of social change that might help in charting a way forward for community development praxis. First, it is orthodox to community development praxis that relationships, with all the characteristics of listening, dialogue, joining and so forth, are crucial. From such relationships, people find shared concerns, pains, dreams, and come together to learn, do analysis and strategise for change. Second, relationship building, dialogue and learning must take account of people's *emotions* – particularly fears, distrust and so forth (as per previous analysis). Clearly the way forward is not *only* a dialogue about 'facts'. Emotions need to be taken equally seriously, and community development practitioners need to be equipped with capacities to engage with people who are aggrieved and feel strongly. Third, it might be helpful to understand social change through the lens of complex systems thinking, in which recent studies have shown that small changes can be significant in shifting the political culture. For example, the work of Chenoweth and Stephen (2012) suggests that reorienting the world views and practices of 3.5% of the population is critical to shifting ideas. Such research and complex thinking provides a window of hope, because small experiments can make a difference, and thinking emergently, such experiments can impact on many people. Perhaps only shifting a small percentage can shift the gesture of politics.

Taking all this into account, this study also draws on the micro-mezzo-macro-meta level framework of community development as theorised in the recent book *Participatory Development Practice* (Kelly and Westoby, 2018). Within this framework the key praxis of community development requires community practitioners to do micro-level work – which is to be in dialogue with people they meet in places they work. This micro level dialogue involved listening, learning and engaging with the world view of the people. Building from such dialogue, the mezzo-level work brings people together or engages with existing groups in circles of learning, making sense of the world. Here is the possible place of popular education (see Marjorie Mayo in Chapter Five). The macro-level work is engagement and support of place-based people's organisations, as key infrastructure of civil society. Such places 'hold' the bottom-up and the participatory programmes that emerge from the micro- and mezzo-level work. Finally, meta-level work is the practice that works 'beyond the local', linking local issues to broader regional, national or international movements. It would seem that a community development response to right-wing populism needs to attend to all four levels – dialogue, circle-work, people's organisations and social movements. This argument will now be grounded.

Thinking about a response – community development praxis

In his classic novel *Grapes of Wrath*, Steinbeck (1939) makes the poignant comment, 'alone I am bewildered'. This is the cry of people atomised, isolated, alone, trying to make sense of their world. Alone and bewildered, people are clearly vulnerable. The case has been made of multiple vulnerabilities, from risk society, structural violences, emotional fear and anxiety, all manifest in the four big Ds. At the same time a theory of social change for community development has been offered.

If the analysis provided is accurate, how can community development respond? I am tentative in making any certain claims, or signposting with any clarity. Assuming there is agreement that people have legitimate grievances – and thus will turn to 'something' for change – what can community development offer that right-wing populism cannot?

If people alone are bewildered, they turn to others to make sense of the world – that essential movement understood in community development orthodoxies as the movement from 'I' to 'we'. However, there are many forms of 'we' that are profoundly dangerous. For example, research shows how 'mob mentality – the propensity for groups of people to shed the inhibitions of societal and moral standards' (Woldford, 2014) – is dangerous. Rarely has the mob 'done good' in history. Right-wing populism, as a form of organised 'we', also appears to be elusive in terms of generative futures, particularly if judged by social and ecological imperatives for justice.

So, the challenge is to conduct relevant work of enabling people to overcome their isolation and accompanying bewilderment, become a 'we', get organised and mobilised for different purposes. Here are my proposals.

First, our work in re-emphasising social life: To say it again, one of the key consequences of the 30+ years of economically oriented policy (economic rationalism, neoliberalism, risk society and so forth) is the undoing of society (implying a growing individualism and consumerism) and the resultant fragmentation of community – sometimes described as atomisation. One of the problems of atomisation and fragmentation is that more and more people are isolated and bewildered. Furthermore, as already suggested, people who are isolated and feel alone are vulnerable to joining the kind of 'Us' versus 'Them' antagonism that populisms offers.

In response to this 'Us' versus 'Them' politic, a community development praxis pushes in a different direction, either connecting people back into embodied and online social networks – creating the social activities that enable people to connect – or building on organic movements in which people are rebuilding community (for example, downsizing, community garden movement and so forth). Crucially this kind of community building, reasserting the primacy of the social over the economic, requires a nuanced and sophisticated understanding of intersectionality and multiplicity. It is to avoid 'community as unity' (as per the work of Nancy, 1991; Derrida, 2001; Gibson-Graham, 2006), while recognising the anxiety-induced need for 'ethno-traditional' communities (Kaufmann, 2018). The work in re-weaving community as sites of the social and ethical decision making (Gibson-Graham, 2006) is crucial in undermining the conditions that make right-wing populism thrive.

Second, clarity about the importance of 'community' as a site of democratic struggle and the crucial role of popular education: However, re-emphasising or rebuilding the social is not enough. Crucially, critical or radical community development can insert popular education practices, or political education into some of these social networks, ensuring there are spaces for a revival of deliberative democracy and historical-political education at local levels. These deliberations and educational efforts are important for people to make sense *with others* of the unfolding democratic and potentially demographic crises. The stories within Marjorie Mayo's chapter offer good examples of this.

Importantly, while popular education can occur in an embodied way as people in localities sit 'in circles' learning and deliberating about key issues, the key issues are uniquely now local *and* global (that is, meta-level). For example, three of the most significant political questions of our time are to do with: solutions to global climate change, solutions to mass migration, and also innovating new models of ownership and regulation of big data. Like land in earlier history (signifying a division between the aristocracy and commoners) and the means of production in the most recent history (signifying a division between capitalists and proletariat), data is now the defining feature of power. Those who own data own the future, and unless citizens find places to learn and deliberate around such issues, new patterns of domination and inequality will become entrenched with little community or social resistance. The new age of surveillance capitalism will become entrenched (Zuboff, 2019).

The French philosopher Jacques Derrida (2001) argued that 'community' is a significant site of struggle – there are people *for more boundaries*, excluding 'the other', and those *for hospitality*. This site of community is then part of our struggle as practitioners and could form the basis of a popular education campaign, of grassroots education focused on these crucial local–global issues. Community practitioners at the front line of place-based work can support visions for hospitality, and platforms that enable authentic deliberation. Importantly, such education should *not* be prescriptive, pushing onto people a utopian vision of 'welcoming diversity', but should be dialogical, starting with people's experience and stories.

Where are the space and places in which people are learning? If community development practitioners dream of supporting a politics of inclusion and hospitality, if we support a praxis of mobilising around collective solutions to complex social, cultural and technological challenges, then there is a need to reorient the work towards place-based embodied popular education.

Third, building a countervailing organisational force: Popular education is not just about political learning and platforms for learning, it is also about organising. And organising is crucial as one way of building a countervailing organisational force.

Not everyone is willing to go on a dialogical learning journey. For example, a story from Nowra, Australia in the *Griffith Review* (Adcock, 2017) is illustrative. In this story, many homeless people had moved onto the camping site in the town showgrounds. There they could access toilets, showers and electricity. But eventually angry local residents organised to have them removed. In the *Griffith Review* account, there was a very vocal town council meeting where the angry 'anti-homeless people' had a strong voice, and the mayor was forced to act on their behalf. The 'voice' of the people perhaps? Local populism in play?

But the real problem was that angry loud people got their way because there was no organised countervailing force. All the local service providers and community practitioners were consumed with the problem of housing provision, and no one had done any organising work that could ensure there was a different resident voice at the town council meeting.

It is suggested that every place has those willing to learn under the conditions of dialogue, care, respect. We need to work with those people and build an organised countervailing force in place to fight (and I mean fight, because it is sometimes a dirty fight) against those who wilfully choose in favour of exclusion and dehumanising and are, at times, willing to do violence to others.

Of course, such organising needs to occur locally, with progressive people's organisations, but such organisations also need to be linked into the meta-level work already mentioned – particularly in the formation of networks, federations and coalitions, ensuring local issues are also articulated into policy-oriented and institutional activity. Increasingly, this meta-level work also needs to enter the local–global nexus of practice.

Fourth, be pro-state and pro-politics: Finally, community development practitioners need to move beyond a cynical feeling about the state, and instead be advocating 'for the state', not confusing state capture by corporations, or institutional racism, sexism, ableism and so on, as a problem of the state per se. While we rebuild associational life at a local level, as per the first point, we should also advocate for the 'social state' through forming or participating in social movements that have a broader scope, whether it be regional, national or international. In a forum on the issues of community development's response to right-wing populism hosted in my home town of Brisbane recently, one person suggested that neighbourhood and community centres should form a new national civic movement named something like 'communities for political integrity'.

This study specifically points to the 'social' state, signalling the role of the state in addressing its own internal racisms, alongside structural marginalisation – in terms of both redistribution and recognition (Fraser and Honneth, 2003), which is the best way to avoid the conditions that are ripe for right-wing populism. Although we could add 'just transition' to redistribution and recognising in acknowledgement of climate change.

Conclusion

Community development practitioners do need to engage locally and globally, bringing our particular skills in creating spaces, places and platforms for associational life, filled with dialogical and agonistic conflict. It is our job to create the places where people can put aside their rage, and learn the disciplines of conversation and deliberation, heard, while not affirmed as necessarily right. In a nutshell, the work of reconnecting. These are the basic qualities of liberal democracy also infused with a radical egalitarian spirit, and a cohesive society.

The recipe for a truly *popular* agenda – which is what a critical and radical community development praxis would dream of – lies in how apparently divergent discontent is cohered into a set of public demands; how communities and people learn to mobilise and organise inclusive campaigns around those demands; how to construct alliances and federations (meta-level work) through careful negotiation around grievance and common purpose; and how, in turn, the language of anger and outrage can be harnessed for the 'common good', and not the malignant appetite of any corrupted populist leader.

References

Adcock, B. (ed) (2017) 'Rush to judgement: stigmatising the homeless in Nowra', in J. Schultz (ed), *Perils of Populism*, Griffith Review 57, Brisbane, Australia: Griffith University, pp 59–69.

Banks, S. and Westoby, P. (eds) (2019) *Ethics, Equity and Community Development*, Bristol: Policy Press.

Beck. U. (1992) *Risk Society*, London: Sage.

Buber, M. (1947) *Between Man and Man*, London: Routledge Classics.

Chenoweth, E. and Stephen, M. (2012) *Why Civil Resistance Works: The Strategic Logic of Nonviolent Conflict*, New York: Columbia University Press.

Derrida, J. (2001) *On Cosmopolitanism*, New York: Routledge.

Eatwell, R. and Goodwin, M. (2018) *National Populism: The Revolt against Liberal Democracy*, UK: Random House.

Finchelstein, F. (2017) *From Fascism to Populism in History*, Oakland: University of California Press.

Fraser, N. and Honneth. A. (2003) *Redistribution or Recognition: A Political-Philosophical Exchange*, London: Verso.

Frazer, P. (2017) 'When everybody does better', in J. Schultz (ed), *Perils of Populism,* Griffith Review 57, Brisbane, Australia: Griffith University, pp 70–79.

Freire, P. (1972) *Pedagogy of the Oppressed*, London: Penguin Books.

Gibson-Graham, J.K. (2006) *A Post-Capitalist Politics*, Minneapolis: University of Minnesota Press.

Grayling, A.C. (2017) *Democracy in Crisis*, London: Oneworld.

Hage, G. (2000) *White Nation: Fantasies of White Supremacy in a Multicultural Society*, New York: Routledge.

Hage, G. (2003) *Against Paranoid Nationalism: Searching for Hope in a Shrinking Society*, Annandale, NSW: Pluto Press.

Hall, S. and Jacques, M. (1983) *The Politics of Thatcherism*, London: Lawrence Wishart in association with Marxism Today.

Kaufmann, E. (2018) *Whiteshift: Populism, Immigration and the Future of White Majorities*, London: Allen Lane/Penguin Books.

Kelly, A. and Westoby, P. (2018) *Participatory Development Practice, Using Traditional and Contemporary Frameworks*, Rugby: Practical Action Press.

Ledwith, M. (2015) *Community Development in Action: Putting Freire into Practice*, Bristol: Policy Press.

Marazzi, C. (2011) *The Violence of Financial Capitalism*, Los Angeles, CA: Semiotext.

Mouffe, C. (2018) *For a Left Populism*, London: Verso.

Nancy, J.L. (1991) *The Inoperative Community*, Minneapolis: University of Minnesota Press.

Rasool, E. (2018) 'Is populism creating a crisis for democracy?', *The Daily Maverick*, 8 June, [online] www.dailymaverick.co.za/opinionista/2018-06-08-is-populism-creating-a-crisis-for-democracy/

Schultz, J. (2017) 'Grooming the globe: denying fairness, complexity, humanity', in J. Schultz (ed), *Perils of Populism*, Griffith Review 57, Brisbane, Australia: Griffith University, pp 7–10.

Steinbeck, J. (1939) *The Grapes of Wrath*, USA: The Viking Press.

Tiffen, R. (ed) (2017) 'The restoration impulse', in *Perils of Populism*, Griffith Review 57, Brisbane, Australia: Griffith University.

Westoby, P. (2018) 'Community development's response to "sham" right-wing nativist populism: contributions to a Thinkery', *New Community*, 15(5) Issue 60: 19–24.

Westoby, P. and Dowling, G. (2013) *Theory and Practice of Dialogical Community Development: International Perspectives*, Abingdon: Routledge.

Wolford, B. (2014) 'Mob mentality: the brain suppresses personal moral code when in groups', [online] www.medicaldaily.com/mob-mentality-brain-suppresses-personal-moral-code-when-groups-288342

Zizek, S. (2017) *The Courage of Hopelessness*, Brooklyn, NY: Melville House.

Zuboff, S. (2019) *The Age of Surveillance Capitalism*, London: Profile Books Ltd.

FIVE

Community development and popular education in populist times

Marjorie Mayo

Community-based education has a long history within community development narratives. These histories have included the contributions of community-based learning to movements for colonial freedom in Africa, India and elsewhere in the Global South, just as they have included contributions to community development narratives in Britain and elsewhere, in the Global North. These interconnections between community-based learning and community development predate even the seminal contributions of the Brazilian popular educator, Paulo Freire, focusing on enabling communities to understand the underlying causes of their problems, developing critical consciousness as the basis for promoting collective action for social change (Freire, 1972). The relevance for community development theory and practice has been set out explicitly in key texts such as *Community Development: A Critical Approach* (Ledwith, 2005) and *Participatory Practice* (Ledwith and Springett, 2010).

More recent discussions of the contested notion of popular education highlight these interconnections still further, going on to distinguish popular education from 'merely populist' approaches, in that it is 'rooted in the real interests and struggles of ordinary people, overtly political and critical of the status quo (and) committed to progressive change' (Crowther et al, 2005: 2). It forges a direct link between education and social action. Far from being populist, in fact, it has been argued that popular education has actually been taking off in direct response to the growth of far right populism and increasing authoritarianism in recent years.

This chapter starts from the potential contributions that popular education can make, building on the legacies – and lessons – from the past; enabling communities to respond more effectively to the challenges that they face in the contemporary context; developing collective strategies for social justice and community solidarity; and promoting the politics of hope rather than exacerbating the politics of hate. These are ambitious aims, and not without their own inherent tensions; definitions of popular education have been and continue to be contested, and so have definitions of populism, in their turn.

Having explored these questions in theory, the chapter moves on to consider ways in which popular educators have been engaging with communities to address contemporary challenges, exploring the underlying causes of the growth of far right populism, as well as developing alternative strategies in response. In practice, working collectively for more inclusive forms of community development and social change, popular educators can provide tools to enable communities to deepen their knowledge and critical understanding of the problems that they face. Most importantly, popular educators can provide the support that communities need in order to engage with the emotions that underpin the growth of far right populism, along with the growth of racism, xenophobia, misogyny, anti-Semitism and Islamophobia, just to mention the most pervasive forms of prejudice, discrimination and oppression involved. The chapter includes examples for illustration, dating back over previous decades. However, while recognising the achievements of popular education, the chapter concludes by highlighting some of the remaining tensions and the continuing dilemmas.

Contested definitions

Popular education has been defined as starting 'from the real and systematic inequalities and injustices that currently exclude many people from anything but a nominal notion of citizenship' along with 'listening to and articulating those voices which have been silenced and excluded from the public business of civic and political life' (Crowther et al, 2005: 3). This involves a 'bottom-up' process, starting from ordinary people's own interests, aspirations and lived experiences. Furthermore, 'learning is essentially about making knowledge that makes sense of their world and helps them to act upon it, collectively, in order to change it for the better' (Crowther et al, 2005: 4) – key dimensions of community development processes.

This type of definition provides a useful starting point. Like so many contested definitions, however, it raises further questions in its turn. In reality, as Liam Kane explains in the same collection of papers (Crowther et al, 2005), popular education is interpreted in a myriad of ways, diverse and sometimes contradictory understandings that need to be confronted (Kane, 2005: 32). Who exactly are the ordinary people? And do they have real interests in common? Who is to define these, and how to take account of differences within as well as between communities and social movements? The concluding section returns to these questions.

Like popular education, populism has been a contested concept, in its turn, with varying approaches, based on widely differing political perspectives. Historically, populism has been applied to very different movements in Europe and elsewhere, including both Latin and North American countries (Lazaridis et al, 2016). It has been argued that there have been soft versions of populism and hard versions of populism, with populisms also of the political left (Mouffe, 2018) as well as populisms of the political right, the term being applied to differing movements, ideologies and political practices (Laclau, 2005). Not all populists come from the far right, then, although that is the focus of this particular chapter, reflecting the challenges that the far right poses in Britain today. But not all of those on the far right could be described as populists, either. Far from it, in fact.

Despite any such differences, populisms have tended to share a common approach in that they identify with the 'people' as against the elites (Laclau, 2005; Lazaridis et al, 2016). Populism tends to emerge in crises of representation, Laclau suggests, when formal political processes fail to meet social demands. In such contexts a section of the community (the underdog) may then present itself as representing the whole community – the people versus the elite or the establishment.

In times of challenge, populism has also been associated with emotional appeals to notions of identity, such as national, ethnic or religious identities (including white nationalist identities), typically framed in terms of the contrast between 'us' and the 'others'. The 'others' may be minority communities, including newcomers, such as migrants and refugees, especially those from different cultures and religions. And the 'others' may be elites, politicians, the plutocracy, or in the case of the United States, the 'Washington insiders' (Panizza, 2005: 3).

Combating such views with appeals to the 'facts' simply misses the point here. Especially if the 'facts' come from distrusted sources. People reply with comments such as, 'They would say that, wouldn't they'? And 'who needs experts anyway?' Myth-busting exercises about the impacts of immigration have been challenged for precisely such reasons. Those already opposed to immigration may simply refuse to believe the counter-arguments, even when these arguments are supported by seemingly irrefutable facts. So where does such scepticism come from?

There is not the space in this chapter to explore the theoretical underpinnings of the rise of far right populism in detail. But to summarise, theoretical roots would seem to be traced from aspects of postmodernist thinking, as Harvey, among others, has suggested. Harvey himself welcomed the contributions that postmodernism had been making to the study of contemporary capitalism in the context of neoliberal globalisation (Harvey, 1990). He was appreciative of the radical potential of postmodernist critiques of previously accepted approaches. And he valued postmodernist emphases on the importance of addressing social divisions in terms of gender, sexuality and race – although he himself continued to locate these in relation to the centrality of class divisions in capitalist societies.

However these positive aspects of postmodernism had their downsides, in Harvey's view. Anti-authoritarian iconoclasm could be deployed for radical ends. Conversely, postmodernism could lead to the 'suspicion of any narrative that aspires to coherence', challenging all basic propositions and all consensual standards of truth and justice, of ethics and meaning (Harvey, 1990: 350). If nothing is to be believed, then anything goes? Responses to the postmodern critique of meta-narratives could include an over-emphasis on localism and competition between the fragments, Harvey continued, with identity politics taking over from class politics, rather than enriching class politics with more complex understandings of the intersectionalities between class and other forms of discrimination and oppression.

There are significant elements here with resonance in terms of understanding far right populism. Such approaches have been linked with forms of anti-intellectualism that mark a return to pre-modernist or pre-Enlightenment thinking, others have similarly argued (Wodak, 2015: 2). If anything goes, then any interpretation is as valid as any other. So why fuss about the 'facts'? Wodak asked: if identity politics should come to supersede class politics, with identifications based upon feelings and emotional attachments, where does that leave the working class and working class politics?

So what? Why would this matter if these were no more than academic debates? But what if such views had wider resonance, part of the mood music of the times? How might such attitudes play into wider scepticism about truth claims or indeed about the relevance of arguments based on factual evidence at all? In fraught times, divisions between traditional left- and right-wing politics can give way to fragmentary forms of identity politics accompanied by more general feelings of anger at elites – potentially populist responses. Social media can have particular significance in such contexts, fanning the dissemination of *alternative* truths.

The retreat from class politics has been identified as particularly relevant, in relation to the frustrations of the traditional white working class in Britain. The Runneymede Trust's report *Who Cares about the White Working Class?* (Sveinsson, 2009) explores the causes of these frustrations, set against the background of divisive forms of identity politics. The report challenges the media's focus on competition between different ethnic groups – with the white working class losing out to particular minority communities. This is set against the reality that the most disadvantaged in society are working class people of whatever ethnic background, the poorest fifth of the population who are increasingly separated from the most prosperous majority – rather than from each other – by inequalities of income, housing and education, among others. This is not, of course, how these divisions are necessarily perceived, however.

Meanwhile, 'middle class commentators may be happy to defend white working class interests against the onslaught of politically correct multiculturalism' in the Runneymede Trust report's view, but 'they will simultaneously deride and ridicule the feckless and undeserving poor, who have squandered the opportunities gracefully given to them by the welfare state, and can therefore rightfully be left to wallow in their own poverty' (Sveinsson, 2009: 5). The demonisation of white working class communities has featured in a number of studies in recent years (Jones, 2011; McKenzie, 2015) – demonisation processes that have been amplified on social media, along with television series portraying the 'underclass' as benefit scroungers at best, if not actually dangerous criminals.

There have been challenges to these demonisation processes, of course. Poverty porn has been resisted, as people at the sharp end of austerity have organised to make their voices heard. 'We don't have to accept this attack on our living standards, we don't have to accept the demonization of the various minorities, be they disabled, poor, single parents, immigrants or refugees', as a disabled activist has explained (Sng, 2019). 'We can stand up, join forces, and support one another', she argued. Furthermore:

> We are telling people there is a better way, that life doesn't have to be as hard as it is today, that austerity is a deliberate ideological choice designed to punish the poor for the deliberate actions of the rich, particularly the bankers. (Passmore, 2019)

People can and do engage in popular education for themselves in such ways, as well as engaging with popular education initiatives from outside.

To summarise the discussion so far, popular education and populism are both contested concepts, with varying interpretations. Populists tend to pose the interests and views of 'the people' as being in opposition to those of the 'elite'. They typically appeal to people's emotions and feelings of identity rather than simply relying on rational arguments alone, let alone relying on rational arguments about the underlying causes of increasing poverty and widening inequalities.

Popular educators have also been committed to starting from the interests and views of ordinary people, in parallel. But popular educators take more account of the significance of divisions and conflicts of interest *within as well as between* communities based on the intersectionalities between social class and other forms of discrimination and oppression (Shaw and Mayo, 2016). These different approaches have widely different implications in practice.

The impact of populism, particularly far right populism, has been very obfuscating in fact. People blame others (the 'other') for the destructive impacts of financialisation, globalisation and austerity, undermining the basis for building alliances for collective action to tackle people's problems at local, national and international levels. Popular education, in contrast, has significant contributions to make to community development, drawing upon structural analyses of the structural causes of communities' problems, building community solidarity as the basis for more effective forms of social action for transformative change.

In addition to drawing on structural analyses, however, popular educators need to recognise the importance of taking account of people's emotions. And they need to recognise the tensions inherent in starting from where people are at – while aiming to shift communities forwards in more constructive ways. There are dilemmas here for community development practitioners more generally: how to build community solidarity while taking account of differences and conflicts of interest *within as well as between* communities. And how to understand and respect people's feelings and views on the one hand while recognising the importance of challenging negative stereotypes on the other? Psycho-social approaches have particular relevance here, particularly psycho-social approaches as developed by Paul Hoggett and colleagues (Hoggett, 2016).

Taking account of structures of feelings

The notion of *structures of feeling* is one that Hoggett uses to explore the ways in which groups and communities can experience feelings together; collective mood music that predominates in particular contexts over space and time (Hoggett, 2016). Rather than focusing on either the individual or the wider society, this type of approach focuses on the creative ways in which people interact with the wider society as social beings, two-way processes that shape us in our social contexts.

These collective feelings can be positive or negative – or some combination of both, just as individuals' feelings can combine positivity and negativity, love and hate, hope and fear. People speak of 'depressed' communities, for instance, contrasting these communities with places with more positive feelings of community spirit. In turn, writers refer to the *zeitgeist*, the spirit of a particular age.

In the contemporary context, Hoggett focuses on the significance of generalised affects, which he identifies as free-floating feelings of anxiety. These free-floating affects have no apparent focus or target, flitting from one thing to another. But populists can give them a focus, turning them into more specific emotions, particularly of fear, envy and even hatred of the 'other'. This is particularly toxic at present, given the extent of such generalised anxieties, and the precariousness of so many people's lives, especially, although by no means only, affecting young working class people. There is plenty for them to worry about in 21st century Britain and indeed, elsewhere.

Such situations give rise to feelings of weakness and powerlessness, as people can come to believe that others are being treated more favourably, being given the respect that they feel that they themselves deserve – but fail to receive (Clarke et al, 2006). Such feelings of weakness and powerlessness can then become a mixture of bitterness, complaint, envy and shame. In such stigmatised contexts the emotional 'habitus' reflects more generalised feelings of helplessness and hopelessness, shame and despair.

These types of feelings can, of course, be identified in materially deprived neighbourhoods. But such feelings can be identified more widely too, feelings of nostalgia and cultural loss as well as feelings of anxiety about the state of the economy and material insecurities (Demertzis, 2006). There would seem to be resonances here with many of the concerns that have been emerging from studies of the far right in Britain and the USA in recent times. Brexit slogans such as 'Take Back Control' have appealed to wide sections of the population, chiming with feelings of nostalgia for a mythical golden age, an age when Britain – like the USA – was seen to have been great, when shared cultures were valued and communities were believed to have been strong.

Politicians from the far right do not create such feelings out of thin air, Hoggett (2016) explains. But such generalised feelings (or 'affects') can be manipulated. Moral panics can be whipped up by the media – fear can sell copies – and politicians can play upon such fears for their own ends, professing to be standing up for the 'little man' (sic) and/ or the 'silent majority', outcomes that are especially evident in times of stress. Free-floating anxieties and fears can too readily become projected onto the 'other'.

Hoggett points to research which suggests that people who are better informed may be noticeably less affected by populist politicians' rhetoric (Hoggett, 2016). This is not to pose rationality against emotions however. On the contrary. Reasoned responses have their place, but there needs to be engagement with people's passions too, supporting them to move from shame to pride – from grief to the type of anger that mobilises them to take action against injustice. Common interests need to be addressed together, he concludes, while differences need to be recognised and understood through processes of deliberation and dialogue based on mutual respect (Hoggett, 2016).

Popular education in practice

There is growing interest in popular education in the current context, in face of the challenges posed by neoliberal globalisation and the politics of austerity, along with the challenges posed by the growth of far right populism and increasing authoritarianism, as has already been suggested. There have been examples of community-based popular education in response to the election of Donald Trump as President of the USA in 2016, for instance. And there has been an upsurge of interest in popular education in Britain in response to the growth of hate speech and hate crime following the referendum on Brexit in 2016. Young people, but by no means only young people, have been participating in a range of activities to examine the political situations in which they find themselves, as the basis for exploring the scope for developing alternatives. As Kenan Malik has pointed out, there has been a growing backlash against the consequences of free market policies and a sense of alienation from mainstream institutions as the lives of so many young people have been shaped by the financial crash and by the austerity policies that have followed from 2008 (Malik, 2018: 17).

In the context of the growth of the far right and the politics of hate, there is growing interest in understanding the causes as the basis for working towards more hopeful futures. Within the UK, the programmes for 'The World Transformed' (TWT) events that have been organised alongside Labour Party conferences since 2016 illustrate the range of topics that have been debated in the context of such concerns. These events have attracted impressively large audiences, young people getting involved in politics for the first time and older people re-engaging, as the parameters of political debate have been widening beyond the middle ground of the so-called Third Way. This focus on popular education has been seen as central to the construction of alternative approaches. The aim has been to develop a broad movement in support of transformative policies for 'the many not the few', as the 2017 Labour Party election manifesto expressed this (although TWT is not a party political organisation per se, being committed to engaging people and groups across the spectrum of progressive politics).

This inclusivity has been mirrored in TWT's events. The programme for 2018 has been described as offering a similarly wide and participatory set of events, attracting even greater numbers of participants, with four days of socialist politics, art exhibitions, and other forms of community and cultural activity (The World Transformed, 2018). Jointly organised with Global Justice Now, the focus has been on international as well as more local issues, with grassroots activists exchanging experiences and views as well as hearing from well-known names. The World Transformed is just one example, of course. There have been workshops, seminars, courses and informal events elsewhere in Britain and beyond, including the self-education activities that have been accompanying social movements and social movement campaigns, depending upon their particular focus.

Popular education initiatives have addressed people's immediate worries over jobs, education and training, housing and planning, health and the environment, to name just some of the most topical concerns that have been amplified by the far right, exacerbated as these problems have been as a result of the politics of austerity. Popular education initiatives have also been tackling some of the most emotive issues that the far right has been manipulating, engaging with people's underlying anxieties and resentments.

The first story explores popular education and participatory action research as these have been applied via community histories and the arts. These initiatives have included the use of graffiti art, as well as oral histories and archival research, to explore their neighbourhoods' pasts as the basis for developing their hopes for the future. The second story explores the use of popular education, working with young people to tackle racism in football. Their passions for the so-called beautiful game were being engaged to challenge the spread of the more negative emotions of racism, hate speech and hate crime.

Story 1: From the past to the present – popular education, participatory action research and the arts

While so much of the contemporary focus in Britain relates to popular education in response to the far right in the context of Brexit there may be lessons to be learnt from anti-racist popular education initiatives in the past, as well as from New Labour programmes from 2006 onwards, through a range of subsequent initiatives up to 2010. The South Yorkshire hub of the New Labour government's programme to promote Active Learning for Active Citizenship (Mayo and Rooke, 2006) provides illustrations in point. The hub was based in Sheffield, set up as a partnership between the Workers Educational Association (WEA) and Northern College, an adult residential college near Barnsley. Both organisations had long-established track records of working with communities and social movements, including experience of focusing upon international as well as more local issues and concerns.

This was an area that had been changing rapidly, as Ted Hartley, from the WEA, explained in his reflections on his experiences in South Yorkshire (Hartley, 2010). There had been widespread social and economic atomisation, following the loss of jobs in mining and other industries. He associated these processes of atomisation with first Tory and then New Labour free market policy approaches, accompanied as these had been by shifts and changes in major services, as a result of privatisation.

Meanwhile, between 2001 and 2006, Sheffield's black and minority ethnic communities had increased from 8% to 30%. There were refugees and asylum seekers. There were economic migrants from countries that had recently joined the European Union (and so gained the right to work in Britain), countries that included Poland, Slovakia and the Baltic states. And terrorist attacks had been fuelling anti-Islamic feelings, with rising xenophobia in general and increasing Islamophobia more specifically.

Migrants and asylum seekers were being demonised as the 'root of social ills' (Grayson, 2010: 157). This climate of 'common sense racism' and the accompanying growth of support for extreme right political parties (Grayson, 2010: 157) had to be challenged, along with the public policies that were exacerbating the problems.

So how did this approach work out in practice? There were workshops and study visits. There were residential courses, including courses 'to develop anti-racist working, solidarity and strategy' (Grayson, 2010. 162). There were sessions on 'Kicking Out Racism in Your Community', 'Challenging Racism for Community Trainers' and 'Divided We Fall; Resolving Conflict in Communities'.

Meanwhile, there were also residentials for asylum seekers and refugees, including, 'Living in the UK'. There was a course for Refugee Community Organisations (RCOs), 'How to Organise RCOs'. And there were residentials that brought different groups together, to explore their issues and experiences, together. Examples included the sessions that the Northern College and the WEA organised on 'Migration and Europe', including sessions focusing on the rise of far right sentiments across the continent (topics of continuing relevance subsequently).

Subsequent research programmes have likewise provided resources with the potential for challenging the far right. In more recent times this is somewhat ironic, given the challenges inherent in the policy context, including the higher education policy context more generally. The Connected Communities programme is a case in point. The UK Arts and Humanities Research Council launched a cross-research council initiative with the aim of achieving 'new insights into community and new ways of researching community that puts arts and humanities at the heart of research and connects academic and community expertise' (Banks, Hart and Wards, 2019: xii). As part of this programme, one of the participating research councils, the UK's Economic and Social Research Council, funded a five-year project running from 2013 to 2017, entitled: 'Imagine – Connecting Communities through Research'. This was to be a collaborative project involving research partnerships between 'people from communities of place, interest and identity largely based outside universities, and academics largely based within universities' (Banks et al, 2019: xiii) – community–university partnerships backed with public funds, despite the wider context, with austerity policies continuing to impact upon communities and universities alike. Against this background, researchers from a range of disciplines worked with community partners to explore the changing nature of communities, taking account of their historical, cultural, democratic and social contexts over time.

The Imagine project's initiatives connected communities with experiences from the past then, as well as identifying ways forward for the future (Banks et al, 2019). The approach was explicitly based upon community development principles, summarised as starting from people's own experiences, enabling communities to identify their own needs, developing collective strategies to challenge unequal power relationships, promoting social justice and inclusion to improve the qualities of their own lives and those of their communities and the wider societies of which they were part. Their view of co-produced research drew explicitly on similar traditions, focusing on 'participatory and action-orientated research, inspired by radical social movements concerned to democratise knowledge production' (Banks et al, 2019: 23) citing Freire and others, including reflections from previous community development programmes in Britain (Kyneswood, 2019).

As part of this Imagine initiative, projects in the North East of England involved workers and volunteers in each area, 'engaging with residents and service users to explore aspects of the past, present and future of their neighbourhoods', as Banks and her colleagues explained (Banks et al, 2019: 28). Together they used a range of creative methods, such as graffiti art, as well as oral histories and archival research, to explore their neighbourhoods' pasts as the basis for developing their hopes for the future.

One of the most significant themes to emerge related to these neighbourhoods' pasts and local people's concerns with the importance of challenging their areas' stigmatisation. Government-supported Community Development Projects had already challenged the view that these areas' problems were due to the deficiencies of their residents, demonstrating that these areas' problems stemmed from de-industrialisation and the failures of public policies. But decades later, what has been described as territorial stigmatisation (Wacquant, 2007)) was continuing to blight people's lives. As a member of a local history group in North Shields commented, reflecting on the portrayal of such negative stereotypes in a BBC television programme called 'Living with Poverty: The Queen of North Shields in 2013', 'everyone's out of work, no one wants to work, everybody lives on the borderline … it was awful the way it was portrayed' (Banks et al, 2019: 33). Small wonder then that challenging stigma emerged as a major concern for residents who wanted to change the reputations of the areas in which they lived.

Despite the value of these initiatives, these areas' objective realities have remained challenging to say the least. Cultural strategies were never likely to reverse so many decades of industrial decline, accompanied, as they have been, by the limitations of successive public policy responses. Yet cultural strategies – including initiatives to reclaim communities' histories – have particular relevance in the context of the growth of far right populism, replacing alienation, hopelessness and shame with more positive feelings of pride in past achievements and solidarity in the pursuit of alternative futures (Ward et al, 2019).

Story 2: From the past to the present – challenging racism and discrimination in football

Sports have provided opportunities for engaging with people's emotions, just as the arts have, providing ways of offering challenges to the far right. 'Kick it out' and 'Show Racism the Red Card' football both provide illustrations. Racism and discrimination have been only too evident, both on and off the pitch, attitudes and behaviours that have been challenged in a variety of ways over past decades. The 'Kick it Out' and 'Show Racism the Red Card' campaigns have been organising a range of interventions with players, trainers and managers, working with fans along with those involved in the sport professionally, going into schools and formal education settings, as well as developing training materials for popular education initiatives in various contexts. The continuing importance of these approaches has been highlighted only too clearly with the emergence of far right Tommy Robinson's 'Democratic Football Lads Alliance' in 2017, targeting young football supporters with a view to mobilising them for the far right.

Kick It Out was formed back in 1993 as 'Let's Kick Racism Out of Football'. This was a time when racial violence, harassment and abuse were described as being rife in the game – but the authorities were seen as being in denial (Kick It Out, 2017: 1). The campaign therefore set out to raise awareness about inequalities and exclusion and set an evolving agenda for action to enable the authorities, leagues, clubs, players, match officials and fans to tackle these issues (Kick It Out, 2017: 1). The range of activities had included a series of initiatives to promote inclusivity and equalities within professional football along with equalities and anti-discrimination training and education for all those concerned.

There had been targeted campaigns and education programmes to tackle prejudice and hate, including the release of a film as part of Chelsea's campaign to tackle anti-Semitism, for example, a resource that other clubs were being encouraged to use. Equality ambassadors had been raising awareness among young people in schools and junior clubs. And the clubs' community programmes offered important ways to promote equalities and community cohesion more widely. Much has been achieved. Despite these initiatives, however, there have been worrying reports of violence in recent times, reflecting a rise in reported and under-reported hate crimes in the wider society. These are continuing challenges, exacerbated by increasing pressures from far right populism.

At the time of writing, a Black player caused concern when he explained that 'I've had enough. I've got five or six more years left in football and I just can't wait to see the back of it' (Hytner, 2019: 55). The player had just been subjected to monkey chants from the stands in the game between England and Montenegro, part of an ongoing pattern of physical as well as verbal abuse. The situation in some countries would seem to be even worse; perhaps with less having been done in the way of popular education in these situations.

The evaluation of 'Show Racism the Red Card's' 'Routes' project pointed to similar conclusions (Rodgerson, 2018). This particular initiative had set out to provide specialist anti-racism educational interventions through schools and formal educational settings in Tyne and Wear, targeting young people aged between 13 and 18 years who had been identified as being at risk. This was an area that was known to be targeted by far right extremists.

The project was based on the recognition that racism is multifaceted and so needs to be tackled with flexibility, taking account of 'young people's sense of identity, sense of place in their communities and in the wider political and economic context' (Rodgerson, 2018: 5). Their concerns had to be addressed in 'a safe, non-judgemental space, in order to foster young people's self-expression and critical thinking skills' (Rodgerson, 2018: 5). And rather than telling young people what to think, the approach encouraged 'the exploration of where our ideas come from', via 'the development of critical thinking skills'. Young people's need for safety and respect had to be met, in other words, taking account of their own sense of identity, before the wider issues could be effectively addressed. This approach seemed to be working. Qualitative feedback from the young people and education providers involved offered some evidence that the project was 'being valued, needed and that objectives are being met' (Rodgerson, 2018: 5).

These initiatives were about far more than challenging the far right on the streets, activists argued, although that was certainly necessary too. Rather it was about engaging with people, building a movement for change. And this involved being clear 'what it is we stand for', putting out strong messages about what 'we are *for*, not just what we are *against*', through popular anti-racist education, working for social solidarity and social justice agendas.

Conclusion

Popular education can contribute to the development of challenges to far right populism, enabling people to develop more critical understandings of the issues that concern them most, sharing strategies to address these collectively. There are however continuing tensions and dilemmas. For a start, the very definition of popular education has inherent tensions and challenges, as has already been suggested. Who exactly are the 'ordinary people' who are to be the focus of popular education to enable them to take their interests forward in the first place? And do they have real interests in common? Who is to define these, and how to take account of differences within as well as between communities and social movements? (Kane, 2005). These are fundamentally problematic notions underpinning the very concept of popular education – and most especially so in the context of far right populism.

There are continuing tensions inherent in popular education in practice too, starting from where people are at, validating the legitimacy of their concerns while aiming to move people on. Whose perspective needs to provide the focus for moving on and why? When to challenge people's existing beliefs? And when and how to confront their prejudices?

Whose knowledge really counts and on what basis? How do we define the boundaries between respecting people's existing knowledge on the one hand and colluding with more populist approaches on the other, accepting 'common sense' explanations without challenge, when people blame the 'other' rather than unpacking the underlying structural causes of their problems? Here too popular educators need to use their judgement, recognising the inherent dilemmas that may be involved.

Another set of tensions relates to the realm of emotions, the feelings that have been underpinning people's reactions to neoliberal globalisation and the effects of austerity in recent years. How can we work with people's emotions productively? Working with emotions is potentially challenging whatever the situation, let alone in the context of far right populism, surrounded by feelings of anxiety, powerlessness, resentment, shame, fear and hatred of the 'other' – a context in which expressions of racism, anti-Semitism, misogyny, Islamophobia and xenophobia have been becoming increasingly normalised. Coping with such emotions requires resilience; the ability to contain your own feelings as well as to contain the feelings of others (Hoggett et al, 2009). These requirements pose continuing challenges, then, with no immediate prospect of becoming redundant in the contemporary context.

There are implications here for those concerned with the education and training of popular educators and participatory action researchers.

Universities and colleges need to ensure that they provide their students with safe spaces for ongoing cycles of reflection and action within their programmes of learning, taking account of the importance of the emotional dimensions involved. Employers need to recognise the importance of providing support as part of continuing professional development for their staff. And activists need to develop their own support strategies, finding ways of looking after themselves and effectively managing the stresses that they experience. They need to do this as individuals, and as members of mutual support networks, sharing experiences and reflecting on these together as the basis for imagining alternative futures.

Dreams and utopias are essential components of any educational practice with the power to unmask what Paulo Freire has described as the dominant lies (Freire, 1996), just as they have been essential components when it comes to sharing scenarios for transformative futures. Hope was an ontological need, he argued. But even this was not enough. It was *critical* hope that was needed for the fierce struggle to build a better world. Which is why popular education and participatory action research are more relevant than ever, supporting movements for justice, solidarity and social transformation.

References

Banks, S., Armstrong, A., Bonner, A., Hall, Y., Harman, P., Johnston, L., Levi, C., Smith, K. and Taylor, R. (2019) 'Between research and community development: negotiating a contested space for collaboration and creativity', in S. Banks, A. Hart and P. Ward (eds), *Co-Producing Research: A Community Development Approach*, Bristol: Policy Press, pp 21–48.

Banks, S., Hart, A. and Wards, P. (eds) (2019) *Co-producing Research: A Community Development Approach*, Bristol: Policy Press, p xii.

Clarke, S., Hoggett, P. and Thompson, S. (eds) (2006) *Emotion, Politics and Society*, Basingstoke: Palgrave Macmillan.

Crowther, J., Galloway, V. and Martin, I. (eds) (2005) *Popular Education: Engaging the Academy*, Leicester: NIACE.

Demertzis, N. (2006) 'Emotion and populism', in S. Clarke, P. Hoggett and S. Thompson (eds), *Emotion, Politics and Society*, Basingstoke: Macmillan Palgrave, pp 103–22.

Freedman, D. (2011) *The Assault on Universities: A Manifesto for Resistance*, London: Pluto.

Freire, P. (1972) *Pedagogy of the Oppressed*, Harmondsworth: Penguin.

Freire, P. (1996) *Pedagogy of Hope*, London: Bloomsbury.

Grayson, J. (2010) 'Borders, glass floors and anti-racist popular adult education', in M. Mayo and J. Annette (eds), *Taking Part?*, Leicester: NIACE, pp 156–68.

Hartley, T. (2010) 'Proving a point: effective social, political and citizenship education in South Yorkshire', in M. Mayo and J. Annette (eds), *Taking Part?*, Leicester: NIACE, pp 141–55.

Harvey, D. (1990) *The Condition of Modernity*, Oxford: Blackwell.

Hoggett, P. (2016) *Politics, Identity and Emotion*, London: Routledge.

Hoggett, P., Mayo, M. and Miller, C. (2009) *The Dilemmas of Development Work*, Bristol: Policy Press.

Hytner, D. (2019) 'Rose rages at racism', *The Guardian*, 5 April, p 55.

Jones, O. (2011) *Chavs*, London: Verso.

Kick It Out (2017) *Football in Pursuit of Equality (E), Inclusion (I) and Cohesion (C)*, Kick It Out.

Kane, L. (2005) 'Ideology matters', in J. Crowther, V. Galloway and I. Martin (eds), *Popular Education: Engaging the Academy*, Leicester: NIACE, pp 32–42.

Kyneswood, B. (2019) 'Co-production as a new way of seeing: using photographic exhibitions to challenge dominant stigmatising discourses', in S. Banks, A. Hart and P. Ward (eds), *Co-Producing Research: A Community Development Approach*, Bristol: Policy Press, pp 155–80.

Laclau, E. (2005) 'Populism: what's in a name?', in F. Panizza (ed) *Populism and the Mirror of Democracy*, London: Verso, pp 32–49.

Lazaridis, G., Campani, G. and Benviste, A. (eds) (2016) *The Rise of the Far Right in Europe*, Basingstoke: Palgrave Macmillan.

Ledwith, M. (2005) *Community Development: A Critical Approach*, Bristol: Policy Press.

Ledwith, M. and Springett, J. (2010) *Participatory Practice: Community-Based Action for Transformative Change*, Bristol: Policy Press.

McKenzie, L. (2015) *Getting By: Estates, Class and Cultures in Austerity Britain*, Bristol: Policy Press.

Malik, K. (2018) 'No reds under beds, but the young are awake to the flaws of capitalism', *The Guardian*, 21 January, p 17.

Mayo, M. and Rooke, A. (2006) *Active Learning for Active Citizenship*, Crown Copyright.

Mouffe, C. (2018) *For a Left Populism*, London: Verso.

Panizza, F. (2005) 'Introduction: populism and the mirror of democracy', in. F. Panizza (ed), *Populism and the Mirror of Democracy*, London: Verso, pp 1–31.

Passmore, K. (2019) 'Bristol', in P. Sng (ed), *Invisible Britain: Portraits of Hope and Resilience*, Bristol: Policy Press.

Rodgerson, C. (2018) *Routes, Executive Summary and Local Context*, Show Racism the Red Card.

Shaw, M. and Mayo, M. (2016) 'Class, inequality and community development: editorial introduction', in M. Shaw and M. Mayo (eds), *Class, Inequality and Community Development*, Bristol: Policy Press, pp 3–22.

Sng, P. (ed) (2019) *Invisible Britain: Portraits of Hope and Resilience*, Bristol: Policy Press.

Sveinsson, K. (ed) (2009) *Who Cares about the White Working Class?*, London: Runneymede Trust.

The World Transformed (2018) The World Transformed programme, [online] https://theworldtransformed.org

Wacquant, L. (2007) 'Territorial stigmatization in the age of advanced marginality', *Thesis Eleven*, 91: 66–77.

Ward, P., Banks, S., Hart, A. and Pahl, K. (2019) 'Conclusion: imagining different communities and making them happen', in S. Banks, A. Hart, K. Pahl and P. Ward (eds), *Co-producing Research: A Community Development Approach*, Bristol: Policy Press, 203–9.

Wodak, R. (2015) *The Politics of Fear*, London: Sage.

SIX

Social-media-weaponised populism and community development

Jacques Boulet

This chapter examines the resurfacing of populism and its much-discussed and documented adoption and enactment by leaders and citizens. More specifically and in the Freirean (1970) 'problem posing' tradition, this chapter discusses reasons for this (re-)emergence and its effects on people's daily lives and their participation in community life against the wider political–economic background, two areas central to much community development theory and practice.

Trying to understand the genesis of contemporary 'populism(s)', the study focuses on the 'populus', the 'people', both as 'objects' of populist impositions and processes and as their 'subjects', indeed, their co-producers. The first question posed is: what is going on with and around people – especially their modalities of 'being' and 'relating' – rendering them more 'prone' to being influenced by populisms and become populisms' 'accomplices'? Second, what role do social media play in this imposition/complicity dialectic? Indeed, social media powerfully invade and interpenetrate all levels and processes of the political economy, of people's everyday experiences and their subjective-affective lives, and they infest the mediating institutions operating 'between' the virtual global and the imperceptible here-and-now. Finally, a third question: what is the effect of such socially mediated populism on communities and on efforts to (re)develop and maintain them? Some ideas about ways to resist the (combined) assault of populism and social media and restart the project of democracy conclude the chapter.

Understanding modern populism(s): revisiting Arendt, Orwell and others

I wonder what Hannah Arendt would say about politics, power, the 'mob' and the 'masses' today, nearly 70 years after *The Origins of Totalitarianism* (1951) appeared. She saw the rise of totalitarianism occurring in a context where social pathologies had accumulated, eroding the conditions for a viable public life and destroying the necessary balance between personal autonomy and collective will. For Arendt, pathologies rendering populations amenable to 'totalitarian' ideas in the early part of the 20th century included the violent spread of imperialist capital(ism) and colonial suppression and how the ruling classes had transformed the state into an instrument to protect and further their own interests. This de-legitimised political institutions and undermined the principles of citizenship and deliberative consensus central to democratic political process. Add economic problems (the Great Depression), civil unrest and the sense of insecurity caused by disruptions of order and stability people believed they had lived in, and they were open for single, clear and simple ideas about reasons and responsibilities for all ills and evils. Populist leaders painted a path towards a secure future, promising protection against all danger, but demanding to be followed without questioning. Trump's mantra to 'Make America Great Again' (MAGA) offers the clearest contemporary instance of such substance-less promise.

The characteristics Arendt ascribes to those falling for the totalitarian leader or 'system' are instructive: the 'masses' are a quintessentially totalitarian phenomenon, being vast in number but isolated in nature. Totalitarian society creates an immense collection of atomised individuals or people who have been so beaten down that they become apathetic, offering their unconditional loyalty to the totalitarian regime. She suggests that 'identification with the movement and total conformism seem to have destroyed the very capacity for experience, even if it be as extreme as torture or fear of death' (Arendt, 1951: 308). Key features of the totalitarian state include its system of indoctrination, propaganda, isolation, intimidation and brainwashing, instigated and supervised by a secret police, transforming classes and rendering thoughtful individuals unable to make sound political decisions.

Discussions of other instances of populism often include George Orwell's successive 'anti-totalitarian' works *Animal Farm* (1945) and *Nineteen Eighty-Four* (1949). From Orwell's own democratic socialist perspective, both evoke the Soviet Union's communist regime, while Aldous Huxley's *Brave New World* (1932) anticipates scientific developments allowing radical transformations in reproductive technology, documenting the potential of psychological manipulation and classical conditioning, combining to create a rather unpalatable 'utopian society'. Together they present a dystopian mix of features regularly presented by proponents of liberal/social 'western' democracies as a negative foil to contrast against their own assumptions, beliefs and pretentions. A key character in *Nineteen Eighty-Four* illustrates the tenuous nature of that assumed contrast: 'The party told you to reject the evidence of your eyes and ears. It was their final, most essential command' (Orwell, 1949: 178), a sentence comparable to 'democratically elected' President Trump's statement in a speech at a Veterans Convention in Kansas (The Philadelphia Enquirer, 2018): 'What you're seeing and what you're reading is not what's happening.'

Still, many observers of contemporary 21st century political affairs, including populists, would baulk at the link this study seeks to establish between Arendt's 1930s 'totalitarianism' and present-day 'populism(s)'. Indeed, the key features ascribed to the Hitler and Stalin regimes seem to be hardly present in the overt forms she experienced herself, including their genocidal consequences.[1] Yet anyone wondering why politics today is so polarising and dumbfounded about the results of 'democratic' elections of a growing number of populist and nationalist governments and leaders will find startling parallels with the political movements emerging a century or more ago. Today, we are clearly experiencing a revival of reactionary governments in a growing number of nations, including Trump's US, Brexit-dominated UK, several European and Latin American countries, including Turkey, Hungary, Poland and Brazil, and certainly in neoliberal Australia. Here is what Henri Giroux (2018, 2019) thinks about the parallelism:

> While there is no perfect fit between Trump and the fascist societies of Mussolini, Hitler, and Pinochet, 'the basic tenets of extreme nationalism, racism, misogyny, and a hatred of democracy and the rule of law' are too similar to ignore (Johnson, 2018). In this instance, neoliberalism and fascism conjoin and advance in a 'comfortable and mutually compatible project and movement that connects the exploitative values and cruel austerity policies of casino capitalism' with fascist ideals (Gilroy, 2000). These ideals include: the veneration of war; anti-intellectualism; dehumanisation; a populist celebration of ultra-nationalism and racial purity; the suppression of freedom and dissent; a culture of lies; a politics of hierarchy, the spectacularisation of emotion over reason; the weaponisation of language; a discourse of decline; and state violence in heterogeneous forms. Fascism is never entirely interred in the past and the conditions that produce its central assumptions are with us once again, ushering in a period of modern barbarity that

appears to be reaching towards homicidal extremes (Bottici, 2017). (Giroux, 2019)

Many similar statements are being made in Australia. At the time of the 2019 federal election, columnist Jacqueline Maley (2019a) quotes John Williams' statement that the (previous prime minister) 'Howard became a "mild populist" who spoke for so-called "middle Australians" [now the "quiet" Australians], who were uneasy with Asian immigration and, later, the idea that Islamic terrorism might somehow be imported to Australia via boat people'. After the re-election of the conservative Morrison government, she comments (Maley, 2019b):

> When an emboldened government that rejects transparency collides with the erosion of public confidence in democracy, freedoms will die. And they will die quietly, behind closed doors, without even enough information for a proper post-mortem.

Kemal Rijken's (2019) overview of the rise of far-right conservative parties and their gradual entry into governments in Europe shows how their dogmatic structure and philosophy prevent the governments they have been part of from engaging in the necessary compromises when governing a country. Failure to compromise contributes to the neoliberal process of 'moving' the political 'centre' ever more to the right and, aided and abetted by the manipulative influence of modern communication systems (discussed later), this, in turn, damages the centrist parties themselves. In addition, 'movements' like the Tea Party (US), the *gilets jaunes* (France), the neo-fascist and neo-Nazi groups and parties have appeared in many nations, alongside the nationalist tropes generated by Trump (MAGA), the Brexit phenomenon and parties like One Nation in Australia. Globally, rejection of migration and refugees widens and racism deepens (Miller, 2018), combining the voices of resentment ('we are the forgotten people' and 'we no longer count in our country') with those of the deniers of climate change (just one of the 'inventions' of the well-off city 'elites') (Han, 2018a, 2018b; Hearse, 2019). Politics is thus reduced to a *cultural conflict* between (left) 'intelligentsia', protesting from their prosperous city comfort zones, and the 'forgotten' groups, especially in the regions, fearing under- and unemployment, feeling loss of control over their lives and livelihoods and grasping at any straw promising certainty, guidance and 'greatness'.

Examining the intricacies of the 'culture wars', Peter Limberg (2018) prefaced his article with a 1992 election quote from Pat Buchanan, considered by many (e.g. MacLean, 2017) the prototype of the 'new' populist leader and agitator:

> My friends, this election is about more than who gets what. It is about who we are. It is about what we believe, and what we stand for as Americans. There is a religious war going on in this country, a cultural war as critical to the kind of nation we shall be as the Cold War itself, for this war is for the soul of America.

Critical of the reductionist 'cultural' approach in such statements, Anton Jäger (2018) and Jan-Werner Müller (2016) hold on to the underlying class structure on which culture 'wars' and populism rest and from which they emerge. Similarly, Walden Bello (2019) covers a century of what he calls global 'counterrevolutionary' attempts, while Buyung-Chul Han (2018b) updates Michel Foucault's (1976) analysis of power to the digital age. Discipline is no longer solely a matter of the institution; the new panopticons are the social media where individuals submit to self-discipline or to 'sadness by design' (Lovink, 2019). In contrast to prisoners, who – at least – had the freedom to lose themselves in thought, the political economy of capitalism intends to exploit our private and shared emotions to better sell us often unneeded consumer goods, the social media imposing a totalising form of control.

Indeed, social media sell us 'regimes of truth' governing knowledge, life, relationships and the ways in which individuals construct their subjectivity between a precarious sense of 'self' and a precarious sense of a 'collective' they no longer feel part of. Australian cartoonist Leunig (2019) neatly illustrated the shifts in populist 'operations' in a cartoon with the caption: 'Big Brother is now telling you you're amazing, incredible, awesome and beautiful, and you don't need to be more than you are right now because you are enough.'

The 'populism' of the social media

How do social media influence our daily lives, our emotional and relational 'household', public and community life and a meanwhile globalised political economy? Trying to comprehensively understand their workings and effects is not easy, as information is spread across disparate publications and sources and comes to us in fragments seemingly only relevant to specific areas and from specific perspectives, a dispersion making it difficult to detect the relationships and mutual causalities of factors operating at various levels.

From a more encompassing philosophical/ethical and critical viewpoint, Laurence Tribe (1973) offers an entry point, written at a time when the ecological consequences of technological progress started to emerge: for example, Rachel Carson's *Silent Spring* (1962). While Tribe's title, 'Technological Assessment and the Fourth Discontinuity: The Limits of Instrumental Rationality', today sounds somewhat bombastic, its warning seems even more relevant. Tribe suggests that after the Copernican, the Darwinian and the Freudian 'discontinuities',

> a fourth great discontinuity – that between man [sic] and his machines ... must be bridged if man is to live in harmony with his tools, and hence with himself. The only alternative to such unified coexistence, according to this view, is the dilemma of either rejecting man's technologies in Luddite panic – or becoming their slaves. (Tribe, 1973: 617)

Referring to Weber's (1954) distinction between '*purpose*-rational' and '*value*-rational' ('*Zweckrational*' and '*Wertrational*'), Tribe (1973: 660) concludes that:

> if we make no effort to progress ... in the direction of a constitutive rationality that will enable us to someday do better, it is hard to see what can prevent technology assessment from remaining purely technological ... the ... notion of technology ruling man [sic] by its autonomous imperatives becomes frighteningly plausible.

What would Tribe now make of our being swept up and inundated by the tsunami of 'social' media, starting a mere decade after he wrote his article? He would heartily agree with John Naughton's call for a '21st-century Martin Luther to challenge the church of tech'. Referring to himself as a 'recovering utopian', 25 years after his initial 'bedazzlement' by the internet's promises of empowerment, democracy, enlightenment, his article's first paragraph, like Luther's featuring 95 theses, is sobering:

> A new power is loose in the world. It is nowhere and yet it's everywhere. It knows everything about us – our movements, our thoughts, our desires, our fears, our secrets, who our friends are, our financial status, even how well we

sleep at night. We tell it things that we would not whisper to another human being. It shapes our politics, stokes our appetites, loosens our tongues, heightens our moral panics, keeps us entertained (and therefore passive). We engage with it 150 times or more every day, and with every moment of contact we add to the unfathomable wealth of its priesthood. And we worship it because we are, somehow, mesmerised by it. (Naughton, 2017)

Apart from connecting people and facilitating social intercourse across space and in 'real time', social media and electronic technologies are regularly credited with being instrumental in the growth and strength of protest movements; they get people together for 'flash-mobs' or gather 'clicks' for petitions, condemnations, protests and expressions of unhappiness about local/state/federal/global politics and economics. Indeed, 'clicktivism' has now spread widely as a useful – if not always successful – armchair-and-desk/laptop/mobile form of participation in local-to-global affairs, offering a sense of collectivist action, precisely the space populism also claims.

An early voice warning against illusions about democracy, freedom and liberty being brought on by the electronic media is Evgeny Morozov (2011). He carefully distinguishes between threats to our privacy and how they are related but not identical to the threats to our democracy. A subtitle in his final chapter, 'Taming the Wicked Authoritarianism', specifically denies Zuckerberg's claims that Facebook's purpose is to 'make the world more open and connected' (Hoffmann et al, 2018). Morozov (2017: 319–20) urges cyber-realists to stop believing that democracy will be run from Silicon Valley, concluding: 'a world made of bytes may defy the law of gravity but absolutely nothing dictates that it should also defy the law of reason' (or the laws of love, solidarity and justice).

Following up on his earlier *Rich Media, Poor Democracy* (2000), Robert McChesney (2013) confirms Morozov's warnings; he shows how the political economy of the internet is dominated by a handful of monopolies, making their owners hyper-rich while colonising the cyberspace, destroying credible journalism in the process and leaving fertile ground for new types of 'thought leaders' (Drezner, 2017), 'influencers' and TED-talkers, reshaping the 'world of ideas'. Drezner suggests that three factors have 'caused' this reshaping: erosion of trust in expertise and knowledge; increasing political polarisation; and the growing power of the plutocracy; to which i^2 would add a growing receptivity for populist memes and tropes. A recent report for the UK

Institute for Strategic Dialogue (ISD) by Davey and Ebner (2019: 14) documents 'the extent to which extreme-right concepts such as the "great replacement" theory and calls for "remigration" have entered mainstream political discourse and are now referenced by politicians who head states and sit in parliaments'. To illustrate this: the *New York Times* published three articles analysing Trump's 'Twitter use' (McIntire and Confessore, 2019), the 'ultimate weapon of mass dissemination'. As to the disseminated content, Tim Dean (2019) has lost faith in 'free speech', because the '"Anti-social" media ... have gone to great lengths to build new technologies that promote the worst features of bad faith discourse', thus undermining one of the central preconditions for democracy to work and for communities to engage in political discourse leading to effective action for positive social change.

In over 1,000 pages, Shoshana Zuboff (2019) and Tim Wu (2016) aptly 'summarise' the connection between the global and everyday/ experiential processes of Lovink's (2019) totalising forms of control. Zuboff describes how tech companies gather our personal data online, selling them to the highest bidder, whether government or retailer. In 'surveillance capitalism', profit depends not only on predicting but on modifying our online behaviour and the decisions we make in our economic and political 'choices' – however predefined they already are anyway. Resonating at once with Arendt, Tribe and Foucault, Zuboff talks about 'totalitarianism as a new species of power' which has shifted from the direct violence occurring during the first half of last century, to 'instrumentarian power', operating through behavioural modification, aided and abetted through technology and the social media (Zuboff, 2019: 354–60). Wondering how this fusion of capitalism and the digital will shape the values defining our future, she suggests that the real choice we need to make is between allowing the power of technology to enrich the few and impoverish the many, or to harness it for wider distribution of the potential social and economic benefits of capitalism. Like Tribe, Zuboff suggests that the existential issue at hand is whether we will be masters of the digital or its slaves.

Christl and Spiekermann (2016) equally document social-media-generated power imbalances leading to systematic discrimination, companies hurting consumers, warning that in the long term we may witness the 'end of dignity'. For Franco Berardi (2010: 100), this end has already been reached through 'semiocapitalism': 'the goods that are circulating in the economic world – informational, financial, imaginary – are signs, figures, images, projections, expectations', robbing their 'consumers' of the human capabilities setting us apart from other species while giving us many additional responsibilities.

In his history of 'attention seeking', Tim Wu (2016: 215–16) warns that 'the first great harvester of human attention, it must never be forgotten, was religion. The impulse to idolise has not faded in our secular age, only gone seeking after strange gods'. The digital age has introduced the 'establishment of the celebrity-industrial complex', leading Wu (2016: 243–4) to argue for a 'human reclamation project … in which we must act, individually and collectively, to make our attention our own again, and so reclaim ownership of the very experience of living', certainly a necessary precondition for any form of community engagement.

While Zuboff sees the spectrum of totalitarianism and populism moving from violence-based to 'instrumentarian' (by 'policy' and 'virtually' – almost subcutaneously – penetrating the life-worlds of individuals and communities), it still features plenty of violent and often murderous state repression of journalism and opposition (the Saudi power cartel's murder of journalist Khashoggi being a recent example, the police violence against Extinction Rebellion demonstrations another – Dodd, 2019). Feeling like a 'fox in the henhouse', *Observer* journalist Carole Cadwalladr (2019) used a TED talk to tell the assembled billionaires, 'the Gods of Silicon Valley: Mark Zuckerberg, Sheryl Sandberg, Larry Page, Sergey Brin and Jack Dorsey', that 'they had broken democracy'; she had:

> walked among the tech gods last week. I don't think they set out to enable massacres to be live-streamed (Myanmar, Christchurch). Or massive electoral fraud in a once-in-a-lifetime, knife-edge vote (Trump, Brexit, Cambridge Analytica). But they did. If they don't feel guilt, shame and remorse, if they don't have a burning desire to make amends, their boards, shareholders, investors, employees and family members need to get them out. (Cadwalladr, 2019)

Coincidentally, the G20 meeting in Osaka agreed to demand that the tech gods stop filming and otherwise aiding and abetting terrorism and terrorists (G20 OSAKA Declaration, 2019), leaving me wondering whether the assembled politicians included state terrorism in that demand. With *The Citizen Lab* (2018), i believe not.

The omnipresence of social media in our everyday lives distances us from what is happening directly around us (sometimes dangerously so), while 'putting us in touch' with an abundance of things, events and people everywhere else. While locals (may) know everything about Trump and Brexit shenanigans, international soccer and Beyoncé's new underwear and can admire beautiful 'influencers' in G-strings in front of the remnants of the Chernobyl disaster (Squires, 2019: 12), active participation in politics and involvement in local communities has not benefited from this virtual omnipresence. The use of the relational language of 'liking', 'following' and 'snapchatting' with potentially thousands of far-flung unknowns and barely knowns mimics the intimacy of relational closeness, while the constant production and exchange of 'selfies' aids and abets the presumed centrality of the attention-seeking but often insecure individual person (Gilroy-Ware, 2017); the relational shallowness offers easy 'followers' for populists, 'attention' for self-advertising politicians and 'performative self-presentation' for identity politics alike.

The personal and social promises and predicaments of the social media are being discussed widely, the latter meanwhile confirmed by a great deal of research – psychological, neurological, social-psychological and sociological – and by a growing number of writers; even a summary would go beyond the space available in this chapter and it has been offered elsewhere (Boulet, 2018a). In our consumerist culture, where 'freedom', choice, self-direction and the making of profit are sacrosanct, even if the personal and community harm caused by the use of certain products is great, their consumption grows unabated. Indeed, internet addiction joins a rather long list of addictions where 'harm minimisation' is the preferred response, rather than addressing and eliminating their real causes. Gambling, drugs and alcohol and now internet and social media (over-)use fills the coffers of corporations, criminals and (via taxes) governments, so dealing with real causes will be avoided at all costs (Boulet, 2018a: 8).

Former Australian politician Carmen Lawrence (2015) summarises the connections between the erosion of democratic politics and the way we live our personal lives:

> It seems to me that, almost imperceptibly, we have become enamoured with absolutism with a Western flavour; intolerant of nuance and subtlety, always seeking the ultimate in satisfaction or performance – cascading 'likes' and stars and ratings driving our decisions. Shouting at ourselves in every space and staring at tiny screens, dangerously unaware of the real world around us.

Not only in the political sphere do social media play a deeply transformative role; Elizabeth Anderson (2017) extends arguments about contemporary authoritarianism into our workplaces, wondering why they resemble authoritarian private governments – and why we can't see it. Many employers minutely regulate workers' speech, clothing and manners on the job, often extending their authority to their off-duty lives (aided and abetted by electronics); workers can be fired for their political speech, recreational activities, diet and almost anything employers care to govern.

Authoritarianism is now a feature of the new work culture across institutions and organisations, accompanying changes in organisational structure and process imposed by neoliberalism and supported and orchestrated by IT-based communication and information flows (Zuboff, 2019). Indeed, alongside the promised 'trickle-down' benefits of the neoliberal capitalist economy, distributing the bulk of the value-added through workers' work upwards to shareholders and the managerial class – and bolstered by financial permutations in 'mutant capitalism' (Han, 2018b) – more top-down control over work processes is now electronically possible. Instructions about workflows, service delivery and expected productivity and 'outcomes' (including in the community and social services sectors) now *directly* arrive on workers' desks or mobile electronic gadgets without any need for cooperation, teamwork or consideration as to their adequacy for purpose. Surveillance capitalism operates like a global IT conveyer belt, also allowing for the intrusion of work into what used to be 'off work' time and space (Eggers, 2013, referencing Orwell; Monbiot, 2016; and Lyon, 2018).

To conclude, Nicholas Agar (2019) suggests that in the digital economy, accountants, baristas and cashiers can be 'automated-out' of employment; so can surgeons, airline pilots and cab drivers. Machines are said to do these jobs more efficiently, accurately and inexpensively. However, these developments may result in a radically disempowered humanity; as the digital revolution brought us new gadgets and new things to do with them, developments in artificial intelligence will enable computers to take over not just routine tasks but also the kind of 'mind work' and 'community work' that previously relied on human intellect and direct contact. This threatens human agency, as Henry Mintzberg (2015) foretells the impact on organisations and institutions and the mediated effects on cooperation, collaboration and conviviality:

> Especially for operating around the globe, electronic communication has become essential. But the heart of enterprise remains rooted in personal collaborative relationships, albeit networked by the new information technologies. Thus, in localities and organizations, across

societies and around the globe, beware of 'networked individualism' where people communicate readily while struggling to collaborate. The new digital technologies, wonderful as they are in enhancing communication, can have a negative effect on collaboration unless they are carefully managed. An electronic device puts us in touch with a keyboard, that's all.

Where to community (development)?

Applying Chomsky's updated (2002) analysis in *Manufacturing Consent* to social media and their effect on societies and individual persons, it would be rather easy to declare democracy an illusion, and with it many of the values underpinning community development. Indeed, those who control people through fear, appeal to their greed and are able to grab their attention to manipulate their desires are the ones who – in fact – are dictating policies, societal directions and the intentions of community members alike.

Considering that we are running out of time to prevent our earth becoming inhabitable for humans and for many other species, it would be easy to agree with Berardi (2010: 1) that 'the social civilization is over'; the nature of humans as 'subjects', their consciousness and emancipation can no longer be imagined. The 'Neoliberal precarization of labor and the media dictatorship' have destroyed 'the cultural antibodies that in the past made resistance possible' and – parenthetically – that has inspired community development since its beginnings. He continues:

> My knowledge and my understanding do not show the possibility of any acceptable development out of the present catastrophe. But catastrophe … is exactly the point where we move beyond the present and a new landscape is revealed. I do not see that landscape because my knowledge and my understanding are limited, and the limits of my language are the limits of my world. My knowledge and understanding are missing the event, the singularity that might open onto that new landscape.
>
> So I must act *as if. As if* the forces of labor and knowledge may overcome the forces of greed. *As if* the cognitive workers may overcome the fractalization of their life and intelligence. I must resist simply because I cannot know what is happening after the future, and I must preserve the

consciousness and sensibility of social solidarity, of human empathy, of gratuitous activity, of freedom, equality and fraternity. Just in case, right? (Berardi, 2010: 2)

Sharing his acceptance of our existential uncertainty and the questions with merely tentative answers we face, all I can hope for is that this chapter joins the others in this book as instances of Berardi's 'just in case'. As mentioned before, potential responses need to be aware of the various contextual levels at which social-media-enabled and -enhanced populism 'works' in all its virtual 'incarnations'. José Ramos (2017: 109) proposes a futurist strategy by 'looking back to remember yesterday's future and what happened to make that future'. As community development practitioners, looking at our techno/electronic 'shadow', we need to accept that it is part of the present and the new 'commons' we want to craft together. This requires an exercise in anticipatory innovation, innovating for the commons in a way that *creates* a future rather than taking it away, being cognisant of the interpenetrating 'layers' through which political, economic, institutional and everyday experiential processes 'make' reality.

In November 2019, the Just Net Coalition (https://justnetcoalition. org/digital-justice-manifesto.pdf) launched a *Digital Justice Manifesto* addressing many of the issues touched upon in this chapter and they suggest a strong vision and strategies for reaching 'digital democracy' and breaking the power of the 'big five' including Google, Apple, Facebook, Amazon and Microsoft (GAFAM). Together with warnings by EU Justice Chief Vera Jourova to the US IT giants for making money from coronavirus-related fake news, instead of putting in more efforts to stop the deluge (Chee and Baczynska, 2020), they offer eloquent instances as to where the community activists' efforts need to be aimed.

At the political–economic level, with Agar (2019 – and meanwhile many others assembled in New Economy Networks, such as in Australia (nena@neweconomy.org.au) and internationally the Peer-to-Peer (P2P) global network (https://p2pfoundation.net/) – a 'hybrid social–digital economy' could both harness possibilities and efficiencies of digital technologies being inserted in a localised 'social economy', centred on 'connections between human minds'. Resonating central community development values, in a hybrid social–digital economy, people do the jobs for which feelings and direct social relations matter and machines take on data-intensive work, but humans will have to insist on their personal and social relevance in a digital age.

Christl and Spiekermann (2016) suggest imposing increased regulation, enforcing transparency from outside the 'black boxes', a 'privacy-friendly' legal and technical model for the digital economy and broad-scale knowledge, awareness and education. Rejecting Berardi's inevitability, Zuboff (2019: 521–2) suggests that we need to 'rekindle the sense of outrage and loss over what is being taken from us ... the human expectation of sovereignty over one's own life and authorship of one's own experience ... [turning to] Tom Paine, who called upon each generation to assert its will when illegitimate forces hijack the future'. Tim Wu (2016: 343–4) calls for a 'human reclamation project ... the most vital human resource in need of conservation and protection is likely to be our own consciousness and mental space'. With David Lyon and Wu, i propose a community development strategy of conversations and attempts at disconnecting from the global 'attention harvesters' by locally reconnecting, which will start 'paying communal dividends as well as profiting the individual' (Lyon, 2018: 191–7).

Otto Scharmer (2019) bridges the space between the political-economic and the institutional/organisational levels by proposing that, '[a]s systems collapse, people rise'. As part of the rising global activist movement he detects, he refers to Greta Thunberg's Fridays for Future, the Extinction Rebellion, founded in the UK in 2018, aiming to mobilise non-violent climate action worldwide, Sunrise, a US youth-led movement advocating political action on climate change, and teaming up with US Representative Alexandria Ocasio-Cortez and her proposed Green New Deal. Important for community action strategies, Scharmer identifies four main differences between the 1968 movements and those of 2019: the key figures are young women, not young men; they are arguing for a change in consciousness, not just for a change in ideology; they intentionally collaborate with earlier generations, rather than fighting against them; they are using technology in intentional and *new ways* (Scharmer, 2019: 1). Several of these strategies have been honed throughout earlier movements, experimenting with new organisational and relational forms and formats. I am particularly thinking about the diverse 'Occupy' experiences and the 'Indignados' in Spain, the global move towards re-localisation and municipalisation, for which Arturo Escobar's (2018) *Designs for the Pluriverse* offers a 'value-rational' purpose that Max Weber and Tribe would have agreed with.

Echoing Scharmer, Mintzberg (2015) comments on what is needed for positive organisational change, suggesting that 'we tend to make a great fuss about leadership these days' but that 'communityship' is what we need: 'great leaders create, enhance and support a sense of community in their organizations, and that requires hands-on management ... beyond ... individual leadership, to recognize the collective nature of effective enterprise'.

Finally, the (inter)personal level of community praxis. Naming them 'crises', Peter Limberg (2018) usefully summarises the values eroded through the interacting thrust by populist political formations and the invasions of electronics in all spheres of our lives; they are values community development thinkers/practitioners need to recapture and restore at the centre of their endeavours, introducing them in their conversations with colleagues and their communities so that they may contribute to the vital regeneration of community capability:

- The meaning crisis weakened our collective understanding of what ought to be.
- The reality crisis fractured our collective understanding of what is.
- The belonging crisis took away a genuine feeling of community.
- The proximity crisis removed distance from conflicting views.
- The sobriety crisis reduced our agency and turned us into addicts.
- The warfare crisis transformed our minds into weapons for hidden wars in plain sight.

Joining the growing calls for 'digital detox', Cal Newport (2019: 35–6) urges us to exercise *Digital Minimalism* to gain control over the lure of the little screens by applying three principles: clutter (of IT and social media platforms) is costly; optimisation (of what you really need and like) is important; intentionality (around 'why' you're using the media) is satisfying. In our personal, activist and professional lives, community practitioners need to be more conscious about the personal, social and material costs of our morbid dedication to IT and the social media.

However, necessary resistance against the various shades of populism invading our lifeworlds remains, regeneration of our relational capabilities and our communities should be the most important aspiration for community practitioners – in fact, it may be our best defence against populism. Carefully reconsidering four characteristics of 'community' crucial to regenerating aware and socially productive forms of relating and of 'being' community may be useful here: engaging in enduring shared time; inhabiting shared place/space; celebrating reciprocity; rebalancing self- and collective interest (Boulet, 2018b). And, finally, in this 'community', non-human persons and things need to be included to survive the many human-produced ecological challenges.

Notes

1   Obviously, westerners generally 'forget' or 'externalise' references to the horrors their own nations committed during the four centuries of invasions into and colonisation of the 'first nations' across all other continents, as much as we still 'externalise' what our political–economic impositions continue to do to the earth.

2   Readers will notice that – except at the start of a sentence and in quotes – i resist the capitalisation of the first-person pronoun – the 'perpendicular pronoun' – in recognition of the rather pretentious and simply wrong cultural assumptions in western writing about the centrality of the speaking, writing or thinking author/ subject – or, more generally, of the individual person – in the entirety of the living and changing context and the complexity of the interconnections they report on. In modernist research, such assumptions lead to the paradox of *both* denying subjectivity in the researcher, inter-subjectivity in the research relationship and condemning the 'researched other' to objectification (or a form of 'enclosed subjectivity').

References

Agar, N. (2019) *How to Be Human in the Digital Economy*, Cambridge, MA: MIT Press.

Anderson, E. (2017) *Private Government: How Employers Rule Our Lives (and Why We Don't Talk about It)*, Princeton, NJ: Princeton University Press.

Arendt, H. (1951) *The Origins of Totalitarianism*, London: Penguin Classics.

Bello, W. (2019) *Counterrevolutions: The Global Rise of the Far Right*, Rugby: Practical Action Publishing.

Berardi, F. (2010) 'Precariousness, Catastrophe And Challenging The Blackmail Of The Imagination', *Affinities: A Journal of Radical Theory, Culture and Action*, 4(2): 1–4.

Bottici, C. (2017) 'One question fascism (Part one)', *One Question*, [online] http://stateofnatureblog.com/tag/fascism/

Boulet, J. (2018a) 'The promises and predicaments of the social media: is it Zuckerberg's "community" we're talking about in this journal…?', *New Community*, 16(2): 2–8.

Boulet, J. (2018b) 'Researching is relating in place and time', in M. Kumar and S. Pattanayak (eds), *Positioning Research, Shifting Paradigms, Interdisciplinarity and Indigeneity*, Delhi: Sage, pp 106–41.

Cadwalladr, C. (2019) 'My TED talk: how I took on the tech titans in their lair' (www.ted.com/speakers/carole_cadwalladr), *The Guardian*, 12 April, [online] https://www.theguardian.com/uk-news/2019/apr/21/carole-cadwalladr-ted-tech-google-facebook-zuckerberg-silicon-valley

Carson, R. (1962) *Silent Spring*, Boston: Houghton Mifflin Harcourt.

Chee, F.Y. and Baczynska, G. (2020) 'Social media giants told to stop profiting from coronavirus clickbait', *Sydney Morning Herald*, 3 April, [online] www.smh.com.au/world/europe/social-media-giants-told-to-stop-profiting-from-coronavirus-clickbait-20200403-p54gtr.html

Chomsky, N. (with Herman, E.) (2002) *Manufacturing Consent: The Political Economy of the Mass Media*, New York: Pantheon Books.

Christl, W. and Spiekermann, S. (2016) *Networks of Control: A Report on Corporate Surveillance, Digital Tracking, Big Data and Privacy*, Vienna: AGfacultas Universitätsverlag, [online] http://crackedlabs.org/dl/Christl_Spiekermann_Networks_Of_Control.pdf

Davey, J. and Ebner, J. (2019) *'The Great Replacement': The Violent Consequences of Mainstreamed Extremism*, [online] www.isdglobal.org/isdpublications/the-great-replacement-the-violent-consequences-of-mainstreamed-extremism/

Dean, T. (2019) 'Free speech has failed us', [online] https://ethics.org.au/free-speech-has-failed-us/

Dodd, V. (2019) 'Police take hard line on Extinction Rebellion protesters', *The Guardian*, 24 May [online] www.theguardian.com/environment/2019/may/24/police-take-hardline-on-arrested-extinction-rebellion-protesters

Drezner, D. (2017) *The Ideas Industry: How Pessimists, Partisans, and Plutocrats are Transforming the Marketplace of Ideas*, London: Oxford University Press.

Escobar, A. (2018) *Designs for the Pluriverse: Radical Interdependence, Autonomy, and the Making of Worlds*, Durham, NC: Duke University Press.

Eggers, D. (2013) *The Circle*, New York: Alfred A. Knopf.

Foucault, M. (1976) *The Birth of Biopolitics*, New York: St Martin's Press.

Freire, P. (1970) *Pedagogy of the Oppressed*, New York: Continuum.

G20 OSAKA Declaration (2019) [online] www.g20.utoronto.ca/2019/2019-g20-osaka-leaders-declaration.html

Gilroy-Ware, M. (2017) *Filling the Void: Emotion, Capitalism and Social Media*, London: Repeater Books.

Giroux, H. (2018) *The Public in Peril: Trump and the Menace of American Authoritarianism*, New York: Routledge.

Giroux, H. (2019) 'Rethinking the normalization of fascism in the post-truth era', *Tikkun*, [online] https://www.tikkun.org/rethinking-the-normalization-of-fascism-in-the-post-truth-era

Han, B-C. (2018a) *The Expulsion of the Other – Society, Perception and Communication Today*, London: Polity Press.

Han, B-C. (2018b) *Psychopolitics: Neoliberalism and New Technologies of Power*, London: Verso.

Hearse, P. (2019) 'The global networks of neofascism', [online] https://www.redpepper.org.uk/the-global-networks-of-neofascism/

Hoffmann, A.L., Proferes, N. and Zimmer, M. (2018) '"Making the world more open and connected": Mark Zuckerberg and the discursive construction of Facebook and its users', *New Media and Society*, 20(1): 199–218.

Huxley, A. (1932) *Brave New World*, New York: Harper & Brothers.

Jäger, A. (2018) *Kleine Anti-geschiedenis van het Populisme* [*A Little Anti-History of Populism*], Breda: De Geus.

Johnson, C. (2018) 'The momentum of Trumpian fascism is building: stopping it is up to us', *Truth Out*, [online] https://truthout.org/articles/the-momentum-of-trumpian-fascism-is-building-stopping-it-is-up-to-us/

Lawrence, C. (2015) 'The memory ladder: learning from the past, living with doubt', in J. Schultz and A. Tiernan (eds), *Griffith Review 51: Fixing the System*, [online] https://griffithreview.com/articles/the-memory-ladder/

Leunig, M. (2019) 'Big Brother' cartoon, *The Age*, 2 March, p 32.

Limberg, P. (2018) *The Memetic Tribes of Culture War 2.0*, [online] https://medium.com/s/world-wide-wtf/memetic-tribes-and-culture-war-2-0-14705c43f6bb

Lovink, G. (2019) *Sad by Design, On Platform Nihilism*, London: Pluto Press.

Lyon, D. (2018) *The Culture of Surveillance*, Cambridge: Polity Press.

MacLean, N. (2017) *Democracy in Chains: The Deep History of the Radical Right's Stealth Plan for America*, New York: Viking Press.

McChesney, R. (2000) *Rich Media, Poor Democracy*, New York: The New Press.

McChesney, R. (2013) *Digital Disconnect: How Capitalism Is Turning the Internet against Democracy*, New York: New Press.

McIntire, M. and Confessore, N. (2019) 'Trump's Twitter presidency: 9 key takeaways', [online] www.nytimes.com/2019/11/02/us/trump-twitter-takeaways.html

Maley, J. (2019a) [online] www.smh.com.au/politics/federal/just-when-you-think-politics-can-t-get-any-lower-someone-introduces-a-bodily-fluid-20190215-p50y2h.html

Maley, J. (2019b) [online] www.smh.com.au/politics/federal/afp-raids-add-to-picture-of-a-morrison-government-emboldened-20190607-p51vkq.html

Miller, N. (2018) 'A new racism: The rise of anti-Semitism is fuelling a frightening new wave of prejudice in Europe', *The Age*, 8 September, pp 20–22.

Mintzberg, H. (2015) 'Networks are not communities', *Druckerforum*, [online] www.druckerforum.org/blog/?p=1024

Monbiot, G. (2016) *How Did We Get into This Mess? Politics, Equality, Nature*, London: Verso.

Morozov, E. (2011) *The Net Delusion: How Not to Liberate the World*, London: Allan Lane/Penguin.

Morozov, E. (2017) *Freedom as a Service: The New Digital Feudalism and the Future of the City*, New York: Farrar, Strauss and Giroux.

Müller, J.W. (2016) *What Is Populism?*, Philadelphia: University of Pennsylvania Press.

Naughton, J. (2017) 'Why we need a 21st-century Martin Luther to challenge the church of tech', *The Guardian*, 29 October, [online] www.theguardian.com/technology/2017/oct/29/why-we-need-a-21st-century-martin-luther-to-challenge-church-of-technology-95-theses

Newport, C. (2019) *Digital Minimalism: On Living Better with Less*, London: Penguin Business.

Orwell, G. (1945) *Animal Farm*, London: Penguin/Random House.

Orwell, G. (1949) *Nineteen Eighty-Four*, London: Penguin Classics.

Ramos, J. (2017) 'FuturesLab: anticipatory experimentation, social emergence and evolutionary change', *Journal of Futures Studies*, 22(2): 107–18.

Rijken, K. (2019) *Eigen Volk. Hoe het rechtsnationalisme Europa veroverde* [*Our Own People: How Right-wing Nationalism Conquered Europe*], Amsterdam: Ambo.

Scharmer, O. (2019) 'As systems collapse, people rise: seven faces of an emerging global movement', Presencing Institute, [online] https://medium.com/presencing-institute-blog/as-systems-collapse-people-rise-seven-faces-of-an-emerging-global-movement 204df6f06e27

Squires, W. (2019) 'Instagram empowers? What rot', *The Sunday Age*, 23 June.

The Philadelphia Enquirer (2018) [online] www.inquirer.com/philly/news/politics/presidential/donald-trump-vfw-speech-kansas-city-what-youre-seeing-reading-not-whats-happening-20180724.html

The Citizen Lab (2018) [online] https://citizenlab.ca/2018/11/open-letter-to-francisco-partners-continued-misuse-of-nso-groups-pegasus-technology/

Tribe, L. (1973) 'Technology assessment and the fourth discontinuity: the limits of instrumental rationality', *Southern California Law Review*, 46: 617–60.

Weber, M. (1954) *Economy and Society*, Cambridge, MA: Harvard University Press.

Wu, T. (2016) *The Attention Merchants: From the Daily Newspaper to Social Media, How Our Time and Attention Is Harvested and Sold*, London: Atlantic Books.

Zuboff, S. (2019) *The Age of Surveillance Capitalism: The Fight for a Human Future at the New Frontier of Power*, London: Profile Books.

SEVEN

Alinsky revisited: 'rubbing raw the resentments of the people'

Peter Szynka

Introduction

The renowned American community organiser, Saul D. Alinsky (1909–72), was under observation by the Federal Bureau of Investigation (FBI) on suspicion of being a communist or of preparing hate crimes and nurturing racial conflicts. These suspicions were at least partly based on his statements about 'resentments'. It turns out that 'resentments' is one of his more important analytical terms to describe the powerlessness among disadvantaged and vulnerable people. This chapter analyses Alinsky's theoretical background and shows that his understanding of 'resentment' was drawn from the ethics of the Scottish philosopher Adam Smith and the German philosopher Friedrich Nietzsche. It can be shown that Alinsky's conceptualisation of the 'organiser' is the antipode of Nietzsche's 'ascetic priest', who 'first needs to hit the wounds that he is promising to heal' (see Nietzsche, 1967: 126). 'Rubbing raw the resentments' and 'to fan the sores of discontent' are Alinsky's medical metaphors describing his technique to understand frustration and aggression, to cool down emotions and to transform its energy into common action and political negotiation. The 'wounds' in the medical metaphor – should be healed. They were hit before the organisers came and the people have been unable to respond. He tried to empower the people by turning personal discontents and problems into public issues.

In contrast, populist agitators, and particularly right-wing agitators, avoid research clarifying the causes of discontent; they deny facts and create simple solutions. They seek power and money for themselves. They regularly try to intensify hate and aggression and then to direct it against scapegoats. These practices may also violate human rights and international agreements. For community development practice it is necessary to understand the difference between agitation as persuasion, research and support of critical thinking and agitation as seduction, manipulation and the practice of misleading others. In this regard it is important to understand the mechanism of 'resentment'. Community development practitioners must deal with people who suffer from resentments and at the same time they need to unmask techniques and the people who create, amplify and make use of them. Revisiting Alinsky leads to the centre of a problem we are facing in our countries today. What are the lessons to be learned from Alinsky for contemporary community development responses to populism? His analysis and his confrontations with McCarthyism and proto-fascist agitator Father McCoughlin provide examples of ways of meeting the challenges we are facing in Germany today, where new prophets of deceit operating through populist politics again carry out the fine art of propaganda, using the new forms of mass communication and the opportunities of social media.

A German perspective

The aim of the chapter is to contribute a German perspective to the international discussion on community development, populism and democratic culture. What does this mean?

The work of Saul David Alinsky (1946, 1971) not only played an important role within Community Organisation (CO) and Community Development (CD) in the United States; he was also important in reshaping social work in Germany after World War II. Many German students and teachers were given stipends in so-called re-education programmes and in this way reconnected with international discussions and Anglo-Saxon concepts of social work such as case work, group work and community work. Before the international discourse was interrupted by the National-Socialists, German social workers and planners picked up the idea of settlement houses and community centres like Toynbee Hall in London or Hull House in Chicago and established their own community centres in Berlin and elsewhere. They began to establish welfare organisations in order to coordinate private activities of benevolence (Müller, 1982: 35, 73, 135).

In former studies I reconstructed Alinsky's theoretical background (Szynka, 2005, 2006). Alinsky was trained as a sociologist and criminologist at the University of Chicago, known as the 'Chicago School of Sociology', a famous centre of sociological studies on immigration and city planning. I tracked down the appreciation and influence of German sociology in the Chicago School. Alinsky was part of a group which I would call the 'Yiddish Connection'. Alinsky, together with Louis Wirth, a German immigrant, and Edvard Shils, could easily read and translate the work of German sociologists and philosophers like Ferdinand Tönnies, Friedrich Nietzsche and Max Weber.

The study will also consider some German political writers who criticised populist tactics during the time that a democratic culture was developing in Germany. It was around 1848 when the first German parliament was established in Frankfurt. Their experiences fit well into the analysis of Alinsky's theoretical background.

These writers are also relevant to the current situation in Germany. At the time of writing this chapter, a few weeks before the election of a new European Parliament in May 2019, nationalist and right-wing parties are trying to build an anti-European coalition and to obstruct democratic culture with money from obscure sources, and using dubious methods and means. Article 20 of the German Basic Constitutional Law states that 'All state authority is derived from the people' and article 21.1 says that 'Political parties should participate in the formation of the will of the people' but they must publicly account for their assets, for their sources and the use of their funds. This is currently not very easy for some right-wing parties. According to German Basic Law, the Constitutional Court can control the constitutionality of political parties in Germany. A similar regulation on the European level is still missing. This makes it challenging for outside powers trying to interfere. Right-wing populism dominates the ongoing discussion of populism in Germany.

What could we learn from Alinsky? Some years ago, in 2016, the FBI published 458 pages of documents on its investigations into Saul Alinsky between 1940 and 1970. Alinsky was suspected of cooperating with communists and of applying class war tactics in his organisations. He was listed in the Rabble Rouser Index of Chicago and suspected of preparing hate crimes and violence while organising working class and black people in the Chicago Woodlawn neighbourhood and in Rochester, New York. An important aspect of the FBI investigation was analysing Alinsky's statements on 'resentments'. He said on several occasions: 'First rub raw the resentments of the people', 'Fan the latent hostilities of many of the people to the point of overt expression' or 'Provide a channel into which the people can drain their underlying guilt for having accepted the previous situation for so long' (Alinsky, 1971: 116). Then, in November 1970, the FBI deleted Saul Alinsky from the Chicago Rabble Rouser Index (Federal Bureau of Investigation). The FBI argued that Saul Alinsky was a radical but not a revolutionist. In addition, the FBI argued that in his work, Alinsky underlines 'the stupidity of violence in democratic processes' and that he aimed to 'give voice to the common man' (sic) in order to prevent him from throwing 'himself at the feet of a dictator' (Federal Bureau of Investigation, 1970).

It is important to find out more about Alinsky's understanding of 'resentment'. It comprised a mixture of meanings which he derived from Adam Smith's book *Theory of Moral Sentiments* and Friedrich Nietzsche's *Genealogy of Morals*. Adam Smith valued resentment as a gift. He wrote: 'Resentment seems to have been given to us by nature for defense, and for defense only. It is the safeguard of justice and the security of innocence' (Smith, 1853: 135). According to Smith, feelings of resentment and gratitude are two sides of the same coin. They are natural gifts and must be articulated in order to stabilise 'doing good' and to avoid injustice. 'Doing good' is recognised and amplified by gratitude and resentment. According to Smith it is an articulation of critique against injustice and wrongdoing.

On the other hand, Friedrich Nietzsche was sceptical regarding the social function of resentments. He did not apply Smith's theory and used instead the French expression '*ressentiment*'. He states that in history the spontaneous public articulation of resentments has been hindered by superior powers and was regularly oppressed by violence. The '*ressentiment*', according to Nietzsche, was redirected into the individual. There it stays as a hidden emotion of anger and fear. The longer it stays within the individual, the more it poisons their thoughts and behaviour. Finally, it makes people unable to express their wishes or fears, makes them unable to act rationally and opens them to different kinds of manipulation. Nietzsche warns against false prophets, namely the 'ascetic priest', who long ago discovered that he could make political use of people's fears, that he can store their anger within them and that he may direct their rage against scapegoats and political opponents. Nietzsche (1967: 128) wrote: 'He brings salves and balm with him, no doubt; but before he can act as a physician, he first has to hit the wound'. When he then 'stills the pain of the wound, he at the same time infects the wound'. He 'alters the direction of ressentiment' by saying 'you alone are to blame for yourself!' The ascetic priest fights 'against anarchy and disintegration of the herd, in which the most dangerous of all explosives, ressentiment, is constantly accumulating'.

Alinsky takes up Nietzsche's medical metaphor and understands 'ressentiment' as a wound, which has to be healed in order to restore the social function of 'resentment' as described by Smith. He discussed 'resentments' in this way: 'Now, do you think, when I go into a Negro community today, I have to tell them, that they are discriminated against? Do you think I go there and get them angry? Don't you think they have resentments to begin with and how much rawer can I rub them?' (Sanders, 1965: 32).

In 1962 he explained to an audience of the Chicago Chapter of the National Association of Housing and Redevelopment Officials:

> Those who point accusingly to the 'rubbing raw of resentments' ... 'arousing dormant hostilities' in organizational activities reveals an absence of understanding of the elementary mechanics of motivation and behavior. The community organizer digs into a morass of resignation, hopelessness, and despair and works with the local people in articulating (or 'rubbing raw') their resentments. (Alinsky, 1962: 13)

In his statement 'You don't have to take this, and there is something you can do about it!', Alinsky (1962: 13) becomes a catalytic agent transmuting hidden resentments and hostilities into open problems. The very action of elevating these dormant hidden hostilities to the surface for confrontation, ventilation and conversion into problems is in itself a constructive and important catharsis. The alternative would be permitting incessant accumulation and compounding submerged frustrations, resentments and hostilities in large segments of the population, with the clogging of all channels for relief evolving into a nightmarish setting for a probable backfiring of actions generated by irrational, vindictive hate with tragically destructive consequences for all parties.

This shows that Alinsky has no need to 'hit the wounds first', as Nietzsche's figure of the ascetic priest did. Alinsky starts with pre-existing resentments. To 'rub raw', then, would mean to take away the scrub and to clean the wound. 'To fan' would mean to air and cool down the inflammation and to dry the surface of the wound so it can heal. 'To channel' would mean to drain the purulent and infective secrets. So, he conceptualises his organising work in direct opposition to Nietzsche's 'ascetic priest'. In my view, Alinsky's way of dealing with resentments is not to stir up the people but try to understand them. That is, Alinsky talked about their problems and searched for a way to solve those problems cooperatively. The following discussion will come back to this procedure of understanding.

Two ways to respond

Consequently, there are two ways to respond to resentments. First, track down the 'false prophets', who, according to Nietzsche, reverse the direction of the resentment into the individual and so create a precondition for political exploitation. Consequently, there are two ways to respond to resentments. In this chapter I will first track down the 'false prophets', who according to Nietzsche, reverse the direction of the resentment into the individual and so create a precondition for political exploitation. After that, I will explain Alinsky's alternative concept.

In 1844 Heinrich Heine published his poem 'Germany – A Winter's Tale' (Heine, 1844: xxiv). It was translated into many languages.

> O how I detest the trumpery set
> Who, to stir men's passion heated,
> Of patriotism make a show
> With all its ulcers fetid.
>
> (Translated by Edgar Alfred Bowring)

Another translation, by Jacob Rabinowitz, says: 'I've always been embarrassed by the rabble who play on people's feelings, exhibiting their patriotism as a beggar would his running sores'. Heine's original term is '*Lumpenpack*' and refers to Marx's term '*Lumpenproletariat*', meaning the lowest group of working-class people, who are suspected of treason, easy to mislead and to corrupt. Heine also uses the metaphor of the infected wound.

Misleading people always needs others who are willing to be misled, corrupt people need corruptible people. It is a question of demand and supply. Heinrich Hoffmann was a writer, psychiatrist and politician. He was involved in preparing the first German Parliament in 1848 in Frankfurt and he knew well the numerous and different factions of his time. In 1848 Hoffmann published a satirical *Handbook for Rabble Rousers* (Hoffmann, 1848: 7). It was allegedly to teach 'how to become a man of the people within a few days'. He created a typology of five groups of artificial patriots. The first three groups, according to Hoffmann, are more or less innocent or crazy and their performances are easy to see through. They are:

1. The vain Patriot – *Patriota artefecialis vanus* … who is seeking reputation
2. The eloquent speaking Patriot – *Patriota artefecialis loquax* … who delivers fine speeches
3. The foolish Patriot – *Patriota artefecialis confusus* … who confuses the people and provides no direction. (Hoffmann, 1848: 7)

Hoffman warns us against the artificial patriots from the groups four and five.

4. The indebted Patriot – *Lumpacivagabundus artefecialis patrioticus* … who is seeking communist redistribution

5. The displeased, resentful Patriot – *Patriota artefecialis furiosus* ... who, has an apparatus of terrorism at hand with guilotinizing, strangulizing and lanternizing proposals for reformation. (Hoffmann, 1848: 7)

The last words are unusual even in the German language. Hoffman employs neologisms and refers to the many people who were killed during the French Revolution, either brought to the scaffold or hanged with a rope on the lanterns in the city of Paris.

Hoffmann dedicates his booklet to the German people and warns against violence. He tries to raise critical awareness of false leaders (as opposed to natural leaders). He reveals their tricks of posing, making faces and their use of opportunistic symbols to demonstrate that they belong to the ordinary people. And again, Friedrich Nietzsche in 1887. His views are in line with Hoffmann but his language is not satirical but clear and distinct:

> I do not like these agitators dressed up as heroes who wear the magic cap of ideals on their straw heads; I do not like these ambitious artists who like to pose as ascetics and priests but who are at the bottom only tragic buffoons; and I also don't like these latest speculators in idealism, the anti-semites, who today roll their eyes in a Christian-aryan-bourgeois manner and exhaust one's patience by trying to rouse up all the horned-beast elements in the people by a brazen abuse of the cheapest of all agitator's tricks, moral attitudinizing. (Nietzsche, 1967: 158)

In my view, Nietzsche's blaming approach is only topped by the sharp and unmasking words of George Orwell in his review on Adolf Hitler's *Mein Kampf* from 1940:

> It's a pathetic, dog-like face, the face of a man suffering under intolerable wrongs. In a rather more manly way, it reproduces the expression of innumerable pictures of Christ crucified, and there is little doubt, that that is how Hitler sees himself. The initial, personal cause of his grievance against the universe can only be guessed at; but at any rate the grievance is there. He is the martyr, the victim, Prometheus chained on the rock, the self-sacrificing hero who fights single handed against impossible odds. If he were killing a mouse, he would know how to make it seem like a dragon. (Orwell, 1940: 28f)

From these writers, we can learn how false prophets have worked in history. But what could be the alternative way?

The next section will examine the work of Saul Alinsky and the community organising practice which is derived from his work. As stated previously, Alinsky's approach was conceptualised to restore the social function of resentment according to Adam Smith and not to compete with the bad examples in history to create and exploit '*ressentiment*' in the way Nietzsche and others have described and warned against. To better understand Alinsky's approach we have to remember some of the theories that were relevant in the Chicago sociology during his time.

First, William Isaac Thomas and what he has called the 'Definition-of-the-Situation'. 'If a person perceives a situation as real', he wrote, 'it is real in its consequences' (Thomas, 1928: 553–76). It does not matter if that given perception fits the reality. When people believe something is real, they will act on this perception and their actions will form a new social reality. If people act on wrong definitions, the world will not change for the better. So, in order to develop a community, we must begin with the given 'Definitions-of-the-Situation', discuss them in groups and learn about other possible definitions to see whether a given perception is close to truth.

Second, we must remember the German sociologist and long-time co-editor of the *American Journal of Sociology*, Ferdinand Tönnies (1887). His theoretical distinction between community and society was important for the understanding of immigration processes in Chicago. Community, according to Tönnies, is the older form of living together; it is based on emotions and traditions. Society, on the other hand, is based on rational decision and calculation. Alinsky's conclusion was: children learn in their families how to act in their neighbourhood. Grown up, they learn in their neighbourhood how to act in their communities. As adults, they learn how to act in and participate in the modern and open society. Alinsky wrote on immigrant communities of his time: 'these national neighborhoods served in a significant function in providing a harbor, both economic and cultural, from which they could sally forth into the strange American seas' (Alinsky, 1960: 143). He compares the community with a cocoon: 'After the immigrants and their children had germinated for some time in this cultural cocoon, absorbing American information and attitudes in their minds and American money in their pockets, they would emerge and take wings into the non-national American society' (Alinsky, 1960: 143). In this way, Alinsky describes the ongoing transition between community and society. If communities are based on emotions and traditions while the surrounding society is based on decision and rational calculation, there is a need to find a way for the society to understand the emotions and traditions of a given community. On the other hand, it is important for a given community to understand the rules of the surrounding society and to learn to participate and act within the society according to those rules.

Third, we must take Max Weber into account in order to better understand the sense of social actions. We find his earliest reception in the US with Alinsky's mentor Louis Wirth, an immigrant from Germany, and Edvard Shils, who was an early translator. Weber's concept of 'understanding' is crucial for Alinsky's handling of 'resentments'. Weber states that social action is always directed to others. Then he distinguishes four different basic types of social action.

Social action can be:

a. instrumentally rational
b. value-rational
c. traditional
d. affectual. (Weber, 1978: 24–6)

In order to understand the sense of for each type of social action we must therefore know about the underlying motives and energies:

a. instrumentally rational: reasons, goals and purposes
b. value-rational: moral and aesthetical value decisions
c. traditional: the mores, manners and customs
d. affectual: the feelings and emotions.
   (Weber, 1978: 24–6)

Building on Weber's framework, we must therefore listen to others and learn to understand the sense of their actions. This process of careful understanding of emotions, customs and values will lead to rationalisation. Emotions will not be 'heated' and exploited but cooled down, expressed and explained. In such a process an open society may integrate cultures and communities with all their emotions, values and traditions, and enlarge their experience and knowledge.

Finally, we should come back to Nietzsche again and understand the meaning of power. According to Nietzsche, the ancient valuation of power was simply that it is 'good to be strong' and 'bad to be weak'. During a so-called Jewish–Christian 'transvaluation of values' there developed what Nietzsche calls the 'slave morality' or the 'mentality of the herd'. The strength (of the other) then was transvalued as evil, while the weakness (of the Christian community) was transvalued as good. Because the Christian community could not stand against the power of the elites, it draws back from this world and waits for a revenge which will take place in another world.

Alinsky agreed with Nietzsche's criticism of Christian communities and suggested withdrawing from the historical Jewish–Christian transvaluation of values as described by Nietzsche. Furthermore, he never tired of saying that it is important to think not only of another world to come but start with the world as it is. He reminds his audiences that there is also a 'life after birth' and that an individual or a community has to act here and now (Alinsky, 1968: 60). He therefore demands a new redefinition of power and ta return to the ancient view as described by Nietzsche. The communities should overcome the 'mentality of the herd'. Power, according to Alinsky's valuation, is good, but it is not an end in itself. We should be cautious, because power also tends to corrupt (Alinsky, 1971: 48–51). On the other hand, a lack of power is not good. Poverty, in his view, is also and foremost a lack of power. Poor or black people will not get into a better situation without power. Power, according to Alinsky, has two forms: it operates through too much money or many people (Norden, 1972: 74). A people's organisation needs a broad base and should grow. A people's organisation should not only work on a single issue; it needs an informed, democratic and natural leadership. It should step into the arena of politics with clear values, goals and priorities and not shy away from conflicts; it should be able to compromise. Overcoming the 'mentality of the herd' will lead to integration into an open society.

Thus, drawing from these lessons, community organising will usually follow a three-step learning process:

- Listening – The 'art of understanding': to resolve resentments, heal the wounds of immigration, learn about trauma, emotions, values, traditions and plans.
- Research – The 'art of generating reliable information': to develop common 'definitions of the situation' by group discussions, undertaking power analysis by participatory research, be aware of and de-mask false prophets, search for practical solutions.
- Action – The 'art of participation': find and develop natural leadership, train speakers and leaders, go forward to the negotiation tables and don't care about conflicts, be fair.

Takeaways

What may we take away from this re-visitation? Alinsky developed community organising not only from theory. He was not an armchair sociologist. He worked in the field, talked to people and worked within institutions and organisations. He experienced the suffering of working-class people and took part in many conflicts between and within immigrant and ethnic groups. He was acutely aware of the disturbing voices of some firebrand protagonists in the political arena. One of them was Charles Coughlin, also known as 'Father Coughlin – the Radio-Priest'. Coughlin is one of the best researched agitators of the 20th century. He was an ordained Catholic priest and one of the first who moved from his pulpit to a broadcasting studio. In this way he vastly enlarged his audience by using the new media of the time. He was an anti-Semite and a hatemonger. He took money from Nazi Germany and was also sponsored by the contemporary America First Movement. The Catholic Church had great difficulty silencing him. He fits very well into the line of false prophets we have been warned against by Heine, Hoffmann, Nietzsche and others (McClung Lee and Briant Lee, 1939; Löwenthal, 1948).

In comparison with these examples, Alinsky never got tired of arguing that people's organisations have to be broad-based, consisting of people with different ethnic and economic backgrounds; people have to speak for themselves; they must control their anger; they should understand the power structures; and they should not shy away from conflicts in the political arena. In addition, they need to research their issues carefully; consider different views; develop solutions and bring them to the negotiating table. Finally, they should know their interests but should also be able to compromise, because they are not alone in this world.

What happens if we confront Alinsky's strategy of community development with current publications referring to growing populism and democracy. From the numerous possible publications, only a few are taken, which are currently discussed in Germany and Europe.

Let us start with the German author Peter Sloterdijk's *Rage and Time* (Sloterdijk, 2006), which reflects on thymotic, or spirited, energies which can take the form of Nietzsche's '*ressentiment*'. He states that emotions of wrath, anger and rage can be stored like money in a bank. Over time, anger stored within the individual will increase in quality and quantity and so become ready for political exploitation. He cites examples from socialist and nationalist backgrounds and concludes that 'beyond ressentiments' rage will be diffused, because the international socialist movement as well as the different nationalist movements are losing their importance. I do not know if he would repeat this conclusion in 2019, now that nationalist parties are searching for international alliances.

Uffa Jessen, in *Politics of Rage*, also reflects on *'ressentiments'*. He states that political emotions are generally underestimated. He argues that people might feel real pain if their traditions are not respected (Jessen, 2017: 31–3). His understanding of resentment is close to Alinsky's approach.

Now we come to some international writers working on populism: Mudde and Kaltwasser state that all kinds of populism start with the difference between 'the pure people' and 'the corrupt elite' (Mudde and Kaltwasser, 2017: 6). They state that populism may be 'both, a friend and foe' of (liberal) democracy depending on the stage of process of democratisation (Mudde and Kaltwasser, 2017: 20, 83–87).

Philip Manow's goal is to map right-wing and left-wing populism in Europe, and he examines the role of the different European welfare cultures. In the northern and western regions, we find relatively stable welfare systems and the people predominantly fear that the welfare system will be invaded by foreigners because of the 'freedom of labour', guaranteed as one of the Four Freedoms of the European Union. These are described in the European Treaties as the free movement of goods, capital, services and labour within the common market. In southern parts of Europe, we find, according to Manow, more left-wing populism, because people fear a flooding of the markets and decreasing prices for local and regional products because of the European 'free movement of goods'. A more materialistic analysis is surely necessary and could explain why populist parties tend to be Eurosceptic (Manow, 2018).

Francis Fukuyama, in his book *Identity – The Demand for Dignity and the Politics of Resentment*, warns us against groups that are seeking supremacy or superiority and states that human dignity should be highly valued (Fukuyama, 2018). Jan-Werner Müller states that populism is directed against pluralism (Müller, 2016) and also warns against attitudes of supremacy and xenophobia.

Ernesto Laclau and Chantal Mouffe consider that 'populism is … not only an essence to politics, but also an emancipatory force' and that 'Populism can help achieve radical democracy by reintroducing conflict into politics and fostering the mobilization of excluded sectors of society with the aim of changing the status quo' (cited in Mudde and Kaltwasser, 2017: 3).

Such discussions of populism may leave community development practitioners perplexed and helpless. We have to be aware of our value decisions. In doing so we leave the realm of pure science and enter the sphere of practical politics. While pure science is dedicated to truth, political activity has to decide what is right or wrong in a given situation. Mouffe, for example, also does not seek to add another academic contribution; she wants to use analysis for the purpose of 'political momentum' (Mouffe, 2018: 19). Therefore Mouffe's idea of 'reintroducing conflict into politics' is taken up, because it is similar to Alinsky's ideas. A sustainable community development strategy should not shy away from conflicts. Conflicts should not be searched for but researched. Conflicts can be caused by changes in production and redistribution, by climate change or by a disregard of human rights in authoritarian systems. The first task is to understand the underlying conflicts and the people who are involved and affected. Then there is the need to develop a strategy of putting these conflicts on the political agenda and acting within political negotiations using rational arguments. This could also be conflictual, but this fight is for justice, human dignity, diversity and against violence and claims of superiority.

Thus, the art of listening, understanding and organising, drawn from Alinsky's work, can help to overcome the current divisions in our societies. In this way, community development practitioners can hope to take some steps forward in establishing and maintaining the ideal not only of a 'government of the people, by the people and for the people', as Abraham Lincoln said a long time ago, but also a society which has structures and processes in place which ensure that all citizens have the power to participate in decision making that affects their lives.

References

Alinsky, S.D. (1946) *Reveille for Radicals – A Pragmatic Primer for Realistic Radicals*, Chicago: University of Chicago Press.

Alinsky, S.D. (1960) 'The urban immigrant', in T. Mac Avoy (ed), *Roman Catholicism and the American Way of Life*, Notre Dame, IN: University of Notre Dame Press, pp 142–55.

Alinsky, S.D. (1962) *Citizen Participation and Community Organization in Planning and Urban Renewal*, Chicago: The Industrial Areas Foundation.

Alinsky, S.D. (1968) 'Is there a life after birth?', *Anglican Theological Review*, 1968(1): 53–75.

Alinsky, S.D. (1971) *Rules for Radicals – A Pragmatic Primer for Realistic Radicals*, New York: Random House.

Federal Bureau of Investigation (1970) 'Memorandum 2-11-1970', https://vault.fbi.gov/saul-alinsky/saul-alinsky-part-01-of-01/view, p 340.

Fukuyama, F. (2018) *Identity – The Demand for Dignity and the Politics of Resentment*, New York: Farrar, Strauss and Giroux.

Heine, H. (1844) *Deutschland ein Wintermärchen*, München: DTV, 1997. Translations used: Heine, H. and Bowring, E.A. (2007) *Germany – A Winter Tale*, New York: Mondial; Heine, H. and Rabinowitz, J. (2016) *Germany – A Winter's Tale*, Pittsburgh, PA: The Poet's Press/Yogh and Thorn Books.

Hoffmann, H. (1848) *Handbüchlein für Wühler* [*Handbook for Rabble Rousers*], Frankfurt: Ullstein, 1972.

Jessen, Uffa (2017) *Zornpolitik* [*Politics of Rage*], Berlin: Suhrkamp.

Löwenthal, L. (1948) *Falsche Propheten – Studien zum Autoritarismus* [*False Prophets – Studies in Authoritarianism*], Frankfurt: Suhrkamp, 1990.

Manow, P. (2018) *Die politische Ökonomie des Populismus* [*The Political Economy of Populism*], Berlin: Suhrkamp.

McClung-Lee, A. and Briant-Lee, E. (1939) *The Fine Art of Propaganda: A Study of Father Coughlin's Speeches*, New York: Harcourt, Brace and Co.

Mouffe, C. (2018) *Für einen linken Populismus* [*Towards a Left-Wing Populism*], Berlin: Suhrkamp.

Mudde, C. and Kaltwasser, C.R. (2017) *Populism: A Very Short Introduction*, New York: Oxford University Press.

Müller, C.W. (1982) '*Wie Helfen zum Beruf wurde – eine Methodengeschichte der Sozialarbeit* [*How Helping Became a Profession – A History of Social Work Methods*], Basel: Beltz.

Müller, J.W. (2016) *Was ist Populismus?* [*What Is Populism?*], Berlin: Suhrkamp.

Nietzsche, F. (1967) *On the Genealogy of Morals*, translated by Walter Kaufmann and R.J. Hollingdale, New York: Random House.

Norden, E. (1972) 'Saul Alinsky. A candid conversation with a feisty radical', *The American Playboy*, March, pp 70–76, 150, 169–78.

Orwell, G. (1940) 'Review of Mein Kampf by Adolf Hitler', in S. Orwell and I. Angus (eds), *The Collected Essays, Journalism and Letters of George Orwell*, *Vol.II, My Country Right or Left*, Harmondsworth: Penguin (1970), pp 27–29.

Sanders, M.K. (1965) *The Professional Radical – Conversations with Saul Alinsky*, Evanston, IL: Harper and Row.

Sloterdijk, P. (2006) *Zorn und Zeit – ein psycho-politischer Versuch* [*Rage and Time – A Psycho-political Investigation*], Frankfurt: Suhrkamp.

Smith, A. (1853) *A Theory of Moral Sentiments; or An Essay towards an Analysis of the Principles by Which Men Naturally Judge the Conduct and Character, First of Their Neighbours and Afterwards of Themselves*, London: Henry G. Bone.

Szynka, P. (2005) *Theoretische und empirische Grundlagen des Community Organizing bei Saul D. Alinsky: eine Rekonstruktion (1907–1972)* [*Theoretical and Empirical Base of Community Organising According to Saul D. Alinsky (1912–1970)*], Bremen: Akademie für Arbeit und Politik.

Szynka, P. (2006) 'Alinsky's secret reading of Friedrich Nietzsche', in A. Heimgartner (ed), *Faces of Research on European Social Development: Community Work, Civil Society and Professionalization of Social Work*, Vienna: LIT-Verlag, pp 297–303.

Thomas, W.I. (1928) *The Methodology of Behavior Study*, New York: Alfred A. Knopf.

Tönnies, A. (1887) *Gemeinschaft und Gesellschaft* [*Community and Civil Society*], Leipzig: Fues.

Weber, M. (1978) *Economy and Society* [*Wirtschaft und Gesellschaft*], Berkeley, University of California Press.

PART 2

Populism and community development in different contexts

From inclusionary to exclusionary populism in the transformation of US community development

Randy Stoecker and Benny Witkovsky

The transformation of community development in the United States

Community development in the United States, in contrast to most of the world, has been a more specialised and narrowly defined practice – so much so that we have a separate term, community organising, to describe the more political and power-based form of practice included in most other definitions of community development. Using that separation, the post-World War II history of community development in the United States can be defined by a transition from a power-based model emphasising participatory and redistributive community power building, to a neoliberal model emphasising physical rehabilitation and business development.

Community organising as a power-based model of community development in the US arguably can be traced back to European colonisation of the North American continent and its developing culture of voluntary associations (de Tocqueville, 2000) and then the early 20th century settlement house movement (Berry, 1986). Saul Alinsky (1969, 1971) was credited with naming the practice, and his work in Chicago's 1930s 'Back of the Yards' neighbourhood created a recognisable model (Finks, 1984). The Civil Rights Movement is the other crucial source of community organising (Morris, 1984; Evans and Boyte, 1986). Its influence on community organising practice has been as profound as Alinsky's, but it has been analysed more as a national social movement than as local community organising processes with national impact. The accepted founding of the movement, the 'Montgomery Bus Boycott', was built through local African American organisations and networks and created a model used in locality-based actions throughout the south and beyond (Morris, 1984; Evans and Boyte, 1986). From these origins came offshoots that melded Civil

Rights organising with Alinsky-style organising such as the Welfare Rights Movement (Piven and Cloward, 1979) and eventually the famous Association of Community Organizations for Reform Now (ACORN) (Delgado, 1986; Fisher, 2009).

Defined through these examples, community organising is the process of a group of people with a common experience of oppression, exploitation or exclusion – a 'constituency' – coming together to identify their common problems and create organisations to attack the causes of those problems. Such groups use a process of choosing narrowly defined 'winnable' issues and engaging in a variety of strategies and tactics against 'targets' – officials that perpetuate the unfair system and have the power to change important parts of it. However, the goal is to go beyond solving specific issues and more broadly organise people to change the system's rules and get a seat at decision-making tables so as to participate with power equal to elites (Alinsky, 1969, 1971; Minieri and Getsos, 2007).

Community organising normally begins locally in a single neighbourhood (Fisher, 1994), or among rural neighbours (Szakos and Szakos, 2008). But local groups can combine into a larger movement, such as the campaign to end 'redlining' – the refusal of banks and other lenders to provide home loans in supposedly unprofitable neighbourhoods in the 1960s in the US. That campaign began in just a few neighbourhoods, and built into a movement that created new federal regulations forcing such loans into long-excluded neighbourhoods (Squires, 2003). The power-based community organising form of community development, then, focused on removing barriers to local community development.

As community organising became more successful and powerful into the 1960s, it influenced federal programmes such as VISTA (Volunteers in Service to America, a kind of domestic US Peace Corps). VISTA workers used their positions to organise people around urban and rural development issues, often targeting local government for its complicity in development practices that displaced marginalised people or neglected their development needs.

By the early 1970s, however, neoliberal pushback became evident. Governments throttled community organising and activist practices within VISTA (VISTA, 2019). And major philanthropic foundations began shifting money away from community organising groups to newly emerging non-profit community development corporations (CDCs) that focused on building buildings and creating jobs (Stoecker, 1997; Yin, 1998). This signalled the ascendance of the neoliberal construction of the non-profit industrial complex (NPIC) that forced people-power groups to adopt 'business models' to engage in development practices that integrated people into the existing system rather than helping them challenge it (Incite, 2009). Community organising groups' reliance on external funding made them vulnerable to funders' imposed values and restrictions. The result, documented first by Yin (1998) in Cleveland and traced into recent times by McQuarrie (2013: 73), was 'a general rationalization of Cleveland's civil society around narrow practices and market-based conceptions of value'. This shift also occurred in neighbourhood organising as groups shifted from organising for power to defending their turf to exclude others (*Playboy Magazine*, 1972; Fisher, 1994). Though community organising remained a powerful force in particular moments (Fisher, 1994), it exerts less influence over development that it did.

Neoliberal community development in the United States

The result of this transformation was a form of neoliberal community development in the new millennium. Neoliberalism itself is characterised by the glorification and empowerment of the capitalist corporation and the removal of barriers to capitalist profit extraction. That requires dismantling the welfare state (Hartman, 2005; Hasenfeld and Garrow, 2012), undermining environmental and health protections (Castree, 2010), and restricting collective action such as union organising (Dinner, 2017) and community organising. It also requires redefining individuals as completely responsible for their own fate; they must compete in the employment marketplace against each other for jobs, benefits, job security and life amenities. In this setting, workers become commodities to be bought and sold or simply discarded like any other production resource (O'Brien, 2006; Rocco, 2016).

The power of the economic in directing community development cannot be underestimated in this context. As funders restrict community development groups' ability to build collective power and shift the emphasis to economic development technicalities, they transform community-based organisations into technical organisations separated from their constituencies (Stoecker, 1997). And since such technical expertise is expensive, these organisations must spend more time serving funders' needs (Thibault, 2007). This neoliberal 'community development' model has produced the concepts of social capital, asset-based community development and social entrepreneurship. Social capital's neoliberal bias first becomes apparent in the term itself. It is social *capital*, not social cohesion or social bonds. The term 'capital' reduces even social relationships to the economic. Social capital development models take community relationships and transform them from what Marx (1859) called use values – things valued for their direct use – into exchange values –things valued in exchange for other things. Those promoting the concept of social capital emphasise that its purpose is to improve the economic success of the individuals who are being urged to build their social relationships (Fukuyama, 1999). By building their social relationships, members of poor communities can supposedly improve their lot in life, especially if they move beyond 'bonding' social capital (building relationships among community members) to 'bridging' social capital (building relationships with outsiders, and obviously the right outsiders) and 'linking' social capital (building relationships with institutions). They can then 'exchange' their relationships with outsiders for access to financial, material and knowledge resources (Putnam, 2000). Of course, this is not in the end community development at all, but individual development, since those who successfully build and exploit such relationships will consequently be able to leave their impoverished community for a 'better' one. But community development organisations, by recruiting racial/economic elites – that is, white businessmen – to their boards, can also use the strategy. The cost, of course, is that the organisation must be attractive to such elites, limiting its ability to challenge the unfair systems that create such elites (DeFillippis, 2001).

Asset-based community development (ABCD) is another form of neoliberal community development, though its adherents reject such association (Roy, 2017). ABCD asserts that welfare state actors treat people in poverty as having deficiencies that must be fixed by top-down welfare state approaches (van den Berk-Clark and Pyles, 2012). By seeing themselves as possessing 'assets', members of poor communities can supposedly experience self-esteem that will motivate them to pool such assets to solve their own problems (Kretzmann and McKnight, 1993). But the ABCD welfare state critique focuses on the individual, ignoring welfare state actors who see the social system, not individuals, as having deficiencies. ABCD consequently wipes away any analysis of oppression, exploitation and exclusion in favour of focusing on the individual who then is expected to discover and mobilise their 'assets' or 'gifts' to compete in the jobs and benefits marketplace. Even when ABCD takes a community-level approach, the method is consistent with the social capital approach, arguing that the community must mobilise its own assets rather than focus on rebalancing the unequal power relations oppressing its members (Stoecker, 2004). The implication is that those individuals and communities that do not succeed at development have only themselves to blame for inadequately mobilising their assets.

Social entrepreneurship may be the climax of neoliberal community development. The hegemonic assertion of social entrepreneurship is that not only can any individual succeed, but they can use their success to promote the greater good. Such a concept serves two hegemonic purposes. First, it reinforces the notion of the self-made person succeeding in the marketplace on their own wits and fortitude. Of course, the fictional glorification of the entrepreneur is not strictly neoliberal, dating back to at least the mid-19th century stories of Horatio Alger (Nackenoff, 1994). Neoliberalism has added the contemporary cover-up that mystifies how the social entrepreneur extracts profit from workers and redirects us to noticing only the entrepreneur's service to various social and environmental causes (Lazzarato, 2009). Social entrepreneurs are now looked to when affordable housing is needed, jobs are needed, environmental innovation is needed and services are needed (Hamschmidt and Pirson, 2011). There is no analysis of how profit extraction shifts wealth upward, and how neoliberal deregulation allows even more wealth to shift upward. The emphasis on social entrepreneurship as community development is now promoted by funders and policy makers from the disinvested urban north to the Global South periphery (Mayer and Rankin, 2002).

With these new models, the forms of community development itself change. CDCs, which used to be the go-to housing development model in poor neighbourhoods, are being replaced by CDFIs – community development financial institutions (Doshna, 2015). CDCs often produced collectively managed housing with some market controls. CDFIs can circumvent that collective process, as for-profit corporate developers can also access their resources under the banner of social entrepreneurship. Public housing residents are being reconstructed as market actors under the guise of individual empowerment through Hope VI and Choice Neighborhoods programmes (Conte and Li, 2013). Farmers' markets reconstruct the local food system as a literal market system, pitting farmers against each other in a physical marketplace and replacing any motivation for conscious collective decision making for food system development with the 'invisible' or, perhaps more aptly, 'blind' hand of the market. The contradictory result is that prices are often higher in such markets, excluding those who can't pay the price that the market will bear (Joassart-Marcelli and Bosco, 2014). Finally, when there is community development planning, it is more for private rather than public goods, and planners go through the motions of participation, in a context where neoliberalism has already weakened social bonds and reduced desire to participate in the collective good (Long, 2012).

Neoliberal community development, however much it was consciously planned and engineered by economic and political elites, required a specific political milieu to take root and grow. In particular, it required a voting base that would support candidates promoting far-right, anti-democratic, anti-worker and baldly racist policies. This political base – rural, white and male – ends up voting to dismantle the community structures designed to empower them in the hope of some benefit from powerful leaders. This is the exact opposite of the community model that organises people to define and pursue their collective self-interest towards an expanded democracy. How can we understand such behaviour? We can start by thinking about it as a result of the Janus-faced nature of populism that allows it to be either (or both) inclusionary and exclusionary.

The transformation of populism in the United States

The two faces of populism appear regularly and even simultaneously in the United States. Most recently this occurred in the 2016 presidential campaigns of Donald Trump and Bernie Sanders. When Donald Trump was sworn in as President of the United States in 2017, he promised 'January 20th 2017, will be remembered as the day the people became the rulers of this nation again. The forgotten men and women of our country will be forgotten no longer. Everyone is listening to you now' (Trump, 2017). Bernie Sanders, who identified as an independent socialist, struck a similar note in his campaign for the Democratic nomination for president. 'Today, we stand here and say loudly and clearly that enough is enough … This great nation and its government belong to all of the people, and not to a handful of billionaires, their Super-PACs and their lobbyists' (Sanders, 2015) Despite dramatically different political standpoints, both men framed their campaigns as defeating entrenched political interests and returning power to the people. Both promised to overturn politics as usual; both promised to rebuild communities to benefit everyday people.

How could both right- and left-wing politicians use such populist language? The Preamble to the US Constitution's promise to vest power in 'We the People' has provided US populism both a depth and a flexibility that has made it a formidable force in the nation's politics. Calling US populism a force that 'binds even as it divides', Kazin (1998: 2) detailed how leaders throughout US history and across the political spectrum sought to challenge incumbent regimes through promises to take power from corrupt elites and return it to the people. He argues that this rhetoric has proven so stable and accessible because it is written into the founding documents of the nation and the founding ethos of US democracy, enabling politicians to wield it without appearing to suggest any kind of systemic revolution. Recent campaigns echo Kazin's analysis, illustrating how populism can be deployed by both the political left and right, for purposes as divergent as advocating political and financial reform to defending racial segregation.

This flexibility can be seen in the evolution of US populism. Beginning in the late 19th and early 20th century, perhaps the first self-conscious US populist movement wove together critiques of economic elites and racial/ethnic outsiders to organise the rural and urban poor in the form of the People's Party and the Farmers' Alliance (Gerteis and Goolsby, 2005). Similarly, William Jennings Bryan combined calls for economic reform with an acceptance of xenophobia and a hostility towards growing racial, ethnic and religious diversity. Others, like Robert M. Lafollete, were largely silent on racial issues and ultimately won the support of black leaders like W.E.B. DuBois (Brøndal, 2011). Movements in the mid-20th century as diverse as worker mobilisation for welfare expansion in the Great Depression and the anti-Semitic and racist campaigns of Father Coughlin, the Ku Klux Klan and Nazi sympathisers have all been described as populist. By the 1960s, Martin Luther King Jr could identify himself with the tradition of US populism (Boyte, 2008) even as George Wallace and other segregationists did as well. More recently, political leaders as ideologically diverse as Ronald Reagan, Bill Clinton (Bimes and Mulroy, 2004), Barack Obama (Cohen, 2008) and George W. Bush (Foley, 2007) have all been described as populist.

The lack of any firm ideological anchor for populism has helped motivate scholars to classify types of populisms. Ernesto Laclau (1977: 143) distinguished between what he called a populism of the dominant and a populism of the dominated. In the former, appeals to restructure politics in the name of the people are deployed by one dominant class fraction in the hopes of unseating another. Laclau sees this as fundamentally repressive because the ascending class fraction must attempt to control and limit the popular unrest it foments. In the latter, populist politics are used to build coalitions among the working class, to illustrate that the systems of domination and inequality that mark their economic and social lives intersect with political structures. While Laclau's interests were in revolution and socialist politics, it is possible to see a similar dynamic at work in less extreme circumstances.

Judis (2016) similarly distinguishes (but puts elites in a somewhat different role) between what he calls 'dyadic' and 'triadic' populism. Judis associates dyadic populism primarily with left-wing movements as a conflictual, vertical relationship between 'the people' and 'the elite' that also involves critical work among and across groups of individuals to build coalitions and collective political identities. Triadic populism, which he associates with the political right, is built out of conflict between the people and elites, but emphasises how elites have benefited or favoured outsiders and others. In Judis' (2016: 15) words '[right-wing populism] looks upward, but also down upon an outgroup'. Brubaker (2017: 359) illustrates how populism gains complexity and flexibility by invoking three distinct, though overlapping, definitions of 'The People': ordinary people as opposed to elites; sovereign people as opposed to non-citizen outsiders; and culturally/ethnically distinct people as opposed to racial others. Thus, thinking about populism of the dominant or triadic populism, some outsiders control the levers of power and threaten domination, while others seek disruption and instability from below; some elites are allies that should be trusted with more power, while others are corrupt and exploit the true people in favour of outsiders.

We can see variations of these types of populism play out on the local level, such as when Republican politicians took over all branches of government in the state by tapping resentments of Wisconsin residents who had seen their relative income and benefits decline over time and pinned the causes on public sector workers, educators and supposedly liberal government leaders (Cramer, 2016), or when an unlikely coalition of farm workers and dairy farm owners successfully opposed legislation promoted by those same politicians that would have further oppressed undocumented workers (Sommerhauser, 2016).

The emotional aspect of populism takes on extra importance in the absence of a clear ideological focus. For Jasper (2011: 286), '[emotions] motivate individuals, are generated in crowds, are expressed rhetorically, and shape stated and unstated goals of social movements. Emotions can be means, they can be ends, and sometimes they can fuse the two'. Those long-simmering emotions about who belongs and who does not, what is fair and what is not, develop the pool of people open to a populist message. Reactions to particular events, moments that highlight inequality in decision making or exacerbate racial tensions, can spark immediate moments of populist mobilisation. These combine to form a general mood that enables certain types of politics, and makes certain forms of populist mobilisation more or less likely (Cadena-Roa, 2002; Jasper, 2011). Populist leaders use emotional self-styling, whether the presentation of an unrefined 'everyman' or the righteous anger of the firebrand, to work the crowd and garner support (Brubaker, 2017). Salmela and Von Scheve (2018) detail how both left- and right-wing populist politicians manipulate the 'emotional opportunity structure', sometimes pushing people towards anger and resentment, sometimes towards hope and action. The role of emotion is also evident in Saul Alinsky's (1971: 116) dyadic populism of the dominated community organising model, as he advocates that the organiser 'rub raw the resentments of the people of the community; fan the latent hostilities of many of the people to the point of overt expression'.

Mostly, in the years surrounding Donald Trump's election, the focus has been on the emotions of the triadic populism of the dominant. In her exploration of the political discontent that fuelled far-right Governor Scott Walker's and then President Donald Trump's popularity in Wisconsin, Cramer (2016) outlined what she calls 'rural consciousness': a sense that typical politicians neither understand nor value rural people's lives or beliefs; with a building resentment and anger towards government and politics as usual (Cramer, 2016). Wuthnow (2018: 10) applied a similar analysis to rural communities across the US, documenting what he sees as 'an outrage in rural America [that] is rooted in frustration that a way of life is crumbling and Washington is making things worse'. Vance (2016: 7) argued that the economic instability experienced by so many people produces 'a feeling that you have little control over your life and a willingness to blame everyone but yourself'. This, he argues, prevents people from investing in themselves and their communities and taking steps to make their lives better. Arlie Russell Hochschild (2016: 108–15) details the anger and distrust such people feel towards a government that fails to protect citizens from environmental and economic disaster, along with a prideful feeling of being 'above' government help, to signal their independence from government and moral superiority to those who accept help. This is piled on top of a belief that government has placed the needs of others ahead of them.

These authors describe a set of emotions that can be understood by relative deprivation theory. People's resentments come from their judgements about how their current life compares to a perceived past, how things should be, or the better treatment 'others' receive. From this lens these interpretive conditions produce resentments that can be mobilised (Gurney and Tierney, 1982). Relative deprivation theories of political mobilisation have their roots in an intellectual era where social movements were often lumped in with other forms of collective behaviour such as crowd panics, insinuating that such activism could be similarly irrational, disorganised expressions of collective anger and frustration. More recently such perspectives have been integrated with explanations that emphasise intentional, strategic and organisational thinking that drives social movements (Gusfield, 1994). We embrace the tension between these two perspectives: there are moments when populist politics can be part of strategic community organising, and moments where it can be isolating and disempowering, leaving people open to the claims of demagogues and anti-democratic politicians.

We draw on these ideas to distinguish between what we will call exclusionary populism and inclusionary populism. Exclusionary populism reflects Judis' triadic populism and Laclau's populism of the dominant. It draws on feelings of relative deprivation that use interpretations, however inaccurate, of other 'races' (to mobilise against affirmative action, for example), other income/employment groups (such as public sector workers with benefits and pensions to mobilise against government spending and taxation), and the glorified past (such as factory closings, mining reductions and fishing restrictions to mobilise against government and especially environmental regulation). Inclusionary populism reflects Judis' dyadic populism and Laclau's populism of the dominated. It draws on relative deprivation, but the interpretations of the past are things like comparisons to the time before the obvious effects of climate change to promote better environmental regulation, comparisons to others' focus on groups like economic elites to organise for greater economic and political democracy, and comparisons to a potential future such as a healthy planet free of poverty and oppression. Inclusionary populism focuses its antagonism upward and outward at elites – government and/or capital – threatening the well-being or autonomy of a diversity of people who also have a shared experience of common issues, while building a more inclusive horizontal structure among the constituency.

Both inclusionary and exclusionary populisms claim to support the majority interest and protect the community from outside threats, but the definition of majority, the community and the outside are deeply contested. Exclusionary populism sees the democratic institutions that mandate community input and involvement as roadblocks in the development process and seeks anti-institutionalist strategies to undermine them. Inclusionary populism sees those institutions as insufficient and seeks alternatives and expansion. Inclusionary populism seeks to bring more and more decisions into the political sphere, re-politicising the capital investment and private partnerships that have come to dominate community development. Exclusionary populism seeks to minimise that politicisation as much as possible unless and until those partnerships appear to be questioned.

We can see the transformation from inclusionary to exclusionary populism from the late 20th century to the present. Cas Mudde (2004) distinguishes the populism of the 'New Left' and 'New Social Movements' of the late 20th century with the populism of 'The Heartland' today. Left populism, he argues, focused on democratic inputs and sought more deliberative and participatory forms of communal decision making. The populism of 'The Heartland' is willing to sacrifice broad participation for centralised power as long as the policy outcomes are in the alleged best interests of 'the people' as they define them. Mudde sees the current moment as one in which the populism of the New Left has fallen by the wayside and the populism of 'The Heartland' has become dominant. This trade-off between democratic processes and an emotional promise to represent the interests of 'The Heartland' has been a hallmark of Donald Trump's politics. As Hochschild (2016: 225) argues:

> More than any other presidential candidate in decades, Trump focuses on eliciting and praising emotional response from his fans rather than detailed policy prescriptions. His speeches – evoking dominance, bravado, clarity, national pride and personal uplift, inspire an emotional transformation.

Lamont and colleagues (2017) see Trump's rhetoric and style as minimising the distance between Trump and white working class people, while constructing the distance between both of them and people of other racial and economic backgrounds.

However, the transformation from inclusionary to exclusionary populism is neither complete nor stable. The 2018 US elections showed some massive swings from right to left. And even throughout local, state and national periods of recent right-wing political domination, there have been energetic and at least occasionally successful uprisings against specific policies, such as the airport blockages protesting against Trump's first immigrant ban (Gambino et al, 2017) and the rallies against separating children and parents at immigrant detention centres (Arango and Cockrel, 2018). It is the local level where our interest is focused, to show next how exclusionary and inclusionary populism influence the current practice of US community development.

Populism, neoliberalism and community development

How can we understand the intersections of populism, neoliberalism and community development in the United States? First, populism persists as part of the lifeblood of the body politic, always ready to be accessed around any grievance or resentment, beginning at the community level, and directed at various targets. The exclusion and inequality that is produced through the interaction of capitalism and the state, at the local, state and national levels, creates a pool of people ready to answer any flavour of populists' call, open to assertions that varying combinations of elites and/or outsiders threaten their prosperity, stability and future. Community development practitioners cannot avoid these politics, as their work focuses on those most subject to the appeal of populism across race and the rural–urban divide. Regardless of the community worker's intent, sometimes these constituencies build campaigns on the promise of transforming community power, and sometimes they reinforce the very structures that make exclusionary populism resonate.

Perhaps no one in the community organising form of community development made more of inclusionary populism than Saul Alinsky. Alinsky (1971: 5) warned about the dangers of ideology becoming dogma and embraced not just a non-ideological populism but an anti-ideological one; as he asserted, 'No ideology should be more specific than that of America's founding fathers: "For the general welfare"'. For Alinsky, community organising began with understanding people's self-interest and fanning their discontent until they were ready to organise and act. His theory of class, more sophisticated than he is often credited with, was divided into the haves, the have-nots and the have-a-little-want-mores. The haves were the 'targets' of community organising, and deserving of the label 'the enemy'. The objective goal of good organising was to 'pick the target, freeze it, personalise it, and polarise it' (Alinsky, 1971: 143). Good community organising also had to help people start with an understanding of the world as it is, conceptualise the world as it should be, and then organise for that world. This has all the elements of inclusionary populism: a focus on the dominated, mobilisation of emotion, and use of relative deprivation in relation to a desired future rather than the past.

Alinsky also understood the risk of community organising being used in both inclusionary and exclusionary populist ways. His passions were with the have-nots, whom he saw as most amenable to an inclusionary populism, but he also understood the strategic necessity of engaging the have-a-little-want-mores – the working and middle classes. He described this class as fearful, resentful and ready to turn towards far-right anti-democratic demagogues, warning that 'If we fail to communicate with them, if we don't encourage them to form alliances with us, they will move to the Right. Maybe they will anyway, but let's not let it happen by default' (Alinsky, 1971: xx). He applied this class analysis to the Back of the Yards neighbourhood where he got his start in community organising:

> They've entered the nightfall of success, and their dreams of a better world have been replaced by nightmares of fear – fear of change, fear of losing their material goods, fear of blacks. Last time I was in Back of the Yards, a good number of the cars were plastered with Wallace stickers; I could have puked. Like so many onetime revolutionaries, they've traded in their birthright for property and prosperity. This is why I've seriously thought of moving back into the area and organising a new movement to overthrow the one I built 25 years ago. (*Playboy Magazine*, 1972)

During the period that Alinsky was lamenting the Back of the Yards' turn to exclusionary populism, however, the general trend in the United States may have been more towards inclusionary populism. Fisher (1994) tracked several eras of organising strategies and the politics they reflected and produced. Challenging the assumption that community organising is necessarily a creature of the left or working classes, Fisher outlined a model of 'Conservative Neighbourhood Organisation' prominent during the immediate post-World War II era – to marshal neighbourhood resources to serve the military, to protect against communism, and to oppose racial change in the name of the best interests of 'the people'. However, he saw the 1970s–1980s era as marked by what he called 'A New Populism' that was anti-ideological and in some ways anti-political. It rejected the explicit leftist message of saving communities from capitalism and encompassed a wide ideological spectrum. In his conception, the populists' primary enemy was the 'bigness and unaccountability of power' whether held by government or by corporations. All this was done in the name of protecting communities and their traditional character and building majoritarian coalitions to defend their local, and sometimes parochial, interests.

The question is whether we are beyond the 'New Populism' period, and what the nexus of community structures and populist politics looks like now. The shift away from the community organising form of community development towards the 'bricks and mortar' community development corporation model involved perhaps not so much a shift in populism as the rise of neoliberalism. From the time of the Jim Crow south there was an organised effort from the far right to dismantle democracy, though it didn't start bearing fruit until later in the 20th century. This was, to some extent, an attempt to oppose populism itself (Maclean, 2017). Within the field of community development, funders' shift away from community organising and towards community development corporations (Yin, 1998) signalled a shift away from populism in community development and towards a technocratic and far less participatory form of community development. This anti-populist period climaxed in the destruction of the famous national community organising network ACORN. ACORN was the ideal type of inclusionary populist community organising group (Fisher, 2009). Among all the national community organising networks, ACORN was the most committed to organising the most oppressed people in the country. It was also the most militant. While other organisations toned down their tactics and shifted their base to church congregations, ACORN was the rowdy build-from-scratch, in-your-face, fight-the-power community organising group. Their slogan was 'The People Shall Rule', and they meant it (Fisher, 2009). They were part of a brief resurgence of new populism in CDCs during the early 2000s, exemplified in Toledo, Ohio (Stoecker, 2003), and in Massachusetts with the Ricanne Hadrian Initiative (Greenberg, 2005). ACORN's involvement in registering voters for Obama earned the organisation non-stop legal harassment from right-wing officials, even though the it was cleared of voter fraud (Salent, 2009; Atlas, 2010). But the far right, using Alinsky's classic strategy of choosing a target, isolating it and polarising it, eventually killed ACORN. None of the other community organising networks, with the exception of the National Organizers Alliance, would stand with ACORN and it collapsed from the attacks in 2010 (Atlas, 2010).

The collapse of ACORN, and the rise of technocratic development strategies, left a far weaker infrastructure with which to organise people for progressive action around their frustrations. At the same time, a surplus of right-wing demagogues exploited these unorganised resentments, and exclusionary populism ascended. Initial warning signs showed in disruptions of town hall meetings, with tactics that both participants and observers associated with Alinsky (Taranto, 2009; Weigel, 2009), around the country as the Obama administration tried to craft what eventually became the Affordable Care Act. The seething resentments, left to drift in an unorganised mass along the political currents, then erupted in populist fury in the 2016 elections. In the midst of a pandemic and a resurgent anti-racist movement, it remains uncertain whether inclusionary populism can break through the neoliberal and exclusionary approaches that have recently dominated US politics.

Where next for community development

Have we passed from a stage of neoliberal anti-populism to an era of exclusionary populism? Weyland (2001) identified what he called 'Neoliberal Populism' in Latin America, arguing that, under certain circumstances, populist politics and neoliberal, market-oriented economic development can go hand in hand. Both populists and neoliberals see communities as undifferentiated masses of individuals, mobilising people to confront problems as homeowners, taxpayers and employees, rather than as communities with shared interests. Neoliberal elites see exclusionary populist leaders as potential allies in eliminating traditional government economic and regulatory policies. Exclusionary populist leaders see neoliberal tendencies towards anti-democratic market reforms as a tool to consolidate power. Both, Weyland argues, distrust the decisions of the masses and their elected representatives and favour top-down decision making. This fits with Laclau's (1977) populism of the dominant and illustrates the uncomfortable but still functional coalition between the exclusionary populist Trump and the Republican Party's neoliberal and exclusionary populist factions. This coalition exerts influence partly because the dense networks of associations that enable individuals to engage in local politics and decision making on a relatively equal playing field, and help foster trust among citizens and between citizens and their government, have declined (Putnam, 2000).

The cure for this condition, according to some, is rebuilding local associations. Fallows and Fallows (2018) document what they define as successful local political projects despite a national scene of polarisation and despair. They portray these projects as 'innovative, compromise-minded, optimistic, and working toward practical solutions to the problems of this age'. Similarly, the faith-based community organising networks, and especially the Industrial Areas Foundation, emphasise 'relational organising' and especially the now iconic 'one to one' relational conversation, where working on social change takes a distant back seat as the path to rebuild local community connections (Stoecker, 2009). This approach risks an exclusionary populism, as it looks to the past rather than to the future, and its hyper-localness risks enforcing uniformity rather than building on diversity.

In such a context, those of us who care about community development must make choices. If we follow Geoghegan and Powell (2009), there are three community development choices: a neoliberal version where civil society is subservient to the needs of economic development; a corporatist version that advocates a partnership between the state, market and civil society; and an activist version, where community development is envisaged as local, nodal and global resistance to neoliberalism. The first two approaches are where we are stuck. Bricks-and-mortar development, though often local in its focus, must still maintain subservience to neoliberal capitalist economic development. And with CDC mergers over the past couple of decades (Rohe and Bratt, 2003), that local emphasis has been replaced more and more by the second model where the larger merged CDCs have stronger relationships with capital and the state than with communities.

The third approach provides hope, but is challenging to implement. We exist in a liminal period, where the neoliberal project of controlling populism may have at least temporarily failed and the consequent populist energy has been unleashed. The challenge is that there is a lack of inclusionary populist infrastructure to channel that energy. And, given how much of that energy is distorted by the machinations of neoliberal capitalism, the 'purer' Alinsky-style populism may not be effective. Alinsky had an incisive critique of local inequality and a well-articulated theory of how to organise people to challenge powerful elites but, symptomatic of inclusionary populism generally, less of an idea about what more equal institutions might look like. This ambiguity allows both community organisers and populists to build broad, cross-cutting coalitions, but calls into question their durability. Under what circumstances will a populist movement maintain an inclusive approach? When will a community, once organised and empowered, retreat into exclusionary populism like Back of the Yards?

Some see a firm commitment to a particular ideology or set of policy goals as a guard against this uncertainty. Organising with an explicit commitment to Marxism, environmentalism or anti-colonialism (among others) may better define a group's mission and prevent it from transforming into exclusionary populism. However, we are sceptical of seeing ideology as a cure-all for these problems. First, it is precisely that ideological fluidity that enables both community development and populism to thrive. Without it we suspect many organising efforts would have difficulty gaining traction. Second, people are capable of holding incomplete, contradictory and changing ideological positions, as the stories showing how Bernie Sanders voters went on to become Trump voters (Kurtzleben, 2017). Participating in a movement with an explicit ideological commitment to equality and inclusion does not prevent an individual from holding exclusionary beliefs or supporting regressive policies in the future. Instead, we may need a form of not just inclusionary populism but also one with a populist process for building an economic analysis (Warren-White, 2006) rather than an ideology. This form of community development is local, builds power and envisions an alternative economy. It can take some lessons from the direct action tactics of Black Lives Matter, others from the local alternative development tactics of local food systems activists, and others from those community organising groups such as People's Action that emphasise concrete victories for the world as it should be.

References

Alinsky, S. (1969) *Reveille for Radicals*, New York: Random House.

Alinsky, S. (1971) *Rules for Radicals*, New York: Random House.

Arango, T. and Cockrel, K. (2018) 'Marches across the U.S. Protest Separation of Migrant Families', *The New York Times*, 14 June, [online] www.nytimes.com/2018/06/14/us/protest-marches-family-separation.html

Atlas, J. (2010) *Seeds of Change: The Story of ACORN*, Nashville, TN: Vanderbilt University Press.

Berry, M. F. (1986) 'The settlement movement 1886–1986: one hundred years on urban frontiers. New York', *United Neighborhood Centers of America*, [online] https://socialwelfare.library.vcu.edu/settlement-houses/settlement-movement-1886-1986/

Bimes, T. and Mulroy, Q. (2004) 'The rise and decline of presidential populism', *Studies in American Political Development*, 18: 136–1.

Boyte, H. (2008) *The Citizen Solution: How You Can Make a Difference*, Saint Paul: Minnesota Historical Society.

Brøndal, J. (2011) 'The ethnic and racial side of Robert M. La Follette Sr', *Journal of the Gilded Age and Progressive Era*, 10(3): 340–53.

Brubaker, R. (2017) 'Why populism?', *Theory and Society*, 46(5): 357–85.

Cadena-Roa, J. (2002) 'Strategic framing, emotions, and Superbarrio – Mexico City's masked crusader', *Mobilization*, 7(2): 201–16.

Castree, N. (2010) 'Neoliberalism and the biophysical environment: a synthesis and evaluation of the research', *Environment and Society*, 1(1): 5–45.

Cohen, M.A. (2008) 'Obama's new populism', *Wall Street Journal*, 23 February, [online] www.wsj.com/articles/SB120372786179687357

Conte, J. and Li, J. (2013)'Neoliberal urban revitalization in Chicago', *Advocates Forum*, [online] www.ssa.uchicago.edu/neoliberal-urban-revitalization-chicago

Cramer, K.J. (2016) *The Politics of Resentment: Rural Consciousness in Wisconsin and the Rise of Scott Walker*, Chicago: University of Chicago Press.

DeFilippis, J. (2001) 'The myth of social capital in community development', *Housing Policy Debate*, 12(4): 781–806.

Delgado, G. (1986) *Organizing the Movement: The Roots and Growth of Acorn*, Philadelphia: Temple University Press.

De Tocqueville, Alexis (2000) [1835] *Democracy in America*, Chicago, IL: University of Chicago Press.

Dinner, D. (2017) 'Employment-discrimination law in the neoliberal era', *Indiana Law Journal*, 92(3): Article 5 [online] www.repository. law.indiana.edu/cgi/viewcontent.cgi?article=11254&context=ilj

Doshna, J.P. (2015) 'Community development in the age of neoliberalism: the case of the Pennsylvania Fresh Food Financing Initiative', PhD thesis, Rutgers, State University of New Jersey, [online] https://rucore.libraries.rutgers.edu/rutgers-lib/47357

Evans, S.M. and Boyte, H.C. (1986) *Free Spaces: The Sources of Democratic Change in America*, Chicago: University of Chicago Press.

Fallows, J.M. and Fallows, D. (2018) *Our Towns: A 100,000-Mile Journey into the Heart of America*, New York: Pantheon Books.

Finks, P.D. (1984) *The Radical Vision of Saul Alinsky*, Ramsey: Paulist Press.

Fisher R. (1994) *Let the People Decide: Neighborhood Organizing in America*, New York: Twayne.

Fisher, R. (2009) *The People Shall Rule: ACORN, Community Organizing, and the Struggle for Economic Justice*, Nashville, TN: Vanderbilt University Press.

Foley, M. (2007) 'President Bush, the War on Terror, and the populist tradition', *International Politics*, 44(6): 666–91.

Fukuyama, F. (1999) 'Social capital and civil society', Paper prepared for IMF Conference on Second Generation Reforms, Washington, DC, 1 October, [online] www.imf.org/external/pubs/ft/seminar/ 1999/reforms/fukuyama.htm#II

Gambino, L., Siddiqui, S., Owen, P. and Helmore, E. (2017) 'Thousands protest against Trump travel ban in cities and airports nationwide', *The Guardian*, 29 January, [online] www.theguardian.com/us-news/ 2017/jan/29/protest-trump-travel-ban-muslims-airports

Geoghegan, M. and Powell, F. (2009) 'Community development and the contested politics of the late modern agora: of, alongside or against neoliberalism?', *Community Development Journal*, 44(4): 430–47.

Gerteis, J. and Goolsby, A. (2005) 'Nationalism in America: the case of the populist movement', *Theory and Society*, 34(2): 197–225.

Greenberg, D. (2005) *Ricanne Hadrian Initiative for Community Organizing Documentation and Evaluation Report*, Boston: Massachusetts Association of Community Development Corporations.

Gurney, J.N. and Tierney, K.J. (1982) 'Relative deprivation and social movements: a critical look at twenty years of theory and research', *Sociological Quarterly*, 23(1): 33–47.

Gusfield, J.R. (1994) 'The reflexivity of social movements: collective behavior and mass society theory revisited', in E. Larana, H. Johnston and R. Gusfield (eds), *New Social Movements: From Ideology to Identity*, Philadelphia: Temple University Press, pp 58–78.

Hamschmid, J. and Pirson, M. (eds) (2011) *Case Studies in Social Entrepreneurship and Sustainability: The Oikos Collection, Vol 2*, London: Routledge.

Hartman, Y. (2005) 'In bed with the enemy: some ideas on the connections between neoliberalism and the welfare state', *Current Sociology*, 53(1): 57–73.

Hasenfeld, Y. and Garrow, E.E. (2012) 'Nonprofit Human-service organizations, social rights, and advocacy in a neoliberal welfare state', *Social Service Review*, 86(2): 295–322.

Hochschild, A.R. (2016) *Strangers in Their Own Land: Anger and Mourning on the American Right*, New York: The New Press.

Incite! Women of Color against Violence (2009) *The Revolution Will Not Be Funded. Beyond The Non-Profit Industrial Complex*, Boston: South End Press.

Jasper, J. (2011) 'Emotions and social movements: twenty years of theory and research', *Annual Review of Sociology*, 37(37): 285–303.

Joassart-Marcelli, P. and Bosco, F.J. (2014) 'Alternative food projects, localization and neoliberal urban development: farmers' markets in Southern California', *Metropoles 15*, [online] https://journals.openedition.org/metropoles/4970

Judis, J. (2016) *The Populist Explosion: How the Great Recession Transformed American and European Politics*, New York: Columbia Global Reports.

Kazin, M. (1998) *The Populist Persuasion: An American History*, Ithaca, NY: Cornell University Press.

Kretzmann, J.P. and McKnight, J.L. (1993) *Building Communities from the Inside Out: A Path toward Finding and Mobilizing a Community's Assets*, Chicago: ACTA Publications.

Kurtzleben, D. (2017) 'Here's how many Bernie Sanders supporters ultimately voted for Trump', *National Public Radio*, 24 August, [online] www.npr.org/2017/08/24/545812242/1-in-10-sanders-primary-voters-ended-up-supporting-trump-survey-finds

Laclau, E. (1977) *Politics and Ideology in Marxist Thought: Capitalism, Fascism, Populism*, London: New Left Books.

Lamont, M., Park, B. and Ayala-Hurtado, E. (2017) 'Trump's electoral speeches and his appeal to the American white working class', *British Journal of Sociology*, 68(S1): S153–S180.

Lazzarato, M. (2009) 'Neoliberalism in action: inequality, insecurity and the reconstitution of the social', *Theory, Culture and Society*, 26(6): 109–33.

Long, J.A. (2012) 'Overcoming neoliberal hegemony in community development: law, planning, and selected Lamarckism', *The Urban Lawyer*, 44(2): 345–98.

Maclean, N. (2017) *Democracy in Chains: The Deep History of the Radical Right's Stealth Plan for America*, New York: Viking.

Marx, K. (1859) *A Contribution to the Critique of Political Economy*, translated by S.W. Ryazanskaya, Moscow: Progress, [online] www.marxists.org/archive/marx/works/1859/critique-pol-economy/

Mayer, M. and Rankin, K.N. (2002) 'Social capital and (community) development: a north/south perspective', *Antipode*, 34(4): 804–8.

McQuarrie, M. (2013) 'Community organizations in the foreclosure crisis: the failure of neoliberal civil society', *Politics and Society*, 41(1): 73–101.

Minieri, J. and Getsos, P. (2007) *Tools for Radical Democracy: How to Organize for Power in Your Community*, San Francisco, CA: Jossey-Bass.

Morris, A.D. (1984) *The Origins of the Civil Rights Movement: Black Communities Organizing for Change*, New York: Free Press.

Mudde, C. (2004) 'The populist zeitgeist', *Government and Opposition*, 39(4): 542–63.

Nackenoff, C. (1994) *The Fictional Republic: Horatio Alger and American Political Discourse*, New York: Oxford University Press.

O'Brien, R.T. (2006) 'Unemployment and disposable workers in Philadelphia: just how far have the bastards gone?', *Ethnos*, 71(2): 165–90.

Piven, F.F. and Cloward, R.A. (1979) *Poor People's Movements: Why They Succeed, How They Fail*, New York: Vintage.

Playboy Magazine (1972) 'Playboy interview: Saul Alinsky', March, [online] https://documents.theblackvault.com/documents/fbifiles/100-BA-30057.pdf

Putnam, R.D. (2000) *Bowling Alone: The Collapse and Revival of American Community*, New York: Simon and Schuster.

Rocco, R. (2016) 'Disposable subjects: the racial normativity of neoliberalism and Latino immigrants', *Latino Studies*, 14(1): 99–117.

Rohe, W.M. and Bratt, R.G. (2003) 'Failures, downsizings, and mergers among Community Development Corporations', *Housing Policy Debate*, 14: 1–2, 1–46.

Roy, M.J. (2017) 'The assets-based approach: furthering a neoliberal agenda or rediscovering the old public health? A critical examination of practitioner discourses', *Critical Public Health*, 27(4): 455–64.

Salent, J. D. (2009) 'Congressional report clears ACORN of voter fraud', *The Seattle Times*, 24 December, [online] www.seattletimes.com/nation-world/congressional-report-clears-acorn-of-voter-fraud/

Salmela, M. and Von Scheve, C. (2018) 'Emotional dynamics of right- and left-wing political populism', *Humanity and Society*, 42(4): 434–54.

Sanders, B. (2015) 'Senator Bernie Sanders presidential campaign announcement', C-SPAN, 29 April, [online] www.c-span.org/video/?326214-1/senator-bernie-sanders-i-vt-presidential-campaign-announcement

Sommerhauser, M. (2016) 'Office of Scott Fitzgerald: Sanctuary Cities Bill not a priority', *Wisconsin State Journal*, 20 February, [online] https://madison.com/wsj/news/local/govt-and-politics/office-of-scott-fitzgerald-sanctuary-cities-bill-not-a-priority/article_e71d653c-dc1f-5a69-a7f4-00f4aa796a22.html

Squires, G. (2003) *Organizing Access to Capital: Advocacy and the Democratization of Financial Institutions*, Philadelphia, PA: Temple University Press.

Stoecker, R. (1997) 'The Community Development Corporation model of urban redevelopment: a critique and an alternative', *Journal of Urban Affairs*, 19: 1–23.

Stoecker, R. (2003) 'Understanding the development-organizing dialectic', *Journal of Urban Affairs*, 25: 493–512.

Stoecker, R. (2004) 'The mystery of the missing social capital and the ghost of social structure: why community development can't win', in R. Silverman (ed), *Community-Based Organizations in Contemporary Urban Society: The Intersection of Social Capital and Local Context*, Detroit, MI: Wayne State University Press, pp 53–66.

Stoecker, R. (2009) 'Community organizing and social change', *Contexts Magazine*, 8: 20–25.

Szakos, J. and Szakos, K.L. (2008) *Lessons from the Field: Organizing in Rural Communities*, New Orleans, LA: Social Policy Press.

Taranto, J. (2009) 'Rules for Republicans, too', *Wall Street Journal*, 17 August, [online] www.wsj.com/articles/SB10001424052970204683204574356512455523766

Thibault, R.E. (2007) 'Between survival and revolution: another community development system is possible', *Antipode*, 39(5): 874–95.

Trump, D.J. (2017) 'The inaugural address', *The White House*, 20 January, [online] www.whitehouse.gov/briefings-statements/the-inaugural-address/

Van den Berk-Clark, C. and Pyles, L. (2012) 'Deconstructing neoliberal community development approaches and a case for the solidarity economy', *Journal of Progressive Human Services*, 23(1): 1–17.

Vance, J.D. (2016) *Hillbilly Elegy: A Memoir of a Family and Culture in Crisis*, New York: HarperCollins.

VISTA (2019) 'VISTA timeline – celebrating 50 years of VISTA service', [online] www.vistacampus.gov/vista-timeline-celebrating-50-years-vista-service

Warren-White, J. (2006) 'From the base: revolutionary left community organizing in the U.S. left roots', [online] https://leftroots.net/from-the-base/

Weigel, D. (2009) 'Conservatives find town hall strategy in leftist text', *Washington Independent*, [online] www.commondreams.org/news/2009/08/12/conservatives-find-town-hall-strategy-leftist-text

Weyland, K. (2001) 'Clarifying a contested concept: populism in the study of Latin American politics', *Comparative Politics*, 34(1): 1–22.

Wuthnow, R. (2018) *The Left Behind: Decline and Rage in Rural America*, Princeton, NJ: Princeton University Press.

Yin, J.S. (1998) 'The community development industry system: a case study of politics and institutions in Cleveland, 1967–1997', *Journal of Urban Affairs*, 20(2): 137–57.

NINE

Populism and environmental (in)justice in Latin America

Marcelo Lopes de Souza

Introduction: the dialectics of populism and authoritarianism and the challenge of environmental justice

With his book *Populism in Brazilian Politics*, published in 1978, Brazilian sociologist Francisco Weffort offered Latin American scholars a seminal – and today an already classical – contribution to the analysis of populism (Weffort, 1978). In fact, it is a fundamental work for all those who intend to reflect on this recurring phenomenon of Latin American politics. 'Populism', however, is a controversial concept, and its content has been appropriated in different ways and with different emphases according to each historical moment and each author's world view. For Weffort, for example, the populist system would be characterised by an anti-liberal and anti-oligarchical bias; a strong degree of disregard in relation to political parties; a nationalist orientation; a clear fondness of industrialisation; and last but not least, a multi-class social composition and cross-class discourse, in spite of most political support coming from the urban workers. Such a picture may perhaps accurately describe regimes and styles of government of the mid 20th century such as that of Getúlio Vargas and Jânio Quadros in Brazil, or of Juan Perón in Argentina, but it is no longer valid without reservations in the 21st century, for reasons that will become clear in the course of the discussion.

Old populism of the mid-20th century has in common with its contemporary expressions the fact that all populist regimes are elected through the mechanisms of representative democracy. In this sense, even if Getúlio Vargas' dictatorial *Estado Novo* or New State (1938–45) already contained clear populist elements, it is the 'democratic' Vargas (1950–54) who fully represents old populism. Populist rulers always tried to seduce the 'people' as voters through government-influenced institutions (such as unions) as well as directly on the basis of massive propaganda, while at the same time searching to restrict direct popular involvement in politics. However, the beginning of the 21st century saw the birth of a different kind of populist government – leftist neo-populism. The emergence of regimes apparently committed to a deepening of 'popular participation' in politics and which do not endorse markedly nationalist values, but simultaneously having as characteristics the co-optation of the masses through welfare programmes and the articulation around strongly charismatic leaders (such as Luís Inácio Lula da Silva, Hugo Chávez, Evo Morales, Néstor Kirchner and Rafael Correa) brought a new trend to the continent. In the context of this trend, left-wing politicians have been elected by the people and do not show strong authoritarian components (with the partial exception of Chávez's Venezuela and above all Maduro's regime). But that does not mean they have *consistently* contributed to the empowerment of the citizens of their respective countries.

Let us turn briefly back to the second half of the 20th century, before we enter the 21st century in a systematic way. Old populism was largely and brutally replaced in Latin America by openly authoritarian and often military regimes in the 1960s (such as Brazil in 1964) and 1970s (such as Chile in 1973 and Argentina in 1976). After the deterioration or collapse of these dictatorships (called bureaucratic-authoritarian states by Guillermo O'Donnell [1996]), markedly liberal-type regimes began to establish themselves: one of the best examples is Fernando Henrique Cardoso's two presidential terms in Brazil (1994–2002). However, the socially negative aspects of neoliberal reforms and adjustment in terms of income distribution and inequality in general soon began to nurture popular discontent in several countries. The frustration accumulated throughout the 1980s and 1990s created the conditions for the leftist neo-populism to emerge at the beginning of the 2000s.

Interestingly, precisely as those authoritarian regimes that dominated the Latin American political landscape in the 1960s and 1970s – and thereafter the liberal governments of the 1980s and 1990s – paved the way for the emergence of leftist neo-populism, the latter has unwittingly collaborated in the growth of the conservative, often authoritarian, tendencies we have seen in several Latin American countries recently. How has this been possible?

Be it due to its concessions to the neoliberal agenda (especially in the case of Brazil under Luís Inácio Lula da Silva and Dilma Rousseff [2003–16]), or due to its vulnerability to chronic and systemic corruption, or to the weakening of autonomous civil society initiatives and organisations (such as trade unions and housing organisations), which were captured ideologically, politically and economically by the state machine – in fact, due to all these factors together – the left-wing populism of the first two decades of the 21st century may have contributed decisively to the emergence of its nemesis in recent years. Indeed, the consolidation of a new wave of conservative populism seems to be a reality, this time with a quite authoritarian discourse and even crypto- or neo-fascist characteristics, as we are witnessing especially in Brazil. Jair Bolsonaro's popularity and election in Brazil in November 2018 can be seen as a turning point in terms of the emergence of right-wing neo-populism as well as of (re)new(ed) authoritarian tendencies within civil society itself.

However, it is still not clear to what extent the Bolsonaro government will be seen in the future as a good representative of the new conservative wave in Latin America. Considering Brazil's huge political weight on the continent, and particularly in South America, it seemed at first reasonable to expect that his victory could slowly influence the political climate at least in some of its neighbours, especially if his government shows a remarkable degree of economic efficiency. Economic success is something that has not yet occurred, but this does not seem to be the sole factor behind the fact that the Brazilian government's political and diplomatic positions have received a cold reception in the current conjuncture: even other conservative heads of government such as Chile's Sebastián Piñera have tried to distance themselves from what has often been regarded as extravagancies and ideological excesses of Brazil's president and his immediate entourage. A perfect example is Bolsonaro's astonishing reaction to the COVID-19 pandemic, which at the moment of writing (April 2020) has oscillated between obscurantist denial ('hysteria') and some kind of underestimation ('just a little cold') in the name of job preservation and ultimately business interests, leading to his increasing isolation both nationally and internationally in his attempts to undermine the efforts of his own minister of health (who has emphasised the importance of social distancing and self-quarantine). Be that as it may, we can see that conservative neo-populism has gradually replaced leftist neo-populism, as much as the latter had replaced the liberal governments of the 1980s and 1990s, and these, in their turn, had replaced the military regimes of the 1960s and 1970s.

At this juncture, we can summarise the characteristics of the three types of populism as follows: **old populism** instrumentalised political parties while it was actually dominated by strong, charismatic leaders who placed themselves above party politics and talked directly and in a very personal way to the 'people'; **leftist neo-populism**, on the contrary, has usually not shown the same disregard for party politics, and what is more, both their strong leaders and ruling parties have welcomed mechanisms of direct 'popular participation' (incidentally, these mechanisms proved themselves useful tools for political co-optation). In contrast to leftist neo-populism, **conservative neo-populism** (the best example being Jair Bolsonaro's government) does not encourage direct popular involvement in politics (in this regard it resembles old populism), while at the same time adopting more or less neoliberal policies that pose threats to both workers' rights and environmental protection (characteristics that make it different from both old populism and leftist neoliberal populism, even if the latter sometimes made significant concessions to the neoliberal agenda, especially in Brazil's case).

Curiously enough, it must be stressed that it was not only within the framework of overtly dictatorial regimes during the 20th century that the struggles for social justice and human rights faced severe obstacles and suffered setbacks. They have also been badly hampered by populism – both right-wing neo-populism with its component of intolerance and conservatism, and left-wing populism, which, by means of co-opting civil society, helps demobilise it and slow down or limit processes of awareness and radicalisation of democracy. The struggles for environmental justice are a crucial example of this.

In Latin America, the expression 'community development' (*desarrollo comunitario* [Spanish]/*desenvolvimento comunitário* [Portuguese]) has historically been linked with ideologically problematic phenomena from an emancipatory point of view: we should not forget that in the 1950s, 1960s and 1970s *desarrollo comunitario*/*desenvolvimento comunitário* was widely used by governments and international institutions to impose a view of 'development' that led to material and cultural dispossession and disempowerment, as a kind of 'socio–spatial engineering' aimed at social control by the state apparatus (see, for instance, Rodríguez, 2014). Nonetheless, the word 'community' as such is very important on the continent. This is so not only because of a long tradition of communitarian organisation, but also due to the ongoing relevance of the 'commons' for many people in the face of threats represented by economic 'integration' (read: dissipation and subalternisation of traditional economic and sociocultural structures) and cultural homogenisation in the wake of globalisation. As Maria Mies (2014: i106) wrote, there is 'no commons without a community'; but in 21st century Latin America, in spite of all progressive rhetoric and some concrete gains in terms of legal rights and economic support, many communities were or have been threatened in different ways by neo-populist regimes, as the 'lifeworlds' (places, ecosystems and territories) of many social groups (Indigenous peoples, peasants, and so on) were or have been contested, challenged and de-territorialised.

The remainder of this chapter will first of all address the main aspects of how left-wing neo-populism has undermined environmental justice in Latin America, and particularly in Brazil. It will then focus more closely on the political and ideological consequences of left-wing populism's contradictions and failure in terms of a deepening of social tensions and struggles. Finally, the conclusion will argue that in view of what was presented earlier in the chapter, and despite its charm from the point of view of most of the international left (but without wishing to deny some social and emancipatory gains), left-wing neo-populism has been ultimately part of the problem rather than of the solution.

Neo-populism's anti-popular dimension seen through the lens of environmental justice

In the name of 'economic development', hydroelectric dams, roads and other infrastructure projects have very often been built against the interests of local populations (for example, peasants and Indigenous people), and without due attention to the environmental impacts. In the name of attracting foreign investment and making money, agribusiness has often been stimulated to the detriment of basic environmental concerns and also of family farming. In the name of export interests (and reproducing, in general, a neo-colonial extractive logic of prioritisation of commodity exports without taking adequate account of environmental vulnerabilities, local/regional social needs and long-term economic consequences), large mining projects have been encouraged, with little care regarding impact assessments and environmental licensing, a situation that has even generated tragedies such as the breaking of the Fundão Dam, in the municipality of Mariana (state of Minas Gerais, Brazil), in November 2015, and the even more terrible bursting of one of the dams of the Feijão Stream, in the municipality of Brumadinho (also in the state of Minas Gerais), in January 2019. Finally, in the name of 'progress', and using the discourse of job creation as an alibi, highly polluting industries have been tolerated and located near poor populations' residential areas, which are truly urban environmental 'sacrifice zones'.[1] The socially unequal distribution of the environmental burdens of economic activities – the core of the concept of environmental injustice – has not ceased and sometimes has not even been mitigated under the sign of leftist neo-populism.

Most of the problems mentioned have much to do with the fact that many Latin American countries have experienced an increasing boom of neo-extractivism in recent years – that is, a 'pragmatic' revaluation of mining activities. Neo-extractivism notoriously causes large-scale environmental degradation, and from time to time results in appalling disasters with tragic consequences. Such disasters include the dam failure in the municipality of Mariana, which killed 19 people, and the similar tragedy in Brumadinho, which cost more than 300 lives. Although the neo-developmentalism (*neodesarrolismo* [Spanish], *neodesenvolvimentismo* [Portuguese]) of the 'progressive' governments in Brazil, Argentina and Venezuela still emphasised, at the level of discourse, the importance of industry and industrialisation, semi-peripheral and relatively industrialised countries such as Argentina and Brazil began to experiment, in practice, from the 1990s on (Brazil) or even from the 1970s and 1980s on (Argentina), processes of de-industrialisation and re-primarisation of the export basket. Typical peripheral countries, such as Bolivia and Ecuador, have not experienced these processes, since the industrial sector has never been very relevant there, either for the formation of GDP or in terms of export items. At the end of the day, all countries have been placing an exaggerated emphasis on mining activities and agribusiness.

As Alberto Acosta reported at the beginning of 2010, in Peru the conflicts around mining activities and oil extraction corresponded to more than 80% of all social conflicts, while in Ecuador the gravest cases of human rights violations took place in areas where transnational mining and oil companies operated (Acosta, 2012: 108). In a nutshell, as Uruguayan Eduardo Gudynas said, '[i]n all countries under progressive governments, the extractive sectors – which include mining, gas and oil – and extensive monocultures oriented to export have been maintained and even strengthened' (Gudynas, 2010: 63) Curiously, this circumstance clearly consolidates a neo-colonial model that, throughout the 20th century, and especially during the second half of the 20th century, Latin America sought to overcome. The main difference between old and new extractivism lies in the fact that within the framework of 'progressive' governments' approaches to neo-extractivism, there is a clear attempt on the part of the state apparatus to use the rent obtained on the basis of extractive activities to finance social infrastructure and reduce economic inequality. However, there are no significant differences between the two types of extractivism in terms of negative environmental impacts. In fact, even in relation to environmental justice, neo-extractivism has played a dubious role.

Despite some undeniable advances and social gains in sectors ranging from public health and education to infrastructure investments, the left-wing populism of the first two decades of the 21st century has represented a phenomenon fraught with contradictions. For example, at the same time as subsidies such as those provided under the Argentine *planes* and the Brazilian *Bolsa Família* programme flow to disadvantaged populations, with positive effects on food and living conditions in general, this form of clientelism does not contribute to professional (re)qualification of the poor and, much less, to raising the political awareness of the workers or to organising them politically. While the interests of marginalised populations seem to be better addressed and the dignity of the poor and minority groups seem to be much more respected, there are many situations in which sacrifices are imposed on vulnerable populations as an apparently inevitable price to be paid in the face of the imperatives of economic development. In light of these imperatives, environmental protection is sometimes treated as a 'luxury' and the interests and rights of people affected by environmental contamination, dam construction, agribusiness pressure on conservation efforts or Indigenous territories are viewed (and sometimes explicitly declared) as matters of minor importance.

In any case, it is necessary to realise that the Latin American countries considered in this chapter form a heterogeneous group not only with respect to the complexity of their economy, their demographic size, the availability of natural resources and the cultural aspects (for example, languages and traditions), but also with regard to politics, from the style of government to the relations between the state and civil society. Ultimately, each case has its own peculiarities, but we can say that in Evo Morales' Bolivia and Rafael Correa's Ecuador[2] the particularly impressive quantitative and cultural relevance of the native peoples and traditional populations reflect or reflected a more sophisticated level of dissimulation and concessions. In contrast, in Brazil, despite some legislative and institutional advances regarding the rights of Indigenous peoples, traditional communities and peasants, the general picture has been different. The overwhelming demographic weight of the urban population (formally more than 85% of the Brazilian population resided in cities and towns in 2010) and the small percentage and low visibility of the interests and demands of the Indigenous peoples and traditional populations have ideologically flanked the brutal processes of socio-spatial transformation that have occurred to the detriment of the ways of life and needs of these groups. The result has been the organisation of campaigns and protests against situations that adversely affect ecosystems and violate the rights of entire populations. These situations are obvious cases of environmental injustice.

Not only because it is the country with which I am most familiar, but above all because it is the country in which the socio–ecological limits and political consequences of 'progressive' neo-populism can best be observed, the Brazilian case will receive special attention in the remainder of this chapter. From the outset, the Lula da Silva government (2003–10) seemed to be more willing to make concessions to agribusiness, mining companies and other big-capital interests than to consistently defend the interests of poor and subaltern groups. This was not only due to economic reasons (such as attracting foreign investments and sponsoring large infrastructure projects), but also to obtaining parliamentary support, taking into account the great weight of mining and agribusiness lobbies in the Brazilian Congress.

The Ministry of the Environment, initially led by Minister Marina Silva – an ex-rubber tapper and comrade of rubber tapper activist Chico Mendes, who became a senator and environmental activist – was put under strong pressure from within the government itself to make several concessions. This was the case, for instance, regarding demands for more tolerance for transgenic soya and maize. As early as in 2003, the Ministry of the Environment was persuaded to accept increasing concessions for transgenic soya and maize production, to the point of agreeing with an amnesty that benefited large-scale farmers who had previously been involved with illegal cultivation of genetically modified crops. The pressures of the large-scale landowners finally resulted in the approval of the new Biosafety Law in 2005 (Law No 11.105 of 24 March 2005), whose regulatory body is the National Technical Biosafety Commission, composed of professionals from different ministries and biotechnology industries, and whose function has been shaped to facilitate, not to hinder, the dissemination of genetically engineered products (Lisboa, 2011: 18–20).

A further example was the transposition of the São Francisco river in the North-East of the country, Brazil's poorest and largely semi-arid region. In spite of a discourse of 'combating the drought' and helping the poor, this 'rearrangement' and supposed 'revitalisation' of the river has actually served more to benefit the strategic interests of supplying water to the Pecém Petrochemical Complex (in the state of Ceará) and for commercial agriculture. These actions resulted in strong resistance on the part of social movements, which denounced the problems resulting for the poor peasants who live at the margins of the river (Lisboa, 2011: 21–2).

Another example was the construction of two large hydroelectric dams on the Madeira river – Belo Monte and Jirau – and another one on the Xingu river – Belo Monte – all three in the Amazon, against which environmentalists, Indigenous peoples and a significant part of Brazilian public opinion mobilised through the press and online campaigns, but without success. At the same time, in the same region, the expansion of cattle herds continued under the Lula government, with serious consequences in terms of deforestation. In addition, the expansion of soybean cultivation in the Brazilian *cerrado* (savannah), at the margins of the Amazon region, also put the rainforest and the communities that live there under increasing pressure, even if, partly, only in an indirect way.

Much of the pressure that came from within the government itself to make environmental demands more flexible (such as several types of concessions and greater speed in relation to environmental licensing) was led by none other than Dilma Rousseff, who was minister of mines and energy between 2003 and 2005 and head of the Office of the Chief of Staff of the Presidency between 2005 and 2010, when she succeeded Lula as President of Brazil. No wonder that the new Forestry Code of 2012, which is extremely generous to large-scale farmers (for example, by means of an amnesty for those involved in illegal logging and through the reduction of environmentally protected areas), was endorsed by Dilma Rousseff's government.

Last but not least, neo-extractivism, whose environmentally and socially negative effects on local communities have been so intensely criticised in Latin America as a whole, has also been the subject of intense discussions by intellectuals, researchers and social movements in Brazil. Santos and Milanez (2014), for instance, have convincingly demonstrated how Lula da Silva's 'progressive' government largely adopted the neo-extractive model while showing at the same time a clear disregard for the voices and interests of local subaltern groups – precisely those that are most affected by neo-extractive processes.

In all these situations, the winners were large (often transnational) corporations, large-scale landowners, construction firms and other representatives of the traditional ruling classes. In contrast, poor farmers, Indigenous populations and residents of communities de territorialised in the wake of the construction of dams or some disaster (as in the case of the dam disasters in Mariana and Brumadinho) are often the clear losers. All this in the name of a dubious 'common good'; all this under the banner of 'neo-developmentalism'; and all this under the auspices of 'progressive' neo-populism.

Even an author sympathetic to the 'progressive' governments that established themselves in Latin America during the first decade of the 21st century, after noting that 'the primacy of liberal-capitalist law that still commands social and power relations implies the deterritorialisation of community territorialities by interpreting the national interest from a colonial perspective that ignores the multiple ethnicities/peoples/ nationalities that occupy the Amazon', was forced to admit that '[t]he governments that proclaim their opposition to neoliberal policies have found it difficult to recognise these territorialities' (Porto-Gonçalves, 2017: 71). The level of scepticism, however, should be higher than that suggested by Porto-Gonçalves: *could* such neo-populist and neo-developmentalist governments have truly been able to embrace these communities and territorialities, given the deep political limits and contradictory dynamics that (have) animated this kind of government?

From leftist neo-populism to neo-authoritarianism?

The debacle of Brazil's Workers Party (Partido dos Trabalhadores or PT) between 2016 and 2018 is the most spectacular example of both the failure of left-wing neo-populism and populism's inability to avoid a comeback of authoritarianism. After 14 years of PT's leftist governments (2013–16), Dilma Rousseff was removed from the presidency after a highly controversial impeachment process (August 2016); former President Luis Inácio Lula da Silva was imprisoned after a not much less controversial legal process (April 2018); and right-wing politician Jair Messias Bolsonaro, a former captain of the Brazilian army, was elected president (November 2018).

From a *liberal* point of view (in the sense of classical liberalism), Brazil's Workers Party indirectly helped organise the right through corruption and '*roubalheira*' (rip-off), as the issues with PT's leftist governments offered the conservative forces plenty of ideological ammunition. Of course, liberals have also denounced the misogynist, homophobic and often racist agenda of extreme right-wing forces – an agenda that has witnessed growing success in an increasingly 'evangelical' country, as the influential neo-Pentecostal churches and their followers show signs of intolerance towards sexual minorities and are frightened by behavioural changes that have produced a higher visibility of feminist, gay and Afro–Brazilian agendas and demands. Some liberal journalists and intellectuals have even noticed and underlined the role that the messianic biases of a portion of the judiciary and of the Public Prosecutor's Office (*Ministério Público*) have had in indirectly helping the extreme right; and a few of them have even been able to realise that the rabid and residual 'anti-communism' of a portion of Brazilian society does not have a basis in reality. But none of these criticisms even touches on a basic factor in the rise of far-right power, namely leftist neo-populism's responsibility for demobilising civil society.

From a left-libertarian perspective, in contrast to the liberal one, left-wing populism, by substituting universalist public policies (agrarian reform and urban reform, for example) for state subsidies, as well as by co-opting unions and social movement organisations, Brazilian civil society has been disorganised and its capacity for resistance weakened. And these aspects are essential for understanding not only the genesis of the ultra-conservative wave in politics, but above all the current powerlessness (and in part blindness) of a large part of the population.

It may be naive to interpret the contradictions of leftist neo-populism as paradoxical. After all, this kind of populism has helped make viable several projects of capital accumulation in Latin American countries, precisely due to its greater facility to break popular resistance and tame hearts and minds in the working class. Despite appearances to the contrary, symbolised by the indignant discourses of the middle classes and capitalists against corruption, both rural and urban businesspeople (from industrialists to bankers to large-scale farmers) as well as a good portion of the middle class, benefited greatly during the governments of the Workers Party in Brazil.

In its leftist variant, populism proved to be more capable of enhancing the role of parties than traditional populism. Although the Brazilian Labour Party (Partido Trabalhista Brasileiro, PTB) was a very important tool for Getúlio Vargas after 1945 (the year the party was founded), the old PTB, even by its belated foundation, never had the socially (dis)organising relevance that PT showed between 2003 and 2016. 'Popular participation' is emphasised in the leftist variant of populism ('participatory budgeting', with all its contradictions and limits, was a good example of this, especially in the context of PT's municipal governments in the 1990s, beginning with Porto Alegre), and authoritarianism was by no means a basic characteristic of this style of government. Despite these caveats, several other elements are in general shared by the old and new versions of populism: the presence of a charismatic leader; the search for the co-optation of unions and popular organisations by the government and the party machine; and the multiple relations of dependence that are created between the popular organisations and the state apparatus.

Leftist populism has made many mistakes, even though its leaders, followers and sympathisers do not view it that way, for what is understood in this chapter as misconceptions are, in their view, essential devices and strategies for seizing state power. Neo-developmentalism, showing only a limited commitment to environmental protection for the benefit of the Brazilian population, was one of these strategies; the concessions to the market and the neoliberal agenda, to the detriment of more decisive redistributive initiatives, was another; and finally there was the perpetuation of ambiguities in the relationship with family farming and the project of agrarian reform ultimately favouring agribusiness. Ironically, the business interests and centrist political forces that have benefited from many gestures of rapprochement and even support from the Partido dos Trabalhadores governments were the same that, over three decisive years (2016–18), turned their backs on the party. It is because of its contradictions and their serious limitations that, in the end, PT's neo-populism can only be considered 'progressive' in this way – with quotation marks.

The obsession with 'governability', expressed by all possible types of legal and illegal bargaining, cost the PT what remained of its credibility. But what should interest the Brazilian population is the fact that, indirectly, for civil society, the hesitations and ambivalences of left-wing populism have taken away much of the people's capacity to effectively resist the dismantling of some institutions that, even if clearly limited by the logic of the state and its hierarchies, bureaucracies and clientelism, can nonetheless be useful. 'Institution' is meant here in the broad sense, comprising both formal institutions directly created or instituted by the government and those that exist more or less outside the government, even if their dynamics very often cannot be understood without reference to the state apparatus for various reasons (trade unions and NGOs, for example). Institutions have been dismantled or weakened in realms as different as the conquest of rights, reduction of social injustice in the countryside and the cities, access to higher education, financing of scientific and technological research, and environmental protection – to mention only a few examples. On all these fronts, great setbacks are now highly likely or have already been experienced under Jair Bolsonaro's conservative government – perhaps a back door to overtly authoritarian adventures.

PT's populism, in short, has largely demobilised Brazilian civil society and the activist citizenry and community organising that go along with genuine community development. In other words, the great 'political–social passive' that left-wing populism leaves as a 'legacy' is the political disorganisation of workers and co-optation of activists, especially in cities. The PT intended (and to a great extent succeeded) in absorbing and directing the popular energies for *its* purposes – including, of course, that of self-perpetuation. The same thing was done with a huge portion of the radical intelligentsia, in the universities and elsewhere. As it almost disintegrated politically and morally, the party carried with it the hopes and the courage of many citizens who believed in its message and leaders. Politico-pedagogically, it left behind it a landscape of ruins.

Conclusion: authoritarianism's inadvertent helpers

Be that as it may, the prospect of substituting left-wing neo-populism for the right-wing variety will surely open a new and even darker chapter in the history of the struggles for environmental justice in Latin America. Right-wing neo-populism has been more inclined to repression than to dialogue, and it is more at ease with suppression of rights than with artifices of co-optation.

The Brazilian case is particularly important and striking, not only because the deleterious effects of neo-populism are evident with regard to ambiguities in dealing with the interests of the working class and with communities of traditional or underprivileged populations, but also because the possible outcomes of large-scale co-optation are clear, as exemplified by the vertiginous growth of conservatism (and even reactionary politics) and ultimately by the election of Jair Bolsonaro in November 2018. Due to Brazil's economic and political importance, this ultraconservative turn can gradually impact on other countries in Latin America, and especially on right-wing activists in South America, in spite of the failures and weaknesses of Bolsonaro's government as perceived even by many conservative politicians.

At the time of writing, Brazil's foreign minister is a fierce climate change denier; the minister of agriculture is an agronomist and a conservative politician who was responsible as a deputy in the Congress, in 2018, for facilitating (through the design of a bill) the dissemination of pesticides in the country; and the minister for the environment is a lawyer whose commitment to environmental protection has been dubious – to say the least. These examples suffice to illustrate the low level of commitment of the conservative Bolsonaro government to an environmental agenda. With regard to human rights, declarations by various members of the government, starting with the president himself, did not allow for much optimism from the very beginning of the government.

The main lesson to be drawn from all these Latin American experiences, and perhaps more clearly from the Brazilian one, is that populism, even in its leftist version, does not consistently empower communities, and by adopting a neo-extractive model and a not particularly critical approach to agribusiness, it threatens local and regional livelihood bases in Latin America. Environmental injustice, which is nothing but the environmental facet of social injustice, has gone hand in hand with all regimes that do not focus on transparency and the consistent empowerment of civil society. This has always been the case with conservative governments, and ironically also came to be largely the case of leftist neo-populist governments, which, moreover, have indirectly paved the way for the new explicitly conservative conjunctures that are now emerging.

As everyone knows, social sciences are not 'exact', but Jair Bolsonaro's administration in Brazil is again a privileged 'laboratory' in relation to what could be regarded as a socio–political 'iron rule', this time a conclusion drawn from the history of humankind in general: apart from extreme situations, when external forces (for instance, in the wake of a war, such as in Europe in 1945) play a crucial role, citizens' self-organising and strong pressure from below are the most decisive factors that can put an end to unpopular governments. Bolsonaro's government has faced increasing pressure from Congress members (and not only from left-wing politicians but also from centrist ones) as well as from many judges and public prosecutors. However, the equally increasing protests and demonstrations by students and several social movements and other civil society organisations have ultimately been more relevant in showing the weaknesses of conservative neo-populism. While politicians (and to a large extent even many judges and public prosecutors) seem interested in the re-establishment of some sort of more or less traditional status quo rather than in a true deepening of democracy, at least a part of Brazil's civil society has apparently grasped that the overcoming of conservative neo-populism cannot be seen as a *non plus ultra* in terms of an emancipatory goal. It is by no means clear that an increasing number of Brazilian citizens will fully understand in the near future that conservative neo-populism (and overtly authoritarian regimes even more) is just the ugliest face of a much larger phenomenon: the contradictions of representative 'democracy' and the capitalist state, particularly in a highly heteronomous and unequal country such as Brazil. Be that as it may, one thing is certain: only civil society's self-organising efforts, which include a truly emancipatory approach to community development, can represent the light at the end of the tunnel regarding the building of a new, more just society – both in relation to environmental justice and more generally.

Notes

1   This term was originally used in relation to the US context (see Lerner, 2010), but Latin America has plenty of examples to offer in this regard. Among many other concrete cases – and restricting myself to one of the most problematic situations, which is that of the populations affected by the oil industry – we could mention the environmental contamination that affects the poor populations of the Matanza-Riachuelo basin in Greater Buenos Aires (see for instance Auyero and Swistun, 2008; Merlinsky, 2013) of the surroundings of the Duque de Caxias refinery in Rio de Janeiro (Raulino, 2013).

2   Evo Morales has been President of Bolivia since 2006; Rafael Correa was President of Ecuador between 2007 and 2017.

References

Acosta, A. (2012) 'Extractivismo y neoextractivismo: Dos caras de la misma maldición' [Extractivism and neo-extractivism: two faces of the same curse], in Grupo Permanente de Trabajo sobre Alternativas al Desarrollo (ed), *Más allá del desarrollo*, Mexico City: Fundación Rosa Luxemburg and Abya Yala, pp 83–118.

Auyero, J. and Swistun, D. (2008) *Inflamable: Estudio del sufrimiento ambiental* [*Flammable: Study of Environmental Suffering*], Buenos Aires: Paidós.

Gudynas, E. (2010) 'Si eres tan progresista ¿Por qué destruyes la naturaleza? Neoextractivismo, izquierda y alternativas' [If you are so progressive, why do you destroy nature? Neo-extractivism, left and alternatives], *Ecuador Debate*, 79: 61–81.

Gudynas, E. (2012) 'Estado compensador y nuevos extractivismos: las ambivalencias del progresismo sudamericano' [New extractivisms and the 'compensating state': the ambivalences of South American progressivism], *Nueva Sociedad*, 237: 128–46.

Lerner, S. (2010) *Sacrifice Zones: The Front Lines of Chemical Exposure in the United States*, Cambridge, MA: MIT Press.

Lisboa, M. V. (2011) 'Balanço da política ambiental do Governo Lula: Grandes e duradouros impactos' [An assessment of Lula's environmental policy: big and lasting impacts], in M. de Paula (ed), *"Nunca antes na história desse país"…? Um balanço das políticas do Governo Lula*, Rio de Janeiro: Heinrich Böll Stiftung, pp 16–31.

Merlinsky, G. (2013) *Política, derechos y justicia ambiental: El conflicto del Riachuelo* [Politics, rights, and environmental justice: the Riachuelo conflict], Buenos Aires: Fondo de Cultura Económica.

Mies, M. (2014) 'No commons without a community', *Community Development Journal*, 49(S1): i106–i117.

O'Donnell, G. (1996) [1982] *El Estado burocratico autoritario: Triunfos, derrotas y crisis* [*The Authoritarian Bureaucratic State: Triumphs, Defeats and Crises*] (2nd edn), Buenos Aires: Editorial de Belgrano.

Porto-Gonçalves, C.W. (2017) *Amazônia: Encruzilhada civilizatória. Tensões territoriais em curso* [*Amazon Basin: Civilization at the Crossroads. Ongoing Territorial Tensions*], Rio de Janeiro: Consequência.

Raulino, S.F. (2013) 'Injustiças ambientais e indústria do petróleo: temor e consentimento nas representações de populações que sofrem efeitos de proximidade da Refinaria Duque de Caxias (REDUC)' [Environmental injustice and the oil industry: fear and consent in social representation among the populations suffering from the effects of proximity to the Duque de Caxias Refinery (REDUC)], *Revista de Educação, Ciências e Matemática*, 3(3): 69–90.

Rodríguez, P.G. (2014) 'Antropología del desarrollo comunitario: Historia y vigencia del desarrollo comunitario en las políticas públicas bonaerenses' [Anthropology of community development: history and validity of community development in Buenos Aires' public policies], *XI Congreso Argentino de Antropología Social* (Rosario, 23–26 July), [online] www.researchgate.net/publication/270051224_Antropologia_del_desarrollo_comunitario_Historia_y_vigencia_del_desarrollo_comunitario_en_las_politicas_publicas_bonaerenses

Santos, R.S.P. dos and Milanez, B. (2014) 'Neoextrativismo no Brasil? Uma análise da proposta do novo marco legal da mineração' [Neo-extractivism in Brazil? An analysis of the proposed new legal framework for mining], *Revista Pós: Ciências Sociais*, 10(19): 119–48.

Weffort, F. (1978) *O populismo na política brasileira* [*Populism in Brazilian Politics*], Rio de Janeiro: Paz e Terra.

TEN

Populist politics and democracy in the UK: implications for community development

Keith Popple

Introduction

There is little doubt that we are living in uncertain and unpredictable times that are marked by significant and profound political and social upheavals and changes in almost all countries and regions of the world. These changes are even greater now that we are dealing with the outcome of the worldwide COVID-19 pandemic. One of the major features of this changing and emerging phenomenon, and a major theme of this edited book, is the rise of populist politics, something which is as notable in the UK as it is elsewhere. As outlined in this chapter, British populist politics, and in particular right-wing populist politics, has been with us for some time and its well-known characteristics have over different time periods had significant implications for communities, for the theory and practice of community development, and for those presently involved in the activity in the UK, where it has suffered substantial financial cutbacks.

After a short working definition of populism which assists locating the issues raised in the chapter, a brief outline is provided of the history of populist politics in the UK, which in modern times dates from the 1930s. In this consideration the study looks at the implications of populism and how, at different times, communities threatened by the outcome of populist activity and policies responded, and how community development has evolved in reaction to this phenomenon. It then offers an overview of the shape and meaning of the present rise in populist politics in the UK, which it is argued can be traced back to the impact of the 2008 global financial crash and the subsequent imposition by successive British governments of economic austerity, all of which has caused considerable economic and social stress in communities. The global crash was followed in the UK with revelations a year later of what became known as the 'parliamentary expenses scandal', which was to change people's view of politicians. Immigration has always been a contentious issue in the UK and it too has fed into the rise of populism.

The outcome of the austerity measures that has led to the contemporary presence of populism in the UK has been a mounting dissatisfaction and a general lack of trust in politics amongst millions in the country. This, together with a hangover from the 'parliamentary expenses scandal' that involved members from both Houses of Parliament, has created a marked degree of scepticism about the workings of the British electoral system. Further, there has been a growing lack of confidence in the system of neoliberal globalised finance capitalism that has left countless communities poorer and economically less secure. People's anger and frustration with these actions have been harnessed by the political right, which during the 2016 Referendum debate focused on the impact of immigration on communities. At the same time the political left experienced populism when Jeremy Corbyn led the Labour Party from 2015 to 2020. The final section notes the unique elements of community development and reflects on the role it can play in these challenging times. The chapter ends by arguing that community development now requires greater funding and recognition while reconceptualising itself in a more radical manner.

Defining populism

Populism is often portrayed as the clash or battle between the 'ordinary', honourable mass of people and the disreputable corrupt elite and is a term that can be used to describe those arguing from either a left-wing or a right-wing position. Nevertheless, as Mudde and Kaltwasser (2017: 5) declare, populism is essentially a contested term with a 'lack of scholarly agreement' and, further, it 'is a label seldom claimed by people or organizations themselves. Instead, it is ascribed to others, most often with a negative connotation' (Mudde and Kaltwasser, 2017: 2).

Nevertheless Mudde and Kaltwasser (2017: 6) define populism as a 'thin-centred ideology that considers society to be ultimately separated into two homogeneous and antagonistic camps, "the pure people" versus "the corrupt elite", and which argues that politics should be an expression of the *volonte generale* (general will) of the people'.

The British political scientist David Marquand similarly interrogates the nature of populism, concluding that 'Populism is not a doctrine or a governing philosophy, still less an ideology. It is a disposition, perhaps a mood, a set of attitudes and above all a style' (Marquand, 2017). While populism is intrinsically neither left-wing nor right-wing, being both radical and conservative, in terms of the fundamental difference between right-wing and left-wing populism, scholars such as Mudde and Kaltwasser (2017), Moffitt (2016) and Mouffe (2018) argue that right-wing populists tend to be 'exclusionary', for example wanting to exclude migrants, or ethnic minorities, or Muslims, whereas left-wing populists have a broader, inclusive concept of 'the people'. With these general definitions in mind, together with the observations from the scholars noted previously, let us move to consider populism in the UK.

The roots of UK populist politics

Although the literature on contemporary populism in the UK is largely underdeveloped, populist politics is not new to the UK – in particular right-wing populism, which has a history dating back to the 1930s. Over the years the core of British right-wing populism has primarily been in response to immigration and in particular non-white immigrants moving into communities that are already under economic stress. What is important for us is to consider is the impact of this right-wing populism on communities and the ways members of these communities and community development have responded.

A case in point is when in 1932 a number of Nazi, fascist and anti-Semitic movements linked together to create the British Union of Fascists (BUF), led by an ally of Hitler, Sir Oswald Mosley. One of the foremost features of BUF activity was its policy of engaging in intimidation and violence in areas of Jewish settlements, particularly in London. It was here, however, that they were frequently confronted by community-based counter movements. Perhaps the most well-known of these encounters took place on 4 October 1936 when thousands of BUF members planned to march through a largely Jewish area of the East End of London. The Jews who had fled persecution in mainland Europe and lived in this economically deprived area residing in extremely overcrowded conditions, were further impoverished when the two main industries they worked in – tailoring and cabinet making – were severely hit by the depression. The Jews had followed previous waves of immigration that had seen Huguenots, Irish and other groups settle in the area. Members of anti-fascist groups and local community members, including supporters of the Stepney Tenants' Defence League, together made up an estimated 20,000 counter-protesters that erected roadblocks in an attempt to stop the

BUF members, who marched wearing their political uniforms (the 'Blackshirts'). After engaging in verbal and physical confrontation, Mosley abandoned the march when it became clear that there would be considerable bloodshed in the ensuing running battles. The Battle of Cable Street, as it is referred to, with its theme 'They shall not pass', is frequently invoked in British politics as a clear example of how a targeted community stood firm against fascist groups and the right-wing populism of leaders such as Mosley (Rosenberg, 2011).

However, it wasn't until the late 1960s, due in part to the increased accessibility of television in people's homes, that populism increased more nationally. Probably the most well-known of the instances where television played a role during that period was when, in April 1968, Enoch Powell, a senior Conservative Party MP, spoke out against immigration with his infamous 'Rivers of Blood' speech which predicted the emergence of racial tension in British cities similar to that witnessed in the United States (Powell, 1968: 99). Parts of Powell's speech were shown the same evening on British television news programmes highlighting his view that non-white immigrants would bring increasing pressure to the already economically poor communities they moved into, so creating the potential for violence between the mainly non-white Commonwealth newcomers and the white residents. Despite being criticised by the British establishment, including leading broadsheet newspapers, the main political parties and the leader of his own party, Edward Heath, who sacked Powell from his influential position as a spokesperson on defence, there was widespread public support for Powell's views – so much so that he was considered to be 'the most admired person' in British public opinion (Dumbrell, 2001: 34). This public support included about 1,000 dock workers, who marched on the Houses of Parliament with slogans such as 'we want Enoch Powell', and a number of mass demonstrations that included trade unionists in London and Wolverhampton, where Powell was an MP (Shepherd, 1998).

Nevertheless, it was non-white immigrants, mainly Asians, living in poor communities that were the victims of Powell's rhetoric, with attacks from emboldened mainly working class whites (www.irr.org. uk/news/the-beatification-of-enoch-powell/). The rising racial and social tension resulted in the Labour government launching the multi-million pound Urban Programme in a matter of a few weeks after Powell's speech. The Urban Programme, which was funded yearly into the 1980s, provided financial support for a range of diverse community-based schemes resulting in the employment of community development practitioners in areas defined in terms of social indicators such as high unemployment and sizeable immigrant concentrations (Edwards and Batley, 1978). At the same time the government funded the expansion of initial community development training and youth work together with the building of youth and community centres: all of which grew out of concern to address social harmony at a neighbourhood level (Gilchrist and Taylor, 2016).

Arguably the most important state-supported community development initiative in the 1960s and 1970s and part of the Labour government's drive to shore up the social democratic ideology was the National Community Development Project (NCDP) that was launched to improve social service delivery and coordinate already operating established community and local authority-based projects (Loney, 1983). The 12 projects which formed the NCDP were to prove to be a milestone in British community development, producing a literature that continues to resonate today (Popple, 2013, 2015; Bank and Carpenter, 2017). The initiative proved to be a thorn in the side of governments, however, as the project teams presented a radical analysis of the challenges facing the communities they were linked with. The teams argued that the impoverished communities they were working in were essential for the continuance of capitalism (CDP, 1977). Needless to say, the government withdrew its funding from the projects, which to their credit maintained their radical analysis.

A decade later Powell's views on racial superiority and the likelihood of intra-community tension were echoed by the National Front (NF), which emerged to become the UK's largest far right party, reaching its electoral height in the mid-1970s when it secured a number of local council seats in elections (Harrop et al, 1980). Members of the NF were known for their intimidation and provocation in communities where migrants resided, in this case overwhelmingly neighbourhoods where Asians lived. Although less overtly radical than the NCDP, the state funded further community development projects in many parts of the country. At the same time, at least two protest and campaigning movements were founded to counter the bullying and terrorising of communities and included the Anti-Racist Alliance (ARA) and the Anti-Nazi League (ANL), both which were active in organising solidarity marches through threatened areas and staging carnivals and festivals in ethnically diverse communities (Popple, 1997). There also emerged Rock Against Racism, a group that organised concerts to celebrate the multiculturalism and diversity of a changing Britain (www.lovemusichateracism.com/about/).

The most recognised right-wing UK populist politician of recent time was Margaret Thatcher, who became leader of the Conservative

Party in 1975, and in 1979 the first British woman prime minister. During her time in office Thatcher's government had a significant and divisive impact on communities throughout the UK. It was during this period that the Thatcher government reduced the social democratic universal approach to welfare and moved to a more selective and residual welfare state and the theory and practice of community development changed its emphasis.

The work of Thatcher, who held office from 1979 to 1990, has been studied by numerous social scientists in an attempt to understand the impact that her ideology and policies had on the British population then and since. One of the most influential of these commentators was the cultural theorist and political activist Stuart Hall, who with others (Hall et al, 1978) accurately forecast the rise of Thatcherism, arguing it would become a turning point in British life. Before Thatcherism, the major political parties were largely agreed on the purpose and scope of the welfare state, a progressive personal tax regime, the nationalisation of key industries and a well-regulated economy – all of which were the central premises of Keynesianism, which had been the dominant economic ideology during the post-war period.

Influenced by the monetarist neoliberal policies advocated by right-wing economists such as Milton Freidman and Friedrich von Hayek, Thatcher represented a new form of popular Toryism with policies appealing in particular to the individual economic interests of sections of the middle and working class. These policies, which were intended to address economic stagflation on the 1970s, included reductions in direct taxation, an increase in indirect taxation, and cuts in state expenditure in areas such as housing and education.

Hall (1980) argued that while Thatcherism was a multifaceted historical phenomenon, it was at root 'authoritarian populism'. Further, according to Barker (1981), Thatcher's views on immigration and in particular non-white immigration was an integral part of a rising racist public discourse, termed 'new racism'. Certainly the election of the right-wing Tory government led to the NF suffering a decline from which it never recovered as those supporting racist policies switched their votes to support Thatcher (Reitan, 2003). In 1978, the year before Thatcher became prime minister, she appeared in a television programme to address public concern over immigration with the now famous line 'People are really rather afraid that this country might be swamped by people with a different culture'. Later in the same interview, using powerful imagery and rhetoric to focus people's minds on outsiders, Thatcher remarked: 'The British character has done so much for democracy, for law and done so much throughout the world that if there is any fear that it might be swamped people are going to react and be rather hostile to those coming in.' Immediately after her comments a survey by National Opinion Polls recorded a spectacular increase in support for the Tories; they shot to an 11-point lead over Labour, which they were previously trailing by two points (Morgan, 2001).

It is important to place Thatcher's rise to power in an economic, political and social context in order to understand it in terms of populism and the impact Tory policies had on communities in the UK. There is little doubt that Thatcherism shaped and reshaped British politics in a manner that no other political leader had previously achieved, in what proved to be a seminal moment in British politics. As we have noted, during the 1970s a successful ultra-right political party, the National Front, established itself and achieved notable local election success. It was, however, countered by much larger active anti-racist movements that sought to protect minorities and the communities they lived in. At the same time, the relative decline of Britain, with the ending of the post-war boom and a period internationally of political and economic turmoil, saw an increasingly polarisation in UK politics. Elements of the Tory party moved further to the right while the labour movement increased its industrial struggles to protect jobs and wages, which resulted in a number of strikes, including those in the postal service and the mining industry. These times provided fertile ground for Thatcher as an emerging populist leader (Mc Smith, 2013).

At the 1979, 1983 and 1987 general elections Thatcher tapped into the electorate's dissatisfaction with what was portrayed as the unwieldy power of the trade unions, the rigidity of a welfare state associated with previous Labour governments, and the apparent limited choice in health care, education and housing, and of course non-white immigration. Although married to a multi-millionaire executive in the oil industry, Thatcher presented herself as a woman of the people, claiming she understood the needs of 'ordinary women' and 'ordinary families', and the nature of changing communities, often presenting herself on television as the populist saviour of the 'little people' against the power of usually uncaring state industries and unresponsive public bodies, and pressure from unspecified outsiders (Blackwell and Seabrook, 1985). Such tropes are typical of right-wing populist leaders, who exploit the tectonic movements that impact on community life as the certainties of the past become replaced by the uncertainties of the future over which people feel they have little or no control.

However, the outcome of Thatcher's populist political programme quickly proved discordant as it was based on individual self-help and market liberalisation and deregulation, which signalled an attack on working class communities and organisations including trade unions. In what became a defining policy of the Thatcher era, council tenants could purchase their homes in the Tory government's drive for a 'property owning democracy'. This policy enriched those who were in a position to purchase their properties, which were sold at a substantial discount, while those unable to purchase were left living in what was usually lower-standard accommodation. Council housing waiting lists lengthened as local authorities were prevented by law from using the finance raised from sales to fund building more homes. This increased the already notable divide between homeowners and those reliant on the rented housing sector. The effect of Thatcher's 'Right to Buy' scheme was that relatively homogeneous housing estates where all households paid rent to the local authority now became communities where residents were divided against each other: between those who paid rent and those who were purchasing their initially council-provided property with a mortgage (Alcock with May, 2014).

With the country divided against itself, Thatcher then employed the technique emblematic of populist leaders and labelled those unable or unprepared to join her new world 'moaning minnies', scroungers, lazy and layabout shirkers. In Thatcher's 'laissez faire' capitalism, where the market trumped the public sector, the Tory government removed state support to key industries such as coal mining, steel making and ship building, leaving thousands of working class communities without employment and reliant on the declining value of state welfare and unemployment benefits. This went alongside significant personal tax cuts for the financially better-off, while those without such support were told to 'get on their bikes' and look for work. The impact on these working class communities cannot be underestimated and is well documented by Jones (2016), who presents a disturbing picture of inequality and class hatred that was amplified by the Thatcher government.

The right-wing populism that Thatcher fed on was typical of approaches by such leaders; it had signifiers primarily based on race and class, and where people and communities were turned against each other. While Thatcher received the rapturous support of the nouveau riche, those working in the newly deregulated finance sector that enjoyed record business and profits, workers engaged in the newly expanding and profitable tech industries based mainly in southern England, and homeowners able to purchase and finance their properties, there were millions of working class people living in communities decimated by the closure of major older manufacturing and mining industries and who were opposed to her ideology and government.

In conclusion, we can see that through the years a racist discourse has been a strong element in right-wing British populism. From Oswald Mosley's 1930s anti-Semitic oratory and leading marches of his 'Blackshirts' followers through communities where Jews lived, to the anti-immigrant racial superiority rhetoric of Enoch Powell, and then Thatcher's use of terms such as 'swamped' in regard to non-white immigrants, we can identify powerful threads of excluding people on the basis of skin colour, and differences in culture, language and religion. Non-white immigrants were presented as unwanted and harmful, although any referenced understanding of how capitalism operates shows that a country's immigrants have provided a powerful engine for economic and social change and a valuable resource in the labour market.

As we have noted, during the periods when the populist right was at its strongest, whether stoked by the racist language of Mosley, Powell or Thatcher, there has been a powerful response in and by communities affected by this rhetoric. Marches, campaigns, demonstrations, concerts and political education have all played a part in countering this hostility and distrust. Similarly, when Thatcher's policies attacked communities in traditional working class areas there was an outburst of action to rebuff the assault on their way of life and their dependency on specific employment. For example, according to Milne (2014), during the 1984–85 coal miners' strike Thatcher was prepared to use the force of the law and the intelligence services to destroy the miners' trade union and the communities they represented.

Throughout the period Thatcher was in power UK community development changed. Before Thatcher was elected in 1979 a large number of state-funded community development practitioners criticised the workings of the welfare state and encouraged government, both local and national, to respond more appropriately to the poor, women and ethnic minorities (Popple, 1994). With the advent of Thatcher, community development shifted its ground and instead of criticising the delivery of welfare, practitioners and academics played a role in defending the welfare state from massive ideological attacks and financial cuts by confident ministers in a government that had secured a large backing from the electorate. As it became increasingly clear that the Thatcher government displayed outright antagonism towards the poor and the services they depended upon, so the anti-statism position of community development became less tenable (Lees and Mayo, 1984). Community development projects lost state funding at the very time evidence was emerging that there was an increasing divide between the rich and the poor, and between those living in the 'North' and 'South' of the UK. The creation of this more sharply divided society was considered to be an essential component of Thatcher's policies (Walker, 1987). It was then that community development became used by the government as a palliative with a range of short-term schemes that were primarily focused on containing the anger felt by communities over unemployment, deprivation, racism, political exclusion and police malpractices (Benyon and Solomos, 1987; Craig et al, 2011).

Jeremy Corbyn and left-wing populism

There was little evidence of left-wing populism in the UK until the election of Jeremy Corbyn as leader of the Labour Party in September 2015 and then again in 2016 after a leadership challenge. In the 2015 leadership election Corbyn gained 59% of the votes cast and in 2016 his vote was 61%. Unlike his leadership challengers who served under the former Labour Prime Minister Tony Blair, Corbyn stood on an anti-austerity ticket and in the 2015 election was considered to be an outsider because of his radical left-wing views. Identifying himself as a democratic socialist Corbyn has a long history of activism inside and outside of the Labour Party, including roles in the Anti-Apartheid Movement, the Anti-Fascist Action, the Campaign for Nuclear Disarmament, and was chair of the Stop the War Coalition from 2011 to 2015.

With Momentum, a grassroots movement supportive of Corbyn, he reached out beyond Labour MPs, his view being that the party needed to be a mass social movement reflecting the real concerns of communities everywhere and in particular those communities and groups that had lost out to neoliberal economic policies. Paradoxically using the Blairite slogan 'For the many, not the few', Corbyn argued that Blair's New Labour largely abided by the Thatcherite neoliberal agenda and that

> 'what most people want: to take on the tax cheats, create a fairer economy, fund a fully public NHS, build more homes, and stop backing illegal wars. For the establishment, those ideas are dangerous. For most people in Britain, they're common sense and grounded in reality.' (Quote by Jeremy Corbyn in Mason and Walker, 2016)

Corbyn continually challenged the view that immigration led to low wages, a lack of affordable housing and a collapse of community. Instead Corbyn and his followers pointed to the excessive power of big business over government policy making, the erosion of workers' rights, the pegging of wages at a low level, and the unabated drive by corporations to minimise costs in order to maximise returns to shareholders, all of which led to widening inequality.

> In Britain, the sixth-biggest economy in the world, over 4 million children live in poverty and hundreds of thousands of families use food banks. As a rising share of national income has gone to owners of capital, pay has lagged behind growth and real wages are now £800 (US$1,060) a year lower than a decade ago. (Corbyn, 2018: 32)

What confirmed Corbyn as a left-wing populist politician is that he argued for a fairer society which had at its centre the inclusion and not the exclusion of people. The Corbyn-led re-energised Labour Party, which during his leadership became the largest political party in the UK and possibly Europe with around 540,000 members (https:// commonslibrary.parliament.uk/parliament-and-elections/parliament/ uk-political-party-membership-figures-august-2018/) drew attention to the falling living standards of millions in the UK, growing job insecurity and shrinking public services. This position resonated with the electorate so much that at the general election in June 2017 the Labour Party, against all expectations, and although not having an overall parliamentary majority, gained enough elected seats to wipe out the Tories' majority in the House of Commons. Corbyn's leadership and the party's popular election manifesto led to a net gain of 30 seats and 40% of the vote, its highest share since 2001 and the first time the party had gained seats since the 1997 election (www.electionresults.parliament.uk).

However, one of the contentious issues that was to haunt Corbyn during his leadership were allegations of anti-Semitism in the Labour Party. In response to these concerns, Labour claimed in 2019 that the party was resolutely addressing matters and had dealt with complaints of anti-Semitism against individual members which led to some 350 resigning, being expelled or receiving formal warnings. This equated to around 0.08% of the party's membership. In the same year nine Labour MPs resigned from the party, saying in part they were doing so because of its poor handling of complaints about anti-Semitism (www.bbc.co.uk/news/uk-politics-45030552).

The widespread concern about anti-Semitism in the Labour Party, including protests from the Jewish establishment, together with a relentless right-wing press attack on Corbyn in which he was frequently misrepresented and mocked, was to damage the party's electoral prospects. It was therefore no great surprise that at the December 2019 snap general election it was the Tory party under the leadership of Boris Johnson that achieved a stunning victory with an 80-seat majority. The main thrust of the Tories' campaign was seeking a clear mandate for leaving the European Union (EU). The Labour Party's share of the vote dropped to 32.1%, with many of the previous Labour-held constituencies that had voted 'Leave' in the 2016 Referendum now voting Tory (www.statista.com/topics/5646/uk-general-election-2019). Corbyn resigned his leadership of the Labour Party and in April 2020 Keir Starmer, who identifies himself as a socialist and is considered to be on the soft left of the party, became the leader. In his acceptance speech Starmer claimed 'Antisemitism has been a stain on our party … and I will tear out the poison by its roots' (www.keirstarmer.com).

In our consideration of Corbyn as a left-wing populist we can see he garnered considerable public support and was instrumental in increasing the membership of the Labour Party in a manner no other leader had ever done. He was able to marshal protests against elements of the establishment and government policies of neoliberalism, arguing for an end to austerity, the reversal of privatisation and demanding billions more investment in public services. The irony of the situation was that when Corbyn stood down as leader in April 2020, the Tory government was in the process of ramping up state spending to unprecedented levels to deal with the impact of the COVID-19. During his time as leader Corbyn continually pointed to the Tories' undervaluing and underfunding of the public sector, including the publicly funded National Health Service. It was at this time when COVID-19 was at its peak in the UK that the public became acutely aware that NHS workers and carers were struggling without sufficient resources and equipment to cope with the thousands who contracted the disease, many of whom were to die as a result. What became clear to the British public was the need to better fund the NHS; a service which continues to be greatly valued and held in high esteem by the population.

In conclusion, although Corbyn's policies and practice were intended to include rather than exclude people, he led the party at a time when a small minority of members voiced and acted on anti-Semitic statements. Unfortunately, this issue was not satisfactorily resolved by the party while he was leader and is likely to be used to divert attention from more positively reflecting on his radical and visionary ideas.

Where and when did the new populism in the UK emerge?

There are a number of economic, social and political factors that have coalesced in the UK to provide productive ground for the populism politics we see in more recent times. Let us consider these different factors.

One of the main factors was the 2008 international financial crash which led to the Labour government taking a number of UK-based banks into public ownership costing the Exchequer £141 billion (Oxfam, 2103). As a result, two years later the Tory-led coalition government introduced 'austerity measures' which were presented to the public as necessary to reduce the state's debts due to the enormous financial bailout to the banks with the intention of maintaining and increasing business confidence and investment. At the same time, and as a part of the mantra that there was no alternative to austerity, the government significantly reduced spending on welfare and public services, asserting that the country was in a period of national emergency (Blyth, 2013). The outcome was that already poor individuals, families and communities were put under greater pressure (Varoufakis, 2017, 2018). There has however been a growing group of leading economists who argue that the real purpose of 'austerity measures' has been political rather than economic. Krugman (2012), for example, argues that the reduction in state expenditure and activity, in particular to reduce the scope of social welfare, has been intended to maintain the power of dominant classes and groups.

Another factor in the re-emergence of populism in the 21st century was, as mentioned earlier, the MPs and members of the House of Lords expenses scandal that broke in May 2009 when The Daily Telegraph began publishing in daily instalments leaked details of expenses claimed by MPs. After considerable public pressure and disquiet, all MPs' expenses and allowances were published on the official Parliament website. This was not before some MPs tried to exempt their expenses from the Freedom of Information Act (2000) which added to the public's anger about what many thought was a cover-up. MPs are allowed to claim certain expenses to assist their work both at Westminster and to cover their travel into and from their constituencies, the cost of employing certain staff and accommodation while in London. However, the published accounts showed the breath-taking nature of claims, including moat cleaning, purchasing porn films, clearing wisteria (a claim made by the future Prime Minister David Cameron), claiming rent for houses actually owned by the MP making the claim, and many other exaggerated and fraudulent claims. The outcome was a number of MPs resigning from Parliament, while others were sacked and de-selected. Public apologies and repayment of expenses were thick on the ground, and several members or former members of the House of Commons, and members of the House of Lords, served time in prison. Needless to say, the scandal left a deep mark on British politics, with the public seriously questioning the honesty and integrity of its lawmakers. It appeared to many to be a matter of one law for MPs and one for the public. To quote William Lewis, who was editor-in-chief of the Daily Telegraph at the time of the scandal, 'the scandal's contribution to the collapse in confidence in our institutions is indisputable. It's a collapse that has led to the car crash that is Brexit' (Lewis, 2019: 24). The third important factor that has provided populism with fertile ground is immigration, which as we have noted is a recurrent theme in British politics.

Migration is a significant factor in a global age where people move to other regions and countries for what are in the main economic reasons and in the 20th century this transformed Britain into a multicultural society (Murphy, 2011). During the 21st century migrants came to the UK from EU countries, which led to increased demands on the welfare, health, care and education services, where paradoxically many of these new migrants were to be employed.

The 2008 financial crisis and the 2010 imposition of austerity measures led to difficulties for individuals and communities, who in turn had a tendency to apportion blame to visible ethnic minority groups including those from the EU. However, the reality was that it was ethnic minority communities that would be the worst affected by government cutbacks and austerity measures. This did not stop right-wing newspapers help create a distorted image of immigration and asylum seekers (Koser, 2016).

Brexit and the implications for democracy

It was against these powerful influences that the British electorate took part in a national referendum to decide whether the UK should continue to be a member of the EU. The result proved to be surprising to many who considered the election would demonstrate the UK's approval of the country's continued membership. In fact, 51.9% voted for the UK to leave the EU while 48.1% voted to remain. (Note: the term Brexit comes from an amalgam of the words British and exit.)

In the period up to and since the referendum it is clear that Euro-sceptic and pro-Europeanists are drawn from across the political spectrum, or in some cases none. What we do know is that immigration, the impact of austerity and the expenses scandal were key issues in the debate around the referendum. It is not my intention here to rehearse the arguments for and against Brexit but rather to link the issues mentioned that emerged as a central concern for those voting to leave the EU with the re-emergence of the far right and the inference for democracy.

As we noted, responses to immigration have been a cornerstone of right-wing populism in the UK for almost a century. Since the 2010 British general election three right-wing populist groups which have at their core controversial and divisive views on immigration have become prominent: the English Defence League (EDL), which protests around the perceived Islamification of the UK; the UK Independence Party (UKIP) that observers comment conflates Britishness with Englishness and appeals to English nationalist sentiment (Hayton, 2016); and the Brexit Party, which was co-founded by Nigel Farage who was at one time leader of UKIP. Since their inception, all three parties have played a role in highlighting immigration and presenting a negative image of immigrants.

The message that these right-wing populist groupings and parties project is that society can be divided into two antagonistic classes – the people and the powerful. There were of course those amongst this diverse class of 'the people', such as immigrants, ethnic minorities and those cheating on welfare, that also received the ire and condemnation of the right-wing populists. During the Brexit campaign in 2016, Farage was leader of UKIP and, despite his privileged background and being a multi-millionaire metals trader in the City of London, used his position to attack the powerful or what he calls the 'metropolitan liberal elite'. Further, in August 2016, during Donald Trump's campaign for election as President of the USA, Farage spoke at a Trump rally in Mississippi, hailing the vote for Brexit as a victory for 'the little people, the real people ... the ordinary decent people'. As Freedland states: 'The implication was that those who had voted remain were unreal and indecent, that they were the big people, the representatives of the mighty and powerful' (Freedland, 2016).

What is to be done: a role of community development?

We have noted that UK right-wing populist groupings and parties have grown in influence and prominence in the last few years. However, their rhetoric and approach has little to do with the notions of liberal democracy. Instead their role has been to peddle conspiracy theories about 'elites', 'rigged institutions' and the 'metropolitan liberal elite' which they claim have 'duped' people. In reality these populist groupings and parties have taken advantage of liberal democratic institutions which over the years have provided the UK with a relatively stable political system.

Evidence indicates that populism is a symptom, not a cause of the problems that the UK has been dealing with in recent years. The question therefore has to be asked as to what can be done to address the problems it has created for communities. Clearly there is much to do on a broad scale at a national level to address these major issues (see for example the work of 'HOPE not hate', the UK's leading anti-fascist network: www.hopenothate.org.uk). Similarly there is an argument to regionalise migration policy to assist in the detoxification of an issue that has such a negative impact on British life (Hatwal, 2018). There is a need to direct massive resources into areas and regions where local institutions such as local pubs, post offices, shops and travel networks that keep communities together have been severely reduced or have disappeared. For too long the needs of communities and particularly working class communities have been ignored and their residents disrespected, as shown for example in the parliamentary expenses scandal. It has been these communities' disconnect from parliament, political parties and the media that has led to the popularity of right-wing populism, which provides simple xenophobic and scapegoating responses to complex issues.

Gilbert (2020) has argued that the austerity which emerged after the 2008 financial crash led to many in the UK working for much lower rates of pay than they would have done. This meant that the high levels of consumption seen in 1980s, 1990s and the 2000–10 decade were no longer possible for these workers. At the same time there was a reduction in public services, rising inequality, 'and the weakening of democracy itself' (Gilbert, 2020: 86). For some the outcome was to turn to authoritarian right-wing programmes that rejected the cosmopolitan political elite and instead look for a sense of national pride, albeit illusionary, which would restore their previous life-chances.

In response, left-wing populism through the Labour Party has recognised the difficulties and concerns of people living in communities left behind and has offered a radical programme which includes fair taxation, new forms of public ownership, keeping communities safe with more facilities such as youth clubs and police officers based at neighbourhood level, and improved funding for schools (Labour Party, 2017). The question now is whether the new leader of the Labour Party, Keir Starmer, will maintain these radical ideas, and whether he is able to achieve electoral success with them.

Community development also has a role to play. It is recognised that community development is approached and funded differently in the four nations that make up the UK: England, Northern Ireland, Scotland and Wales, and as there is no statutory basis for the activity, some areas, regions and countries are financially better provided for than others.

As a value-driven activity, community development stands in opposition to the shouting and posturing associated with the right-wing populism that now permeates aspects of British public life. Unlike right-wing populism, and as I have written elsewhere (Popple, 2015: 114–15), community development has core values of

- equality and anti-discrimination
- social justice
- collective action
- community empowerment
- working and learning together

In all the material I have read relating to right-wing populism in the UK I have not come across these terms. Instead I have found a language that is loud, emotional, often sentimental and rooted in hatred and indifference. It is primarily about the fear of the foreigner, and opposition to different ethnicities, cultures and religions. These groups and parties advocate reducing public services and allowing the market free-reign, so that the rich get wealthier while the poor have to look after themselves. These right-wing populist parties and groupings trade on people's loss of trust in politics, particularly in communities where decades of decline have seen young people leave for lack of reasonable, well-paid employment, where public services are stretched to the limit or removed, and where there is a sense of no hope for a better future.

Due to the impact of austerity, which has seen financial cuts in local authority spending together with the accumulation of years of neoliberal economic policies of deregulation, privatisation, tax cuts for the wealthy and rising and grotesque levels of inequality, community development in the UK has suffered considerable reductions in its funding at the very time when it is needed the most. With the growth of right-wing populism this is particularly important, as community development has as its remit to support communities in tackling local issues, fostering social capital and helping people to develop the skills to work on matters that are important to them.

At the time of writing it is difficult not to feel pessimistic about a future for the version of community development we normally see in the UK. There is evidence that community development funding in the UK is patchy and in many areas is non-existent, which means it cannot effectively address the significant issues that have led to the rise of right-wing populism in communities around the country. If we are serious about the type and scope of community development that we have discussed earlier then substantial increases in funding are required. Enough so that community development can be securely embedded in a range of progressive public services such as education, health, community enterprise and other services that are aimed at improving the life chances of those living in communities that for too long have been neglected and often despised. Further, there is a strong case to significantly increase at all levels the education and training of community development workers and support the advance of a diverse and talented workforce. Whether any of this is likely or possible after the financial impact of the COVID-19 pandemic on the British state finances is of course a different matter.

Importantly there is a need to reconceptualise community development to embrace those often loosely affiliated direct action groups that arise to counter the impact of neoliberal policies and practices. For example, the Occupy Movement, the Hong Kong Umbrella Movement and Extinction Rebellion have evolved as loosely networked, decentralised, grassroots movements which have provided a critical, non-violent action-based response to the excesses of capitalism which has led to massive inequality, increased levels of poverty and the real risk of ecological collapse.

Finally, there is still much to do to raise awareness of the value and effectiveness of community development. Before the impact of the COVID-19 pandemic we witnessed in the UK the reinforcement of neoliberal values and assumptions where individual and corporate greed and wealth was considered good, poorer individuals and communities were disempowered, and minority groups were stigmatised. In the world we have now we need to continue to struggle for a more democratic, equal, prosperous and consensual UK, especially as we have seen how right-wing populist sentiments and activity can evolve and take root.

References

Alcock, P. with May, M. (2014) *Social Policy in Britain* (4th edn), London: Red Globe Press.

Bank, S. and Carpenter, M. (2017) 'Researching the local politics and practices of radical Community Development Projects in 1970s Britain', *Community Development Journal*, 52(2): 226–46.

Barker, M. (1981) *The New Racism: Conservatives and the Ideology of the Tribe*, London: Junction Books.

Benyon, J. and Solomos, J. (1987) *The Roots of Urban Unrest*, Oxford: Pergamon Press.

Blackwell, T. and Seabrook, J. (1985) *A World Still to Win: The Reconstruction of the Post-War Working Class*, London: Faber and Faber.

Blyth, M. (2013) *Austerity: History of a Dangerous Idea*, Oxford: Oxford University Press.

CDP (1977) *Gilding the Ghetto: The State and the Poverty Experiments*, London: Community Development Project and Inter-project Editorial Team.

Corbyn, J. (2018) 'The other path ahead', *The World in 2019*, London: The Economist.

Craig, G., Mayo, M, Popple, K. Shaw, M. and Taylor, M.(eds) (2011) *Community Development in the United Kingdom 1950–2010*, Bristol: Policy Press

Dumbrell, J. (2001) *A Special Relationship: Anglo-American Relations in the Cold War and After*, London: Macmillan.

Edwards, J. and Batley, R. (1978) *The Politics of Positive Discrimination*, London: Tavistock.

Freedland, J. (2016) 'Don't be fooled by these dishonest attacks on the "metropolitan liberal elite"', *The Guardian*, 23 December, [online] www.theguardian.com/commentisfree/2016/dec/23/dishonest-attacks-metropolitan-liberal-elite

Gilbert, J. (2020) *Twenty-First Century Socialism*, Cambridge: Polity Press

Gilchrist, A. and Taylor, M. (2016) *The Short Guide to Community Development*, Bristol: Policy Press.

Hall, S. (1980) 'Popular-democratic versus authoritarian populism', in A. Hunt (ed), *Marxism and Democracy*, London: Lawrence and Wishart, pp 61–73.

Hall, S., Critcher, C., Jefferson, T., Clarke, J. and Roberts, B. (1978) *Policing the Crisis: Mugging, the State and Law and Order*, London: Macmillan.

Harrop, M., England, J. and Husbands, C.T. (1980) 'The bases of National Front support', *Political Studies*, 28(2): 271–83.

Hatwal, A. (2018) 'Devolve immigration policy to the nations and regions to answer the demands of Brexit', in N. Lawson (ed), *The Causes and Cures of Brexit*, London: Compass, pp 103–5.

Hayton, R. (2016). 'The UK Independence Party and the politics of Englishness', *Political Studies Review*, 14(3): 400–410.

Jones, O. (2016) *Chavs: The Demonization of the Working Class*, London: Verso.

Koser, K. (2016) *International Migration: A Very Short Introduction* (2nd edn), Oxford: Oxford University Press.

Krugman, P. (2012) *End this Depression Now!*, New York: W.W. Norton.

Labour Party (2017) *For the Many: Not the Few. The Labour Party Manifesto*, London: The Labour Party.

Lee, R. and Mayo, M. (1984) *Community Action for Change*, London: Routledge and Kegan Paul.

Lewis, W. (2019) 'A very British scandal', *New Statesman*, 3–9 May.

Loney, M. (1983) *Community against Government: The British Community Development Project 1968–78*, London: Heinemann Educational Books.

Mc Smith, A. (2013) 'Margaret Thatcher obituary: The most divisive political leader of modern times', *Independent*, 8 April, [online] www.independent.co.uk/news/obituaries/margaret-thatcher-obituary-the-most-divisive-political-leader-of-modern-times-8564559.html

Marquand, D (2017) 'The people is sublime: the long history of populism, from Robespierre to Trump', *New Statesman*, 24 July, [online] www.newstatesman.com/politics/uk/2017/07/people-sublime-long-history-populism-robespierre-trump

Mason, R. and Walker, P.J. (2016) 'Corbyn hits back after Obama suggests Labour is "disintegrating"', *The Guardian*, 26 December.

Milne, S. (2014) *The Enemy Within: The Secret War against the Miners* (4th edn), London: Verso.

Moffitt, B. (2016) *The Global Rise of Populism: Performance, Political Style and Representation*, Stanford, CA: Stanford University Press.

Morgan, K. (2001) *Britain Since 1945: The People's Peace*, Oxford: Oxford University Press.

Mouffe, C. (2018) *For a Left Populism*, London: Verso.

Mudde, C. and Kaltwasser, C.R. (2017) *Populism: A Very Short Introduction*, New York: Oxford University Press.

Murphy, M. (2011) *Multiculturalism: A Critical Introduction*, New York: Routledge.

Oxfam (2013) *Truth and Lies about Poverty: Ending Comfortable Myths about Poverty*, Cardiff: Oxfam Cymru.

Popple, K. (1994) 'Towards a progressive community work praxis', in S. Jacobs and K. Popple (eds), *Community Work in the 1990s*, Nottingham: Spokesman Books, pp 24–36.

Popple, K. (1997) 'Understanding and tackling racism among young people in the United Kingdom', in J.L. Hazekamp and K. Popple (eds), *Racism in Europe: A Challenge for Youth Policy and Youth Work*, London: UCL Press, pp 13–38.

Popple, K. (2013) 'Reconsidering the 1950s and 1960s: the emergence and establishment of community development in the UK', in R. Gilchrist, T. Jeffs, J.Spence, N. Stanton, A. Cowell, J. Walker and T. Wylie (eds), *Reappraisals: Essays in the History of Youth and Community Work*, Lyme Regis: Russell House, pp 126–41.

Popple, K. (2015) *Analysing Community Work: Theory and Practice* (2nd edn), Maidenhead: Open University Press.

Powell, E. (1968) 'Text of speech delivered in Birmingham, 20 April 1968', *Race*, 10(1): 80–104.

Reitan, E.A. (2003) *The Thatcher Revolution: Margaret Thatcher, John Major, Tony Blair, and the Transformation of Modern Britain, 1979–2001*, Lanham, MD: Rowan and Littlefield.

Rosenberg, D. (2011) *Battle for the East End: Jewish Responses to Fascism in the 1930s*, London: Five Leaves Publication.

Shepherd, R. (1998) *Enoch Powell: A Biography*, London: Pimlico.

Varoufakis, Y. (2017) *And the Weak Suffer What They Must? Europe, Austerity and the Threat to Global Stability*, London: Vintage.

Varoufakis, Y. (2018) *Adults in the Room: My Battle with Europe's Deep Establishment*, London: Vintage.

Walker, A. (1987) 'Introduction: a policy for two nations', in A. Walker and C. Walker (eds), *The Growing Divide: A Social Audit 1979–1987*, London: Child Poverty Action Group, pp 1–6.

ELEVEN

Community engagement policies in the era of populism: Finland

Suvi Aho, Juha Hämäläinen and Arto Salonen

Introduction

Finland, although performing excellently in international comparisons of social cohesion, has seen the steepest decrease in the level of trust in the government among all the OECD countries during the past decade (OECD Country Fact Sheet Finland, 2017). At the same time, right-wing populist rhetoric has strengthened and the populist movement has established its support in the political spectrum. For example, the True Finns party was established in 1995 as a conservative, Christian-socialistic, EU-critical movement placed in the political centre, but electoral victory in 2011 diversified its representatives in Parliament and gave visibility and voice to immigration-critical discourse, which turned the party towards nationalist right-wing populism. To transform Finnish democracy, participatory programmes have been created in order to reach out and engage different groups to join community development practices. These efforts stem both from the public authorities and the renewed Finnish Local Government Act of 2017, as well as from projects undertaken by civil society organisations (CSOs). Further, there is a long tradition of building civil society in Finland, which has often been based on the unique Finnish liberal adult education system. Yet growing inequality is currently deepening the polarisation in political participation. This chapter explores the ways of countering the polarisation and populism by supporting the political capabilities of communities and nurturing deliberative discussion.

The concept of populism in the Finnish context

The concept of populism is slippery. In general, it is a kind of political orientation or practice of policy making confronting the existing political order in the name of the 'people'. Populism is characterised by exclusivist political principles and the denigration of political competitors, yet this strategy has always belonged to politics. Confrontation with other parties and unwillingness to compromise are the distinctive marks of populist parties, including the True Finns. The most important common denominator in discussions of the definition of populism seems to be the populists' resistance to pluralism and their selectivity; that is, only a certain part of the nation represents the true people (Wiberg, 2011: 12; Müller, 2016: 37). Secondly, and this theme is especially prominent in French political science, is the focus on communication and populism, where rather than an 'ism' or an ideology, populism is perceived as rhetoric and a style (Parkkinen, 2017: 277).

In the current Nordic or Finnish forms of populism, xenophobia (and criticism of the EU) can be seen as the common denominator. Nordic populism has been characterised as diluted populism, because supporters differ clearly from far-right or authoritarian government. They value democracy, but are less satisfied with its operability and more suspicious towards minorities and immigrants (Herkman, 2018: 61). Recent research on Finnish populism has dealt mainly with the rise of the right-wing True Finns party, focusing on issues of rhetoric in particular (for example, Palonen and Saresma, 2017). Other aspects and shapes of populism have been considered, but so far there is no comprehensive analysis of populism in Finland. However, a large number of individual studies exist with different kinds of specific perspectives. A recent study, for example, investigates how the term populism has been used in the newspaper *Helsingin Sanomat*[1] in the 2000s, contextualising the interpretations to the current research on populism (Vaarakallio and Palonen, 2017). The election year 2011, which led the True Finns to election success, marks a turning point in Finnish populism, as a phenomenon, as well as in public debate. As often encountered in populism research, in *Helsingin Sanomat*, populist rhetoric is described as cheap; fishing for votes; full of futile promises; a political circus; political simplification; one-sided; and with actual politics as optional.

An article collection edited by Palonen and Saresma (2017: 16) explores populism in the Finnish context and observes the era of Timo Soini (party leader of True Finns from 1997 to 2017) focusing on rhetoric and performative phenomena. Laura Parkkinen (2017) has tracked the general features of populism in Timo Soini's blog and writings. She comments that the language of populism is non-negotiable and rather black and white. Further, though not especially religious, Finnish populism has drawn from religious rhetoric; for Soini, the people possess moral righteousness, and the final battle between good and evil shall break out if changes are not made. Also Veikko Vennamo, the founder and leader of the SMP (*Suomen maaseudun puolue*, Finnish Rural Party) from 1959 to 1979, relied occasionally on the rhetoric of the Old Testament, identifying the true people as suffering; virtuous; chosen people; waiting to be rescued (Parkkinen, 2017: 275–91).

In general, Finnish scholars introduce populism as a research topic manifesting as a multifaceted phenomenon and a field of study applying several approaches (for example, Kovala et al, 2018). This understanding is common in the international community of scholars too. However, as with Finnish scholars, there is no unambiguous concept of populism. This chapter approaches populism as a course of action rather than a theory concerned with ways of being engaged in politics. It is more a set of various political movements than a single political school of thought (Fitzi et al, 2018). Rather than providing a tight definition of populism the approach taken in this chapter is to inspect the nature of populism through scholarly reasoning (Anselmi, 2017; de la Torre, 2018).

Deliberative ideals and trust

While the perceived legitimacy of the political system is a prerequisite to tackling the harmful features of populism, an essential feature of populism is to sustain people's distrust in the political establishment. Populist leaders present themselves as the real voice of the people against established political authority (Hawkins et al, 2018). The only way to resist delusive populism is to debunk populist propositions by making people themselves aware of the real quality of populist pretension through rational argumentation. The cultural foundation for deliberative democracy is citizens who are adept in rational and critical debate on common affairs. It is about a deliberative culture in which people are competent to participate in public debate (Sharon, 2018).

An equally crucial element is citizens' belief in their capabilities 'to influence'. In so far as populism is seen as an attempt to deceive people in order to speak for the political power of populists, it is important to strengthen people's political capability for identifying and resisting this deception. At best, deliberative political communication provides society with appropriate intellectual qualities for increasing people's capacity for civic participation and community development. Real opportunities for participation are needed, and the Finnish effort to oppose populism through civic community exemplifies a way of providing such opportunities.

Populism is characterised by demagogic practices provoking and taking advantage of people's prejudices and dissatisfactions, instead of using rational argumentation. It aims to get endorsement of its own political agenda through a misinforming line of reasoning. However, there are reasons to acknowledge the argument that there is a rational element to populist politics too, in so far as it is a response to people's genuine discontent and alienation from mainstream politics. As the uncertainty and anxiety of the losers of globalisation has been offered as one of the main reasons for the rise of populism (see also Ikäheimo, 2017), it is very dangerous to truncate the independent agency of the populist supporters (for example, Müller 2016). The elderly, less well-educated and working people form the core of populist voters (de Vries and Hoffmann, 2016). Although not based on rational, intellectual and knowledge-based debate as political activity in regard to the solutions to the discontent, populist beliefs provide a channel to express lack of contentment with circumstances and politics.

As noted previously, a significant counterforce against the irrational features of populism is the idea of deliberative democracy, in which the importance of extensive civic debate in public life is emphasised (Bächtiger et al, 2018). A central point of this approach to strengthening people's participation is political debate. The conception of deliberative democracy based on rational argument in public debate, particularly with respect to democratic policy making, has been developed historically in many western countries, including in Finland. In Finland, citizens have statutory rights to be heard and they are encouraged to participate in public debate on common topics at local and national levels. As Jürgen Habermas (1981) states, reciprocal trust is an indispensable attribute of communicative action and decision making. This element develops only in an open atmosphere in which all those who participate in debate aim to promote the common good through rational discourse. Rational communication is realised only if partners believe the associates are honest and aspire to the truth. This kind of participation in public debate must and can be learned, usually in communities. In this sense, countering populism is not only a political issue but essentially a pedagogic issue too. Habermas emphasised that social integration and political participation are connected with the quality of communication in the public sphere (Calhoun, 1992: 5–6). In so far as irrationalism is a fundamental component of populism, the system of public debate based on rational argumentation has the capacity to undermine the populist erosion of democratic political communication.

The Nordic countries have succeeded rather well in combining individual freedom with social security. In theory, the idea of deliberative democracy is connected to the qualities of social justice. In this respect, the Nordic political order resembles, theoretically, John Rawls' (2005) conception of a socially just society bringing the practice of deliberative democracy and the principle of social security together. Wide public responsibility for people's welfare is emphasised, based on comprehensive social rights and the principle of citizens' equality. In general, Finnish society has committed to the principles of a deliberative democracy by providing citizens with wide civil and political rights. Advocacy groups are systematically heard in law drafting; local authorities are legally obliged to promote citizens' participation in policy-making processes at the local level; and civic activities are substantially supported by governmental bodies in terms of civic community engagement policies. Correspondingly, local governments are responsible for organising adequate welfare services according to people's needs. In this way, the civic engagement in community policies links to local social policies.

In Finland, participatory governance has been seen as complementary to representative democracy. It has been introduced as a new kind of civil activity in the field of political participation (Kestilä-Kekkonen and Korvela, 2017) and a new type of governance policies. The main focus has been on citizens' involvement in local policy making (Backlund et al, 2017), suburban and neighbourhood development included (Luhtakallio and Mustaranta, 2017). Much attention is paid to people's opportunities to participate in debate and influence political decision making in different fields of governance, particularly in welfare issues in the local context (Järvinen et al, 2011).

In international comparisons, Finland has been rated as the most stable (Fragile State Index, 2018); safest (Global Law & Order, 2018); happiest (Helliwell et al, 2018 and 2019); and the best-governed (Legatum Prosperity Index, 2018) country in the world. Moreover, Finland belongs to the top five in education (Better Life Index, 2018); gender equality (Gender Equality Index, 2017), lowest income disparity (Alvaredo et al, 2018) and low poverty rate (Poverty Rate, 2018). Objectively, there is little space for discontent. However, there are some instances of dissatisfaction and loopholes in the system of governance which populist politicians utilise in efforts to undermine confidence in Finnish society. Take, for example, the issue of trust. The index of trust concerns the trust of people in the political system, authorities and each other and in Finland high levels of trust in general prevail, relative to other OECD countries (Trust in People, 2018) Paradoxically, the high levels of trust in Finnish society embed a tolerance of the populist aspiration to undermine people's confidence in institutions. This tolerance is an element of open democratic society. An effective counterforce against populism is the deliberative democratic culture that recognises a political opposition's right of voice. This commitment to a political opposition's right of voice provides an opening for populists. Finland has been rather successful in resisting the opportunism of populists, by improving people's social consciousness and encouraging them to engage in public debate and active citizenship through deliberative democracy. Yet as Niemi and colleagues (2018: 306) point out, in spite of a rather stable environment, populism has quite long (though marginal) roots in Nordic countries: in Nordic consensus democracies, it is quite easy to build a confrontation with the ruling elite and public broadcasting companies (Paloheimo, 2012: 327). In a democracy, the diffuse trust of the people is crucial for the legitimacy of the system (see Easton, 1965), but simultaneously, a blind trust of elites is usually not a sign of a healthy democracy (Kestilä-Kekkonen and Korvela, 2017). As Bäck and Kestilä (2009) state: the aggregate-level trends in social capital remain high, but political trust has varied to a much larger degree. In Finland, social trust was high in 1986 and even higher in 1991, but simultaneously political trust declined steeply from 65% to 34%. The evaluations of the trends behind the decline in political trust have been mixed, but in Finland the alleged general pattern of decreasing confidence is visible (Bäck and Kestilä, 2009: 174). Nowadays, though the confidence of people in national government (49%) in Finland still remains above the OECD average (42%), the decrease in confidence of people in national parliament (−27%) has been the steepest in the OECD countries during the last decade (2007–17) (OECD Country Fact Sheet Finland, 2017) . Between 2007 and 2017 the economy reversed, and campaign finance scandals took place, as well as deepening ideological differences between parties. As Newton (2001) states, the relationship with social and political trust is not self-evident. Political trust can mean a variety of things – confidence in political institutions, levels of civic-mindedness, levels of participation, to name but a few.

In Finland, there is no clear aggregate- or individual-level relationship between social capital and political trust. Rather, political trust in Finland is related to political capacity; meaning the *capacity* to understand and analyse the different levels of a political system (Bäck and Kestilä, 2008: 189–90). Several global trends, such as the rise of meritocracy and technocracy, liberalisation of the international economy, increasing individualism and income differences, and the shift of power to the EU level, challenge our political capacity to understand and influence the political system and engage with this system today. The 'local' people (see for example Goodhart, 2017), who may not have gained from globalisation but rather have lost some of their resources, can experience anxieties and feelings of powerlessness, to which populism provides an attractive answer. There are signs worldwide, as in Finland, that liberal democracy is failing to maintain credibility among ordinary citizens (Furedi, 2017).

Short history of populism in Finland

The history of populism in Finland is personified in the activities of Veikko Vennamo, who founded the Finnish Agrarian party (SMP – *Suomen maaseudun puolue*) in 1959. This party claimed to stand for the 'forgotten people' of the countryside, in opposition to the urban elite. Its popularity reached a peak in the 1970, 1972 and 1983 elections, where it gained approximately 10% of the seats in Parliament (Bergmann, 2017: 82). Radical right-wing parties, such as the IKL (*Isänmaallinen kansanliitto*, Patriotic People's Movement) in the 1930s and 1940s only gained modest success in Finland. Rauli Mickelsson (2015) has mapped the ideologies of Finnish populist parties before the 2011 elections, where the True Finns gained their first election victory. The party was established on the ruins of the SMP in 1995, continuing the anti-elitist, conservative values legacy. Party leader Timo Soini, having written his master's thesis on populism, openly accepted the populist label, stating that he wanted to please 'the ordinary man' (Raunio, 2011; Bergman, 2017).

As Jeffrey Kaplan (1999. 8–9) states, the 1990s in Finland would have provided a textbook case and fruitful environment for populists: facing a serious downturn in the economy; immigrants arriving from East Africa to a previously homogenous society; and membership in the European Union partly resulting in economic difficulties for the agricultural economy. Still, no parliamentary or extra-parliamentary success of the populist movement took place at that time. It was not until the beginning of the 2000s that the nationalist youth started to get organised in Finland. An internet forum called *Hommafoorumi* (https://hommaforum.org/) was formed around Suomen Sisu (European Economic and Social Committee, 2019) with a blog Scripta – kirjoituksia uppoavasta lännestä (Scripta – writings from the sinking west) (www.halla-aho.com/scripta/) written by Jussi Halla-Aho, and soon the majority of the *Hommafoorumi* (Case Forum) community joined the True Finns. The nationalist and anti-immigration movement began to have influence on the True Finns, resulting in a landslide victory for show wrestler Tony Halme in 2003 parliamentary elections (Mickelsson, 2015: 148). Studies showed that Halme – someone with 'street cred', using colourful racist language – was able to appeal to many voters, for example in the suburbs of eastern Helsinki, who had not voted for a long time or perhaps never. For the first time, the True Finns joined the government of Juha Sipila after the 2015 parliamentary elections. One concrete consequence of this for NGOs was that the government significantly cut development aid funding and many organisations working with immigration and multiculturalism needed to decrease their work and personnel in Finland.

When Timo Soini announced in 2017 that he would not continue as party leader, the anti-immigration hardliner Jussi Halla-Aho became the new party leader. Soini was involved in establishing the party called *Sininen tulevaisuus* (The Blue Reform). According to Palonen and Saresma (2017: 19–20) the True Finns lost the legacy of Timo Soini in one weekend. During the summer of 2017, after a few theatrical political tricks, The Blue Reform continued in government, and the True Finns shifted to the opposition. In the 2019 parliamentary elections, the True Finns re-established their position, achieving 17.5% support, and secured the position as the second biggest party in Finland. This corresponds to the pan-European trend, in which the average populist (mainly right-wing) vote in the EU stands at 24% (Pihlaja and Sandberg, 2012).

Who supports populism in Finland?

Timo Toivonen (2011) has investigated the structural and political factors behind electoral support for the True Finns in 2007–11. An important finding was the rise in turnout, and even more the rise in the turnout among men supporting the True Finns (Toivonen, 2011: 86–8). For structural factors, the unemployment rate correlated strongly with the change in the electoral support for the True Finns. Statistically significant correlations could also be found with the proportion of people employed as construction and industrial workers, amount of earned income, and the proportion of people with an intermediate-level education. In other words, support for the True Finns grew most in towns where unemployment impacted the industrial (male) workers with relatively good income and low education level (Toivonen, 2011: 90).

A charismatic leader needs to show that they relate to the common people, but also be something else (Parkkinen, 2017: 275). Soini described himself as *maisterisjätkä* (a bloke with a masters degree). In Finnish this means an easily approachable bloke, thus positioning himself in a positive way and as a reliable, harness racing fan, fair, funny and non-hierarchical, yet also an educated man. Semi-religious rhetoric has been effective among voters, who long for the 'good old days' and stability. The figure and speech of Soini challenged the parlance and figure of other stylish, fit and business-like party leaders (Kovala and Pöysä, 2017: 261–3). The present party leader, Jussi Halla-Aho, on the other hand, is a quietly spoken academic with a PhD and a conviction from the highest court for inciting ethnic hatred and blasphemy. The Finnish academic populist leaders, with different personalities and strategies, have proven successful in gaining support from less well-educated (male) voters. Kovala and Pöysä also find that the political emphases, such as on patriotism and power (highlighting the contribution of the defence forces), as well as religious and social conservatism (Soini is Catholic and the True Finns are very hetero-normative) and cultural hostility have especially attracted male voters (Kovala and Pöysä, 2017: 269). In a Gallup poll conducted in 2011, party supporters were asked about their position on racism: 27% of the True Finns supporters identified much or quite a bit with racist features, and a further 36% partly or fully agreed with the statement 'one must acknowledge that certain nations are more intelligent than others' (Koivulaakso et al, 2012: 256).

Critical citizenship through education

Critical citizenship is a fundamental prerequisite for genuine democracy and a constitutive counterforce to political dishonesty, populism included (Puolimatka, 1996). Actually, the provision of adequate intellectual capital through education is needed for the development of critical citizenship, at both individual and collective levels. Since the second half of the 19th century, the Finnish system of adult liberal education has executed welfare-related functions (Niemelä, 2011). The aim has been to provide people with opportunities for meaningful leisure activities, self-development, participation and belonging. Both workers' institutes for working people and folk high schools for young adults aimed to fulfil the mission of enlightenment, including enlightened citizenship.

International comparisons in the field of civic and citizenship education show that a highly developed welfare system does not necessarily work for young people's participation. While Finnish students are on top with respect to academic achievements, they do not participate in civic activities as keenly as young people in most other countries (Schulz et al, 2018: 206). However, Finnish students might have a good cognitive capacity against populism, and the low level of participation may mostly be explained by the attributes of the developed welfare system. For example, in the national report of Finland on the IEA International Civic and Citizenship Education Study 2016 it is speculated that the reason for the relatively low level of social engagement among young people in Finland and in other Nordic countries, in spite of their outstanding intellectual and attitudinal readiness, might be, at least to some extent, that social and political conditions are stable, social security nets are functional and there is no need to struggle for basic rights (Mehtäläinen et al, 2017: 91). However, it is not self-evident that the well-developed welfare system explains the low level of civil participation. Further, Finland is also a promised land for a vast number of civil society organisations (CSOs), and at the European average in voluntary work activity. Organisational culture has favoured compliance with the rules. Apart from political parties and strong trade unions, the core areas of CSOs are other than political (for example, sports and the social sector) (Seppo, 2013).

The Finnish system of education has been developed as an integrated whole covering the human lifespan, consisting of the sub-systems of early education, schools, higher education institutes and adult education. This education system is based on the concepts of life-long learning, equity, trust and responsibility. Most education is publicly funded, education is free at all levels and every student has the right to educational support (Ministry of Education, 2018). The humanistic heritage of the national awakening and civilisation movement at the turn of the 20th century has shaped the later development of liberal education in Finland (Anttonen, 2007). The intended aspiration to enlightenment, aiming to nurture active and critical citizenship, is still the key element of liberal adult education and youth work in theory, policy and practice (for example, Niemi, 2007). This has enhanced the critical social consciousness of people – in terms of intellectual, individual and collective capacity – against political fakery and populism.

New deliberative community engagement policies and practices

As indicated previously, in spite of the vast welfare and educational system, the constitutional rights to participate are only partially actualised. The deliberative methods have not yet been able to erase the inequality in political participation in Finland either. Factors such as level of education, income level and profession have a major impact on the perceived capacity to influence political decision making. As mentioned, political trust has decreased and, additionally, around 40% of Finns doubt the capability of democracy to solve problems. Political participation is especially differentiated among young people: for example, in the 2015 parliamentary elections the polling percentage of young adults (from 25 to 34 years) with a degree was 79%, and with a basic education it was 31% (Valtioneuvoston kanslia, 2018). Growing inequality has direct consequences for political participation, and is further leading to general deficit of empathy and solidarity (Wass, 2016).

Community engagement is a key theme in community development. It involves shifting away from a top-down political approach and it ties universal values to the local context. Engagement refers to socially responsive processes and practices with shared outcomes, aligned with individual, community, civic and institutional benefits. While the key level of participation is the local, enabling structures must be found in municipalities and, even further, in the wider neighbourhoods. Not everyone in the community needs to be involved in the process, but efforts must be as inclusive as possible so that everyone in the community has a chance to engage. Thus, community engagement is about encouraging the community to find and to act towards shared goals (Head, 2007; Johnston, 2018).

Established populism in Finland has brought to the surface issues concerning the failures of and exclusions in community engagement and our participatory civic processes. In order to strengthen the functionality of the representative democracy, modernise the means of direct democracy and tackle the decreasing political trust, there has been an overall shift towards community building and citizen engagement in Finland during the past few years. The new Finnish Local Government Act, which came into force in Finland in June 2017, is more concrete and explicit than the previous law concerning citizen participation. The need for reform arose from the increased individualism, the appearance of new channels for interaction (especially social media), and the unequal participation of different population groups.[2] The new Act encourages multiple methods for community engagement. Several cities have since developed participatory programmes for citizen engagement, brand-new posts have been created to execute the programmes, and at present professional jobs in citizen engagement are becoming more common (for example, Rosenblum, 2008).

In practice, community development has resulted in officials gravitating to interaction with residents and CSOs in a more profound manner. The challenge for the officials is to have the capability and resources to commit to real participatory actions at the early stages of preparation of public decisions. Also, various electronic, map-based and mobile applications and channels have been created to enhance social interaction in the cities. The participatory models reflect the new ethos and perhaps pedagogical experiments regarding how citizens want to be engaged in making the cities accessible and meaningful. As part of the participatory programmes, most of the larger cities in Finland have established working groups in neighbourhoods and districts, where the local officials, associations and grassroots organisations, inhabitants and decision makers come together to create a joint understanding on topical local issues. At best, this might enable greater local influence and concerns being heard in a timely manner. Working groups might also anticipate future needs in service development and public investments in the neighbourhoods. Further, participatory budgeting has become popular in many cities, and people get to decide, for example, what kind of investments will be made in their neighbourhoods or how the money is to be allocated to resident associations.

As participation is becoming more individualised, there is pressure for CSOs to offer more project-oriented and attractive, low-threshold ways for collective engagement (Seppo, 2013). Citizens of the information age can organise themselves and act towards a common purpose in an easier and more diverse way than ever before. This new form of active citizenship is called urban civic activism (Faehnle et al, 2017). Urban civic activism is empowered, for example, by the local participation and interaction model in Helsinki Metropolitan Area, based on local city coaches, business coaches, local forums, participatory budgeting and shared spaces (City of Helsinki, 2018). In other words, urban civic activism is characterised by local-to-local interactions and the sharing of local services that bypass market and state transactions. The positive power of urban civic activism lies in its possibilities for satisfying basic human needs: people can use their own special expertise for common goals, and by doing so they experience inclusion and social participation (Ryan and Deci, 2000; Deci et al, 2013). This is likely to increase the meaningfulness of life. Activities may include, for example, providing the resources needed to solve a local problem through crowdfunding. Urban civic activism can also help organise new services or transfer existing services to the area. Often these services apply different forms of a sharing economy, comprising what might be identified as a fourth sector. In Finland, typical examples of these types of citizen-related activities are food circuits, shared working spaces, local recycling groups and rental services. In the future, blockchain technologies can significantly accelerate urban civic activism, as blockchains make it possible to create an interactive community with trust and without a third party.

Simultaneously, we need to keep in mind that deliberative democracy may appear as a demanding model, requiring that citizens be competent in rational debate on common affairs. Luckily there are many good examples in this field; for example, the Finnish youth cooperative Allianssi, together with the National Workshop Association, have organised training and interventions related to democracy skills, with people working in the fields of workshop activities, unemployment and outreach youth work.

Luhtakallio and Mustaranta (2017: 123–6), who conducted recent action research in a Helsinki suburb, found that the participatory projects conducted by governing bodies do not support participation as a critical and change-enabling action in relation to power structures. They also conclude that participation (which is the requirement for active citizenship) should not be an end in itself, but rather a tool to change things. As Kearns (1992: 32–3) also states:

> the consideration of accountability and awareness of responsibilities should never supersede the main goal of empowering and encouraging people to act by learning new social, political and managerial skills. This implies that in addition to service orientation, active citizenship requires clear demonstration of actual social and individual benefits.

Thus, community engagement projects need to have an impact that can be verified by those participating, otherwise the projects will end up diminishing the trust of the people towards democracy. Further, participatory methods require self-criticality from officials, in order to maintain responsibility, representativeness and legitimacy of the actions (Kestilä-Kekkonen and Korvela, 2017: 27).

Conclusion

Although both reach out to people, the fundamental difference in community engagement practices and populism is how they strive for genuine interaction. Community engagement practitioners aim to support the capacities of all people and encourage inclusiveness, whereas populism in Finland is exclusive by nature. The aims of populists are based on the idea that the nation is a homogenous entity with one true representative (Hirschmann, 1970). Rather than facilitating genuine public will-formation through discussion and deliberative processes, for populists the 'true nation' is a rather symbolic creature (Müller, 2016: 116). Community development officials, together with CSOs and the fourth sector, pursue plurality, discussion and joint prioritisation of actions.

The True Finns have offered a patriotic option in contrast to cosmopolitan internationality and multiculturalism that other parties in Finland promote (with various emphases). They have succeeded in channelling the dissatisfaction (of people who emphasise national values) towards a one-sided political agenda, by positioning themselves, in both the national and European context, as a counterforce to the liberal political agenda, which supports immigration and multiculturalism. Among the voters for populism are many ordinary workers, who find national values and the promotion of the well-being of existing Finnish citizens more important than 'coddling the immigrants' and promoting immigration. The True Finns profile themselves as the true voice of the common people, differing from the agenda of the liberal 'elite', which is described as arrogant and estranged from the people. The economic situation in Europe has remained somewhat challenging over the past ten years, resulting in structural unemployment and fostering dissatisfaction towards Europe-centred political thought. It does not fit well into the nationalistic sense of justice that millions of euros are spent on helping Greece and other pan-European responsibilities – including a liberal immigration policy – while there is plenty of need for help in the home country.

Mechanisms which produce inequality can result in increased political participation, and voting for populist parties can be seen as a form of activation (Hirschmanian voice-alternative[3]) as well as leading to political distrust and withdrawal from political participation (the exit alternative) (Wass, 2016: 35). At best, populism has proved useful in making visible the way in which certain parts of society have not been represented, and brought into focus topics that the public has not been able to discuss, including the level of immigration in Finland and voices critical of the EU.

A recent study by European Economic and Social Committee (Lessenski and Kavrakova, 2019) concludes on the recommendations for tackling the challenges of populism. These recommendations include the same features that we have discussed in this chapter; restoring the public sphere of dialogue and discussion, supporting civil society at local level, investing in formal and informal civic education, and complementing the representative democracy with collaborative elements of participatory democracy.

The need for open discussion of such issues and the role of populist voices in our society is a crucial question for the new century of Finnish democracy. Utilising the subsidiarity principle in communal politics and policy by executing the newly established participatory programmes in cities, villages and neighbourhoods can reinforce people's belief in their capability to influence. The results of the various participatory programmes established in Finland during the past few years are yet to be seen. Instead the appeal of the populism offered by the True Finns has succeeded well in speaking to people. Yet facilitating participatory programmes and public areas in communities for deliberative political discussion may help overcome the deficits in participation.

Notes

[1]   The largest subscription newspaper in Finland and the Nordic countries.
[2]   Association of Finnish Local and Regional Authorities, Democracy Network meetings (2018 and 2019).
[3]   Finnish Sisu: a patriotic and nationalist, immigration-critical movement.

References

Alvaredo, F., Chancel, L., Piketty, T., Saez, E. and Zucman, G. (2018) *World Inequality Report*, World Inequality Lab, Paris: Paris School of Economics.

Anselmi, M. (2017) *Populism: An Introduction*, London: Routledge.

Anttonen, S. (2007) '1900-luvun humanistinen sivistysperintö suomalaisessa kansansivistysajattelussa' [The humanistic legacy of civilization of the 20th century in Finnish folk education], in J. Tähtinen and S. Skinnari (eds), *Kasvatus- ja koulutuskysymys Suomessa vuosisatojen saatossa* [*Rearing and Education Issue in Finland over the Course of Centuries*], Turku: Suomen kasvatustieteellinen seura, pp 613–42.

Bächtiger, A., Dryzek, J.S., Mansbridge, J. and Warren, M.E. (eds) (2018) *The Oxford Handbook of Deliberative Democracy*, Oxford: Oxford University Press.

Bäck, M. and Kestilä, E. (2009) 'Social capital and political trust in Finland: an individual-level assessment', *Scandinavian Political Studies*, 32(2): 171–94.

Bäcklund, P., Häkli, J. and Schulman, H. (eds) (2017) *Kansalaiset kaupunkia kehittämässä* [*Citizens Developing the City*], Tampere: Tampere University Press.

Bergmann, E. (2017) *Nordic Nationalism and Right-Wing Populist Politics*, London: Palgrave Macmillan.

Better Life Index (2018) *Education*, Geneva: OECD, [online] www.oecdbetterlifeindex.org/countries/finland/

Calhoun, C. (ed) (1992) *Habermas and the Public Sphere*, Cambridge, MA: Massachusetts Institute of Technology.

Deci, E.L., Ryan, R.M. and Guay, F. (2013) 'Self-determination theory and actualization of human potential', in D. McInerney, H. Marsh, R. Craven and F. Guay (eds), *Theory Driving Research: New Wave Perspectives on Self Processes and Human Development*, Charlotte, NC: Information Age Press, pp 109–33.

De la Torre, C. (ed) (2018) *Routledge Handbook of Global Populism*, London: Routledge.

De Vries, Catherine and Hoffman, Isabell (2016) *Fear not Values: Populist Opinion and the Populist Vote in Europe*, Gütersloh: Bertelmann Stiftung, eupinions #2016/3.

City of Helsinki (2018) 'Osallisuus- ja vuorovaikutusmalli [Participation and Interaction Model]', [online] www.hel.fi/helsinki/fi/kaupunki-ja-hallinto/osallistu-ja-vaikuta/vaikuttamiskanavat/osallisuus-ja-vuorovaikutusmalli/

Easton, D. (1965) *A System Analysis of Political Life*, New York: Wiley.

Faehnle, M., Mäenpää, P., Blomberg, J. and Schulman, H. (2017) 'Civic engagement 3.0: shifts towards self-made society in Helsinki Metropolitan Region', Yhdyskuntasuunnittelu-lehti 3/2017, [online] www.yss.fi/journal/civic-engagement-3-0-reconsidering-the-roles-of-citizens-in-city-making/

Fitzi, J., Mackert, J. and Turner, B.S. (2018) *Populism and the Crisis of Democracy*, London: Routledge.

Furedi, F. (2017) *Populism and the European Culture Wars: The Conflict of Values between Hungary and the EU*, London: Routledge.

Gender Equality Index (2017) *Measuring Gender Equality in the European Union 2005–2015*, Vilnius: European Institute for Gender Equality, [online] https://eige.europa.eu/gender-equality-index/2019

Global Law & Order (2018) Washington: Gallup.

Goodhart, D. (2017) *The Road to Somewhere: The Populist Revolt and the Future of Politics*, London: Hurst.

Habermas, J. (1981) *Theorie des kommunikativen Handelns [The Theory of Communicative Action]*, Band I–II, Frankfurt am Main: Suhrkamp.

Hawkins, K.A., Carlin, R.E., Littvay, L. and Kaltwasser, C.R. (2018) *The Ideational Approach to Populism: Concept, Theory, and Analysis*, London: Routledge.

Head, B. (2007) 'Community engagement: "participation on whose terms?"', *Australian Journal of Political Science*, 42(3): 441–54.

Helliwell, J.F., Layard, R. and Sachs, J. (2018) *World Happiness Report 2018*, New York: Sustainable Development Solutions Network.

Helliwell, J.F., Layard, R. and Sachs, J. (2019) *World Happiness Report 2019*, New York: Sustainable Development Solutions Network.

Herkman, J. (2018) 'Pohjoismainen malli murroksessa' [The Nordic Model at turning point], in Mari Niemi and Topi Houni (eds), *Media ja populismi: Työkaluja kriittiseen journalismiin* [*Media and Populism: Tools for Critical Journalism*], Tampere: Vastapaino, pp 54–79.

Hirschmann, A.O. (1970) *Exit, Voice and Loyalty*, Cambridge, MA: Harvard University Press.

Ikäheimo, H.-P. (2017) *The Era of Populism – Seasonal Fluctuation or Permanent Change?*, Helsinki: The Finnish Innovation Fund Sitra, [online] www.sitra.fi/en/articles/era-populism-seasonal-fluctuation-permanent-change/

Järvinen, T., Lindell, J. and Raisio, H. (2011) 'Kansalainen hyvinvoinnin ytimessä: Tarkastelussa deliberatiivinen hallinta hyvinvointiyhteiskunnan kontekstissa' [Citizen in the heart of welfare: considering deliberative governance in the context of welfare society], in P. Vartiainen and M. Vuorenmaa (eds), *Kohti sosiaalisesti kestävää hyvinvointia: Vaasan yliopiston julkaisuja*, Tutkimuksia 295, Vaasa:Sosiaali- ja terveyshallintotiede 6, pp 27–40.

Johnston, K.A. (2018 'Toward a theory of social engagement', in K.A. Johnston and M. Taylor (eds), *The Handbook of Communication Engagement*, Hoboken, NJ: Wiley, pp 19–32.

Kaplan, J. (1999) 'The Finnish new radical right in comparative perspective', in Kyösti Pekonen (ed), *The New Radical Right in Finland in the Nineties*, Helsinki: Helsinki University Press,

Kearns, A. (1992) 'Active citizenship and urban governance', *Transactions of the Institute of British Geographers*, 17(1): 20–34.

Kestilä-Kekkonen, E. and Korvalo, P.-F. (eds) (2017) *Poliittinen osallistuminen vanhan ja uuden osallistumisen jännitteitä* [*Political Participation: Tensions between Old and New*], Jyväskylä: SoPhi.

Koivulaakso, D., Brunila, M. and Andersson, L. (2012) *Äärioikeisto Suomessa* [*Extreme Right in Finland*], Helsinki: Into kustannus Oy.

Kovala, U., Palonen, E., Ruotsalainen, M. and Saresma, T. (eds) (2018) *Populism on the Loose*, Jyväskylä: Nykykulttuurintutkimus.

Kovala, U. and Pöysä, J. (2017) 'Jätkä ja jytky populistisena retoriikkana ja performanssina' [Jätkä ja jytky as populist rhetoric and performance], in E. Palonen and T. Saresma, (eds), *Jätkät and jytkyt: Perussuomalaiset ja populismin retoriikka* [*True Finns and the Rhetoric of Populism*], Tampere: Vastapaino, pp 249–71.

Legatum Prosperity Index (2018) [online] https://www.prosperity.com/feed/Social-capital-and-prosperity

Lessenski, M. and Kavrakova, A. (2019) *Societies outside Metropolises: The Role of Civil Society Organisations in Facing Populism*, Brussels: European Economic and Social Committee, [online] https://ecas.org/wp-content/uploads/2019/03/Populism-study.pdf

Luhtakallio, E. and Mustaranta, M. (2017) *Demokratia suomalaisessa lähiössä* [*Democracy in a Finnish Housing Estate*], Helsinki: Into kustannus Oy.

Mehtäläinen, J., Niilo-Rämä, M. and Nissinen, V. (2017) *Nuorten yhteiskunnalliset tiedot, osallistuminen ja asenteet: Kansainvälisen ICCS 2016 – tutkimuksen päätulokset* [*Societal Knowledge, Participation and Attitudes of Young People: Main Results of the International ICCS 2016 Study*], Jyväskylä: Koulutuksen tutkimuslaitos.

Messner, J., Haken N. and Fiertz, C. (eds) (2018) *2018 Fragile State Index* Washington: The Fund for Peace.

Mickelsson, R. (2015). *Suomen puolueet: vapauden ajasta maailmantuskaan* [*Finnish Parties: From Freedom to Weltschmerz*], Tampere: Vastapaino.

Ministry of Education (2018) *Finnish Education System*, [online] https://minedu.fi/en/education-system

Müller, J-W. (2016) *What Is Populism?*, Philadelphia: University of Pennsylvania Press.

Newton, K. (2001) 'Trust, social capital, civil society, and democracy', *International Political Science Review*, 22(2): 201–14.

Niemelä, S. (2011) *Sivistyminen: Sivistystarve, pedagogiikka ja politiikka pohjoismaisessa kansansivistystraditiossa* [*Civilisation: Civilisation Need, Pedagogy and Politics in Nordic Nation Civilisation Tradition*], Keuruu: Kansanvalistusseura ja Snellman-instituutti.

Niemi, K. (2007) 'Kansalaiskasvatus osana suomalaisten nuorisoliikkeiden varhaisvaiheiden eetosta ja toimintaa' [Citizenship education as part of the ethos and action of Finnish youth movements], in Elina Nivala and Mikko Saastamoinen (eds), *Nuorisokasvatuksen teoria – perusteita ja puheenvuoroja* [*Youth-Rearing Theory – Grounds and Statements*], Julkaisuja 73, Tampere: Nuorisotutkimusverkosto/ Nuorisotutkimusseura, pp 64–92.

Niemi, M., Houni, T., Hatakka, N., Välimäki, M., Perälä, A., Suonpää, M., Herkman, J., Kokko, J., Noppari, E, Hiltunen, I., Hautakangas M. and Ahva, L. (2018) 'Kuinka harjata populismia? Askelmerkkejä toimittajille ja yhteiskunnalliseen keskusteluun' [How to brush populism? Step Signs for Journalists and for Societal Conversation], in Mari Niemi and Topi Houni (eds) *Media ja populismi: Työkaluja kriittiseen journalismiin*, Tampere: Vastapaino, pp 304–15.

OECD Country Fact Sheet Finland (2017) [online] www.oecd.org/ gov/gov-at-a-glance-2017-finland.pdf

Paloheimo, Heikki (2012) 'Populismi puoluejärjestelmän vedenjakajana' [Populism as watershed of a party system], in Å. Bengtsson and S. Borg (eds), *Muutosvaalit 2011 [Transitional Elections]*, Helsinki: Ministry of Justice, Selvityksiä ja ohjeita, 16/2012.

Palonen, E. and Saresma, T. (eds) (2017) *Jätkät and jytkyt: Perussuomalaiset ja populismin retoriikka [True Finns and the Rhetoric of Populism]*, Tampere: Vastapaino.

Parkkinen, L. (2017) 'Timo Soini ja kaanaan kieli – pelastuksen politiikkaa ja saarnapuhetta' [Timo Soini and the language of Canaan – the politics of rescue and sermon speech], in E. Palonen and T. Saresma (eds), *Jätkät and jytkyt: Perussuomalaiset ja populismin retoriikka [True Finns and the Rhetoric of Populism]*, Tampere: Vastapaino, pp 273–96.

Poverty Rate (2018) Published by OECD.

Puolimatka, T. (1996) 'Democracy, education and the critical citizen', in Chambliss, J. (ed), *Philosophy of Education*, Abingdon: Taylor & Francis, pp 329–38.

Pihlaja, R. and Sandberg, S. (2012) *Alueellista demokratiaa? Lähidemokratian toimintamallit Suomen kunnissa [Regional Democracy? Procedures of Local Democracy in Finnish Municipalities]*, Valtiovarainministeriön julkaisuja 27/2012, Helsinki: Valtiovarainministeriö.

Raunio, T. (2011) 'Missä EU, siellä ongelma: populistinen Eurooppa-vastaisuus Suomessa' [Where there's EU, there's a problem: populist EU opposition in Finland], in M. Wiberg (ed), *Populismi kriittinen arvio [Critical Evaluation of Populism]*, Helsinki: Edita Publishing Oy, pp 197–220.

Rawls, J. (2005) *A Theory of Social Justice* [Originally published 1971], Cambridge, MA: Harvard University Press.

Rosenblum, N. L. (2008) *On the Side of the Angels: An Appreciation of Parties and Partisanship*, Princeton, NJ: Princeton University Press.

Ryan, R.M. and Deci, E.L. (2000) 'Self-determination theory and the facilitation of intrinsic motivation, social development, and well-being', *American Psychologist*, 55: 68–78.

Schulz, W., Ainley, J., Fraillon, J., Losito, B., Agrusti, G. and Friedman, T. (2018) *Becoming Citizens in a Changing World: IEA International Civic and Citizenship Education Study 2016 International Report*, Cham: Springer.

Seppo, M. (2013) 'Finnish Civil Society Now: Its operating environment, state and status' [KEPA is an NGO platform for global development], Working papers no 39, Helsinki: KEPA.

Sharon, A. (2018) 'Populism and democracy: the challenge for deliberative democracy', *European Journal of Philosophy*, First published 24 September, [online] https://doi.org/10.1111/ejop.12400

Toivonen, T. (2011) 'Perussuomalaisten nousun taustoista' [The background behind the rise of the True Finns], in M. Wiberg (ed), *Populismin kriittinen arvio* [*Populism Critical Review*], Helsinki: Edita, pp 82–93.

Trust in People (2018) *Social Capital: Fairness, Inequality and Intergenerational Mobility*, Brussels: European Commission.

Vaarakallio, T. and Palonen, E. (2017) 'Populismin käsite 2000-luvulla' [The concept of populism in the 2000s], in *Jätkät and jytkyt Perussuomalaiset ja populismin retoriikka* [*True Finns and the Rhetoric of Populism*], Tampere: Vastapaino, pp 45–68.

Valtioneuvoston kanslia (2018) *Eriarvoisuutta käsittelevän työryhmän loppuraportti* [*The Final Report of the Inequality Working Group*], Helsinki: Valtioneuvoston kanslian julkaisusarja 1/2018.

Wass, H. (2016) 'Johdanto: yhdenvertaisuus ja poliittisen osallistumisen eriytyminen' [Introduction: equality and differentiation in political participation], in H. Wass and K. Grönlund (eds), *Poliittisen osallistumisen eriytyminen – Eduskuntavaalitutkimus 2015* [*The Differentation of Political Participation – Finnish National Election Study 2015*], Helsinki: Ministry of Justice. Publication 28/2016, pp 29–44.

Wiberg, M. (ed) (2011) *Populismi kriittinen arvio* [*Critical Review of Populism*], Helsinki: Edita.

TWELVE

Populism and community organising in Hong Kong

Fung Kwok-kin, Hung Suet-lin, Lau Siu-mei,
Wong King-lai and Chan Yu-cheung

Introduction

This chapter explores the potential responses of community development practice to the proliferation of populist practices in Hong Kong. Populism is an under-researched area in the community development field in Hong Kong, despite the increasing prominence of populism globally and the rising popularity of populist practice in Hong Kong since its return to China in 1997. Studies of populism, particularly right-wing populism, have developed the 'globalisation loser' hypothesis (Kriesi et al, 2008; Ramiro and Gomez, 2017). According to this hypothesis, disadvantaged groups, which in the present context include young people, who are frequent users of community development programmes, support right-wing populism. Currently, community workers in Hong Kong are unprepared to respond to this phenomenon. This study is the first stage of a research project examining the implications of populism for community development practice in Hong Kong.

The rest of this chapter is organised as follows. The next section presents a review of the literature on populism, its core features and types, and the meaning of right-wing populism. The social context that has facilitated the growth of populism in recent years is analysed. To contextualise the study, the productivist welfare regime of Hong Kong and the resultant characteristics of community development services in Hong Kong are outlined. The subsequent section presents the research methodology and the findings. The implications of the proliferation of right-wing populism and populist practices for different types for community development are then discussed.

Studies of populism

Studies of populism have revealed its existence in the US since the early 20th century in the form of agrarian populism (see Kazin, 1998; Emejulu and Scanlon, 2016). Left-wing populism has been a feature of South American countries since the mid-20th century (Seligson, 2007; Waller et al, 2017). Among European countries, Ireland is renowned for the populist discourses in its political arena (Suiter, 2016; Ramiro and Gomez, 2017), but populism has been marginal in other European countries since World War II, as right-wing populism was the dominant ideology leading to that war, at least in Germany and Italy (Gonzalez-Vicente and Carroll, 2017; Ottmann, 2017). However, the past decade has witnessed the rise of populism in general and right-wing populism in particular. European countries, including France, Germany, the Netherlands, Norway, Sweden, Greece, Spain and the UK have experienced substantial increases in the number of voters supporting parties that have explicitly adopted populist programmes, particularly parties with right-wing populist orientations (Rooduijn et al, 2014; Ottmann, 2017). The success of Donald Trump in the US presidential election is an indicator of the increasing significance of right-wing populism in the political arena of the American continent. This change is remarkable, as the attention has been on South American countries relating to the proliferation of left-wing populism since the 1970s (Motta, 2011; Waller et al, 2017). The rising popularity of populism can also be seen in Asian-Pacific countries, including Australia and New Zealand (Westoby, 2017; Macaulay, 2019). Given the prevalence of populist discourses and practices, Mudde (2004) has proposed the concept of a populist zeitgeist, although his work focuses on European countries.

The rise of populism as a social phenomenon has led to an increasing number of studies of its nature and changing forms. In the past decade, there have been at least three analytical approaches to populism. First, Wodak (2015), Macaulay (2019) and others analyse populism as a discourse. For example, Wodak (2015) uses discourse analysis to examine the linguistic dynamics in the construction of a common identity, or 'homogenous demos' in nativist terms, which defines various social groups such as migrants, Muslims, women and ethnic minorities as 'Others'. Through the different linguistic process, 'the Haiderization of Europe' and 'the normalisation of exclusion' sustain right-wing populism among the general public. Second, studies inspired by the work of Ernesto Laclau and his later work with Chantel Mouffe (2018) argue that populism has no referential unity because it is ascribed to a social logic whose effect cuts across many phenomena, and is quite simply a way of constructing the political (Laclau, 2005). Populism thus reflects the intrinsic logic of politics or political mobilisation itself: different isolated unsatisfied demands or, in their terms, 'democratic demands', are articulated or transformed into a 'popular demand' or resultant requests for change by a 'unified people' against a 'common enemy', both of which are constituted through the mobilisation process. In other words, the collectives or the people exerting the demands and the demands themselves are both constituted by the populist process (see Laclau, 2005; Marchart, 2012). The dynamics within the political process are the foci of this approach.

The third approach is the ideational approach developed by Mudde and Kaltwasser (2017), which considers populism a 'thin-centred' ideology 'that considers society to be ultimately separated into two homogeneous and antagonistic groups, "the pure people" versus "the corrupt elite," and which argues that politics should be an expression of the volonté générale (general will) of the people' (Mudde, 2004: 543). Thus, populism is a type of ideology which assumes that society consists of two antagonistic groups, the ignorant but benign people and the corrupt elite, and maintains the importance of popular sovereignty. The corrupt elites, who include cultural elites like intellectuals, journalists and various professionals; economic elites like capitalists; and political elites like politicians and government bureaucrats, betray the interests of the general public.

Although populism upholds the importance of popular sovereignty, it emphasises the ignorance of the general public and its inability to hold the corrupt elites accountable. Even liberal democratic institutions cannot protect the interests of the general public. To some, it is the limitations of the liberal democratic institutions that allow the corrupt elites to usurp power. To defend the interests and the popular sovereignty of the general public, populism depends on individual leaders of various kinds, usually charismatic ones, to fight for the powerless general public. Thus, people-centrism, anti-elitism and popular sovereignty are the core components of different versions of populism viewed through an ideational lens (Mudde, 2004; Albertazzi and McDonnell, 2008). Macaulay (2019: 544) argues that due to its characteristic of 'a restricted core attached to a narrower range of political concepts', populism has limited ability to 'advance a 'wide-ranging and coherent programme for the solution to crucial political questions; and must be combined with other "full" host ideologies' (Stanley, 2008: 95–6). This is the reason it is labelled a thin-centred ideology. Relevant to this study, studies analysing whether the critical distinctions between right-wing and left-wing populisms are their populist components or the host ideologies have proposed two theses: the 'populism trumps (underlying) ideology thesis' and 'the ideology trumps populism thesis'. The former emphasises that right-wing and left-wing populism are similar, whereas the latter stresses that 'the host ideology is more important than populism per se in explaining the essence of left and right-wing populisms' (March, 2017: 300). A number of studies have supported the latter thesis, based on the thin-centred nature of populism as an ideology (for example, Otjes and Louwerse, 2015; Mouffe, 2018). In other words, the host ideologies are the significant difference between right-wing and left-wing populism (see Emejulu and Scanlon, 2016; Ramiro and Gomez, 2017).

It is not possible to provide detailed discussions of the virtues and weaknesses of the three approaches in the limited space of this chapter. Briefly, the strengths of the discursive and political logic approaches are in identifying how populism is constructed, particularly right-wing populism, with the former focusing on the linguistic processes and the latter focusing on the political mobilisation process (see Wodak, 2015; Macaulay, 2019). In addition, the discursive approach offers detailed analyses of particular texts and documents, and has developed measurement indicators for identifying types of populism in large textual datasets (see March, 2017). The political logic approach fails to differentiate right- and left-wing populism, as it sees both as simply the constitutive results of a political process (see Zizek, 2006; Gerodimos, 2015). As the focus of this study is the responses of community workers to right-wing populism, we adopt the ideational approach, which has the capacity to differentiate between right-wing and left-wing populism. Thus, this study uses the definition of populism proposed by Mudde (2004) that was cited earlier.

Viewed through the ideational lens, right-wing populism champions the people against the elite or establishment by accusing them of favouring a third group such as immigrants (in general), Muslims, Jews, refugees or simply people of African origin or from other ethnic minorities. Right-wing populists also tend to accuse and discriminate against other minority groups such as those who represent the LGBTQ people (Duarte, 2017: 37).

Thus, the anti-elitism of right-wing populists involves discrimination against third groups, which is not intrinsic to populism, but a characteristic of right-wing populism (Macaulay, 2019). Active promotion of popular sovereignty, which is a core component of populism, ensures the effective exclusion of 'Others'. Such a discriminatory orientation underlies right-wing ideology rather than populism per se. Thus, left-wing populism 'champion[s] the people against the elites or establishment that hold or impose a system of oppression. Normally it tends to advocate for people's rights, and to raise the critical consciousness of society against the status quo' (Duarte, 2017: 37). It does not discriminate against a third group, and most often promotes active inclusion of multiple groups (see also Mudde and Kaltwasser, 2017). Thus, left-wing populism criticises the socioeconomic establishment/elites for their oppression and exploitation of the general public including 'Other' groups.

Social context for the proliferation of right-wing populism

As noted earlier, populism is not a new phenomenon (see Ziai, 2004; Gonzalez-Vicente and Carroll 2017). Different types of populism have been identified on the European, American and Asian continents (Canovan, 2004; Westoby et al, 2019). The left-wing populism in South American countries has attracted academic interest since the 1990s (for example, Waller et al, 2017). The focus of this study, right-wing populism, has become more prevalent in various European, American and Asia–Pacific countries over the past decade. Context is important for a proper understanding of the emergence of the populist phenomenon, and the various meanings of particular populisms in specific countries (see Van Kessel, 2011; Noble, 2017).

Populist ideologies have become so prevalent in these countries that they have made inroads into different political institutions, including presidential offices, as in the recent US presidential election, and parliaments, as happened in the UK, France, Greece and other countries (Ottmann, 2017; Macaulay, 2019). Testifying to its impact, studies reveal that a number of mainstream political parties have incorporated populist discourses into their documents and public speeches and have even adopted the agenda items of populist parties (for example, Bale et al, 2010; Turner, 2010). Whether or not such acts demonstrate the beginning of a populist zeitgeist, as Mudde (2004) controversially argues, the significance of this thin-centred ideology in these countries is beyond question. Taking into consideration the emergence of left-wing populist parties as their rivals to compete for political votes in these countries, further changes to the political arena and within and outside the political institutions can be expected globally.

Many studies have explored the factors promoting the growth of right-wing populism in different social contexts. Nevertheless, there is no consensus on which factors are critical. Studies highlight the social and economic impacts of globalisation (for example Taguieff, 2005; Nordgren, 2017). The economic restructuring towards a service-dominated economy alongside the development of globalisation in European, North American and Asia-Pacific countries has generated growing social polarisation and rising insecurity in employment. It has also led to a growing proportion of people in precarious jobs (Nordgren, 2017), as well as the emergence of the super-rich and a large-scale increase in migrants and refugees competing for low-paid jobs. In addition, the recent wave of globalisation has been accompanied by financial crises of all kinds (Lindgren et al, 1999). These devastating social and economic changes have substantially affected middle- and low-income groups. Austerity policies in some European countries that were a response to the outbreak of various financial crises following the Global Financial Crisis of 2008/9 have worsened the already difficult situations within the affected countries (see Kriesi et al, 2012; Ottmann, 2017). High unemployment rates have particularly affected young people (Ramiro and Gomez, 2017). The emergence of new poor or working poor and the rising uncertainty in the economic fortunes of middle-income groups are among the impacts identified in various studies (see Armstrong, 2018).

These adverse socioeconomic changes have decreased the popularity of neoliberalism in various countries, particularly those with liberal welfare regimes (Esping-Andersen, 2013). Welfare retrenchment and the restructuring of the workforce have further reduced the opportunities for low-income and disadvantaged groups. In countries that have adopted corporatist welfare regimes or social democratic welfare regimes, studies have identified a growing mistrust of migrants' reliance upon welfare provisions (for example, Duarte, 2017). The complexity of the developed welfare systems in these countries makes it difficult to determine the impact of welfare provisions on economic equality (see Derks, 2006). Arguments that migrants unfairly exploit these welfare systems have emerged. The tolerance for diversity has substantially diminished (Fazzi, 2015). Rising ecological risks, which have been caused by the globalisation process and neoliberalist changes in the Global North, have further nurtured the dissatisfaction of middle-income groups (Nordgren, 2017).

Studies reveal that growing dissatisfaction with recent socioeconomic changes is not confined to low-income and disadvantaged groups. Frustration with mainstream political parties and current governments has grown in scale, and the legitimacy of democracy has been substantially weakened (see Gonzalez-Vicente and Carroll, 2017). Studies suggest that the low-income and disadvantaged groups who are viewed as losers in the globalisation process are the major supporters of populist parties, particularly right-wing populist parties. The anti-elitism promoted by the leaders of the populist parties is understandably appealing to this group (Motta, 2011; Pauwels, 2014). The anger of these 'loser' groups is increasingly directed towards the growing number of migrants competing with the low-income and disadvantaged groups for already limited job opportunities, not to mention the increasing number of women joining the workforce, inspired by growing gender equality. Right-wing populist leaders stimulate and reinforce such third-group hatred to increase their votes. The studies putting forward this view have developed the 'globalisation losers thesis' to account for the growing power of right-wing populist parties in European and North American countries (see Kriesi et al, 2012). Studies of the dissatisfaction of middle-income groups have put forward the 'protest vote thesis' (Mair, 2013). According to this theory, people with higher levels of education and income are supporting populist parties to express their discontent with the mainstream parties and the status quo. Nevertheless, these hypotheses need to be confirmed by future studies.

Hong Kong's social context facilitates populism

Previous studies have identified the adverse effects of globalisation on Hong Kong (for example, Lee, 2005; Fung and Forrest, 2011; La Grange and Petrorius, 2016; Fung, 2017). The economic restructuring from an export-oriented manufacturing economy to a service-dominated economy, which started in the mid 1980s, has brought most of the adverse socioeconomic changes identified in the Global North to Hong Kong. In the current service-dominated economy, four industries contribute to economic growth: finance, housing, trade and tourism (see Enright et al, 1999). Most economic sectors in Hong Kong are dominated by giant corporations (see Castells et al, 1990). For example, giant developers dominate the real estate industry and giant commercial banks are powerful players in the finance industry, and these corporations maintain close relationships with the government. Such state–business relations have, in fact, mediated the de-industrialisation processes (Chiu et al, 1997). At the end of the colonial era in 1997, the Basic Law, promulgated by China, created an executive-led government for the Special Administrative Region (SAR). The state's highest executive was to be chosen by a group of

1,200 electors by 2014: major business interests are overrepresented in this group. The legislative council operates under an electoral arrangement through which the interests of businesses and related professionals are protected. The prevalence of neoliberal ideology within the government and among the middle class is all too evident in Hong Kong. It is under such a political–economic configuration that the government has promoted its status as a market productivist welfare regime (Fung, 2017).

Using the welfare regime framework developed by Esping-Andersen (2013), a number of studies have classified the welfare regimes of countries in East Asia as productivist (see Holliday, 2000; Fung, 2017). This kind of welfare regime subordinates social welfare/protection to economic growth, and looks upon economic growth as the fundamental source of welfare improvement for citizens (Holliday, 2000), thereby promoting the productive function of social policy. Different studies classify productivist welfare regimes in East Asia differently (Tang, 2000; Kwon, 2005; Peng and Wong, 2008). Hong Kong is a typical example of the market productivist welfare regime: trade openness and limited democratisation nurture the attitude that redistributive and risk-pooling welfare policy is detrimental to market efficiency. The attitude of the government towards health, education and housing programmes is more positive, as they are regarded as contributing to economic growth by improving the quality of labour or addressing the needs of the productive workforce (Tang, 2000). The government is critical of social security and personal social services, given the work incentive implications of the former and the view that users of the latter are unproductive workers (Holliday, 2000; Fung, 2017), even though these policies sustain social stability and legitimise the government (Gough and Wood, 2004).

The continuing economic changes are associated with volatile unemployment rates, the deterioration of employment conditions, particularly low-income jobs, the emergence of the working poor and growing social inequality (see Lee, 2005; Lee and Chou, 2016; Oxfam, 2018). The Gini coefficient deteriorated from 0.476 in 1991 to 0.539 in 2016 (see Hong Kong Government, various years). These levels of inequality create a high potential for social riots and unrest. In addition, a series of financial crises have affected Hong Kong in different ways. The Asian financial crisis in 1997 brought the collapse of Hong Kong's booming housing market and slowed down economic growth for about a decade (Fung and Forrest, 2011). The Global Financial Crisis of 2008/9 led to rocketing housing prices due to the fiscal policies of the US, the UK and China, which led to a tremendous flow of foreign portfolio investment into Hong Kong's financial and housing markets. The affordability indicator, that is, the price-to-income index, of homeownership units in 2017 had already risen to 19:4 (Research Office, 2018) while, for comparison, it was 9:3 in 1997, when the housing market was already regarded as unaffordable (Chiu, 2007), indicating that even high-income households find purchasing a home difficult.

The adoption of the market productivist welfare regime, along with the continuous neoliberalisation of personal social services, has resulted in supply failing to catch up with the demand for services, leading to the further segmentation of service provision among members of disadvantaged groups (Tsui et al, 2013; Fung, 2014). The government's public housing policy has catered to the housing needs of the public by promoting homeownership. There has been a continuous decline in the supply of public rental housing units, while the policies to promote homeownership have led to a stagnant supply of average-sized houses from 2000 to 2012, and the supply has remained limited since then (see Forrest and Yip, 2014; Lau and Murie, 2017). Private rental housing has become the main source of housing, not only for low-income households but even for average households (Fung, 2012). The emergence of split flat units, which are individual private rental units sub-divided into smaller units, illustrates the extreme shortage of affordable rental units in Hong Kong (Leung and Yiu, 2019).

These adverse socioeconomic changes have affected various social groups, particularly young people and those living below the poverty line, including elderly people, single mothers and disadvantaged communities (Cheung and Leung, 2015; Hung and Fung, 2015; Chan and Chou, 2018; Hung et al, 2019). Since the mid-1980s, the outflow of capital from Hong Kong to mainland China due to its low production costs had led to the de-industrialisation of Hong Kong, which has been accompanied by an inflow of migrants from the mainland, as low-income women seek family reunions with husbands in Hong Kong (for example, Ho et al, 2014; Wong et al, 2017). Most of these husbands are owners, or more commonly workers, in small and medium enterprises that were transplanted to China (Ho et al, 2014). These immigrants from mainland China have been accused of taking jobs away from low-income groups and/or exploiting the already limited welfare provisions in Hong Kong (see Ho et al, 2014). Although they look the same as people from Hong Kong, the different accents of their native Putonghua language make them easily identifiable by hostile others. This racist attitude is particularly prevalent among low-income groups (see Cheung and Leung, 2015). To facilitate continual economic growth, the SAR government facilitated the inflow of tourists from mainland China in 2012. This was further increased by food contamination crises in mainland China, as tourists came to Hong Kong to purchase milk powder and safe food. Inappropriate management of the tourist inflow further reinforced the already racist attitudes of Hong Kong people to people from mainland China. The frustration with the difficulties of satisfying even basic needs, including housing needs, combined with growing racist attitudes towards migrants and tourists from the mainland, has meant that large numbers of social groups in Hong Kong have a social context that resembles that of countries in the Global North.

The racist attitude towards mainland migrants is further reinforced by the slowing of the democratisation of the SAR government since its return to mainland China in 1997. Since 2003, an increasing number of protest movements have been pushing for further democratisation, organised by the pro-democracy movement, with college students and youth among the most active participants (see Chan et al, 2017; Ip, 2018). Concomitantly, there have emerged pro-establishment movements that demonstrate against the pro-democracy movements and support the SAR government (Hui and Lau, 2015; Tang, 2017). The racist attitudes towards mainland Chinese have been reinforced by these political conflicts. The emergence of political organisations demanding the independence of Hong Kong, with youth and college students as active participants, demonstrates the increasing intensity of the political conflicts between Hong Kong and mainland China (Chan, 2016; Kaeding, 2017). The 'Hong Konger' identity was developed through the practices of these political organisations (So, 2015; Kaeding, 2017). Viewing mainland Chinese as the establishment to be fought against is one of the agendas proposed by these associations. The Umbrella Movement in 2014, which was triggered by the refusal of the SAR government to increase the democratisation of the election of the SAR governor, further weakened the legitimacy of the SAR government, and reinforced the conflict between Hong Kong and mainland China (Ortmann, 2015; Yuen, 2015). Riots in the urban core of Mongkok in 2016, with youth as the main participants, testified to the weak legitimacy and tense relationship between the youth and the SAR government (see Chan, 2016; Ip, 2018).

Community development and populism in Hong Kong: the study

There are few studies of populism within the community development field (for example, Emejulu and Scanlon, 2016; Westoby et al, 2019). In view of the values promoted by community development, and its role in adult education in general and in Hong Kong, this study responds to the call to explore the effects of right-wing populism on community development in different parts of the world by Kenny and colleagues (2018). Previous studies have identified the role of the privatisation/neoliberalisation of social welfare (for example, Motta, 2011; Nordgren, 2017) and the impact of racism and sexism on right-wing populism (Nikku and Azman, 2017; Noble, 2017). These results demonstrate the negative impact of these factors on the interests of low-income and disadvantaged groups, who are the service users of community development programmes, and indicate the practical significance of studies of the populist phenomenon.

This chapter reports on the findings of the first stage of a qualitative research study that is a follow-up to the qualitative research project 'Neoliberalisation's Impact on the Community Development Services in Hong Kong', which was conducted by the authors in 2014 (see Fung, 2017). This follow-up study involves a secondary analysis of media reports and documents relating to populist discourses and practices in Hong Kong from 1997, the year when Hong Kong returned to China, to 2018. It also includes in-depth interviews with project officers and frontline workers in five community development projects in 2018 (see Table 12.1). In view of the small number of the sampled projects and the failure to interview other, potentially disinterested projects, the findings of this study cannot be used to represent the entire community development field in Hong Kong. As the first stage of a research project on community development and populism, the findings offer insights into the effects of populism, particularly right-wing populism, on the field of community development.

Secondary data analysis: populism in Hong Kong

Racist attitudes towards mainland Chinese have been prevalent in Hong Kong since before the return of Hong Kong to China in 1997. Nevertheless,

Table 12.1: Distribution of the interviewed samples

Project no:	1	2	3	4	5
Centre/Proj/Non*	C	C	P	N	N
Subvention#	S	S	S	F	F

* C is a community centre; P is an NLCDP; N is a short-term project.

S refers to reception of continuous subvention from government; F refers to short-term funding attained through winning through competitive bidding.

the current focus of racism is on low-income women who come to Hong Kong to reunite with their husbands. They are mostly travelling from the mainland due to the cross-border movement of industrial capital, particularly small and medium enterprises that wished to benefit from the low labour and input costs of mainland China (Enright et al, 1999). In the context of rising unemployment rates and increasing social inequality, these immigrants from the mainland are accused of competing for the already limited low-wage jobs, and exploiting the residual social welfare (see Ho et al, 2014; Hung and Fung, 2015). Following the continuous defeats of political campaigns for democratisation since 1997 and the proliferation of associations promoting Hong Kong's independence, the emergent racist discourses against mainland Chinese as immigrants and tourists have been integrated into the political discourses promoted by these associations (So, 2015; Ip, 2018). Terms like 'locusts' are used to describe the mainland Chinese, suggesting they are stripping Hong Kong of its resources (Hui and Lau, 2015).

The political discourses on social media and new communication channels like internet radio suggest that the SAR government and the central government in mainland China are working together to slow down or even stop the democratisation of Hong Kong. This kind of anti-establishment criticism is accompanied by the call for popular sovereignty, either through further democratisation or Hong Kong's independence (see Kaeding, 2017). The former is usually the preference of those within the pro-democracy camp, whereas the latter is usually found among associations for Hong Kong independence. Simultaneously, views criticising intellectuals and rational approaches for failing to bring about substantial political change/democracy for Hong Kong are also found in these anti-establishment discourses (Chan, 2016; Ip, 2018). Terms like '*zuo jiao*' or 'left plastic/orthodox leftists' are used to criticise those who argue for the need to identify strategies for political change (see Hui and Lau, 2015). These terms imply that such people are stupid for believing in the power of arguments and reasoning to bring about political change, rather than recognising the urgent need for direct action. In contrast, terms like '*Yongwu*' or brave action are used to signify not only the value of action, but also the implied bravery and courage of those taking action (see Hui and Lau, 2015). The ridicule of the leftists is arguably based on the stereotype of the leftists making complicated analysis and/or the close networks between the leftists and members of the political associations. Those supporting brave actions even advocate for violence against their opponents, which include the establishment, the intelligentsia and, to some, the mainland Chinese (see Ip, 2018). Since 2012, campaigns against tourists from mainland

China have included calls for violent action to drive the mainlanders out (Tang and Yuen, 2016). Social actions or protests involving direct confrontation with the police, who are regarded as the 'repressive tools' of the SAR government or establishment, are normal components of the brave action arguments. Confrontations with the police and even attacks on tourists have been reported. Foul language is also found among those promoting anti-establishment and/or exclusionary views (Ip, 2018). This is particularly prevalent among those sharing their views on internet radio channels and social media. The belief that foul language demonstrates the genuineness of a person's statements is one reason behind such language (see Emejulu and Scanlon, 2016). The politeness of the intelligentsia is ridiculed as a sign of their hypocrisy and their lack of courage (Hui and Lau, 2015).

The authors admit that these first-stage findings of the secondary data analysis do not capture the quantitative measurements of these different discourses. Nevertheless, they are clearly identifiable in the news reports, social media and internet radio channels. The discourses used are in some ways contradictory. For example, the anti-establishment views to support popular sovereignty, if we exclude the discussion of mainland Chinese, resemble the right-wing populism identified in the Global North. These views are mainly expressed by associations supporting Hong Kong's independence. The discourses that combine anti-establishment views with the aim of achieving popular sovereignty through fighting for democracy could be considered akin to left-wing populism, although the anti-intelligentsia orientation is not consistent with such a classification. Further research is needed before these categories can be clarified. Nevertheless, this early analysis shows that right-wing populism can be clearly recognised in Hong Kong. Against rationality, the adoption of confrontational actions against the police, the exclusion of mainland Chinese, sometimes through violent means, and deliberate use of foul language are among the characteristics of this discourse. However, the coexistence of both right-wing populism and pseudo-left-wing populism in Hong Kong is a characteristic that demands further research. Youth and low-income groups are among the most active participants, joining anti-tourist campaigns, posting on social media and joining associations supporting Hong Kong's independence.

Qualitative interviews: attitude of workers towards populism in Hong Kong

Due to space limitations, only the results of the study can be highlighted. The limited research on populism in general and right-wing populism in particular in the community development field in Hong Kong is reflected in the interviews with senior management and frontline workers. Until the interviewers clarified the meanings of 'populism' and 'right-wing populism', all of the interviewees focused on the participants' confrontational actions and the use of foul language. Once given the definitions, they broadened their foci to characteristics other than the violence and the forms of discourse identified. In addition, most interviewees said they needed to explore the concepts to better equip themselves to help their service users understand the phenomenon. Thus, limited awareness within the community development field in Hong Kong of the significance and meaning of populism, particularly right-wing populism, is revealed.

The interviewees also confirm the coexistence of right-wing and pseudo-left-wing populism, which are highlighted earlier, and the ambivalent attitudes of workers towards the different populist discourses. In general, neither managers nor frontline workers can clearly differentiate right-wing populism from other types of populism without the help of the interviewers. Nevertheless, they do not support right-wing populist views, although they have ambivalent attitudes towards pseudo-left-wing populism. The association between pseudo-left-wing populism and fighting for continual democracy for Hong Kong accounts for the ambivalent attitudes.

In addition, even though interviewees lack faith in the SAR government's ability to pursue democratisation, they have different orientations towards the adoption of conflict as a method of achieving social change. Specifically, those sharing a conflict perspective towards social change are more sympathetic to pseudo-left-wing populism. Furthermore, the characteristics of populism, including anti-intellectualism and use of foul language, are among the reasons for the workers' ambivalent attitudes.

Apart from these concerns, all of the interviewees said that community development helped disadvantaged groups to understand the populist phenomenon, although they differ in how they think community development plays its part. They identify several methods, including providing opportunities for direct contact between different ethnic groups, civic education, participation, debriefing, resource support and partnership in collective problem solving. Nevertheless, some interviewees highlighted the need to be realistic about the lack of political interest among disadvantaged groups and the effects of neoliberal funding models on personal social services, which have weakened the sustainability of community development efforts in Hong Kong.

Conclusion

This study considers the social context of the development of populism in general and right-wing populism in particular in different countries in the Global North. The literature on right-wing populism helps to identify its key components and the criteria for differentiating it from left-wing populism. Understanding the contextual influences on the development and meanings of right-wing populism provides the necessary guides for exploring the social context and identification of right-wing and pseudo-left-wing populism in Hong Kong. Using secondary data analysis and follow-up interviews with both officials and frontline workers at five community development projects involved in the provision of collective problem-solving activities, this study confirms the existence of right-wing populism and pseudo-left-wing populism in Hong Kong. The limited awareness of the workers in the community development field, their ambivalent attitudes, their belief in community development as a way to help disadvantaged groups understand populism and the challenges raised by disadvantaged groups' lack of interest in political issues and the neoliberalisation of personal social services are revealed. These findings are preliminary and point to the need for further research and analysis on the prevalence of right-wing populism, and the exact nature of the pseudo-left-wing populism, which focuses on democratisation rather than the exclusion of mainland Chinese in Hong Kong, and the attitude of community development workers towards it.

References

Albertazzi, D. and McDonnell, D. (2008) 'Introduction', in D. Albertazzi and D. McDonnell (eds), *Twenty-First Century Populism*, London: Palgrave Macmillan, pp 1–11.

Armstrong, S. (2018) *The New Poverty*, London. Verso.

Bale, T., Green-Pedersen, C., Krouwel, A., Luther, K.R. and Sitter, N. (2010) 'If you can't beat them, join them?', *Political Studies*, 58(3): 410–26.

Canovan, M. (2004) 'Populism for political theorists?', *Journal of Political Ideologies*, 9(3): 241–52.

Castells, M., Goh, L. and Kwok, Y.W. (1990) *The Shek Kip Mei Syndrome*, London: Pion.

Chan, C. P. (2016) 'Post-umbrella movement', *Contemporary Chinese Political Economy and Strategic Relations*, 2(2): 885–908.

Chan, L.S. and Chou, K.L. (2018) 'Poverty in old age', *Ageing & Society*, 38(1): 37–55.

Chan, W.Y., Cattaneo, L.B., Mak, W.W.S. and Lin, W.Y. (2017) 'From moment to movement', *American Journal of Community Psychology*, 59(1–2): 120–32.

Cheung, C.K. and Leung, K.K. (2015) 'Chinese migrants' class mobility in Hong Kong', *International Migration*, 53(2): 219–35.

Chiu, L.H. (2007) 'Planning land and affordable housing in Hong Kong', *Housing Studies*, 22(1): 63–81.

Chiu, W.K., Ho, K.C. and Lui, T.L. (1997) *City-States in the Global Economy*, Boulder, CO: Westview Press.

Derks, A. (2006) 'Populism and the ambivalence of egalitarianism', *World Political Science*, 2(3): 175–200.

Duarte, F. (2017) 'The challenge of right-wing populism for social work', *Social Dialogue*, 17(5): 36–8.

Emejulu, A. and Scanlon, E. (2016) 'Community development and the politics for social welfare', *Community Development Journal*, 51(1): 42–59.

Enright, M., Scott, E. and Leung, E. (eds) (1999) *Hong Kong's Competitiveness beyond the Asian Crisis*, Hong Kong, China: Hong Kong Trade Development Council.

Esping-Andersen, G. (2013) *The Three Worlds of Welfare Capitalism*, Hoboken, NJ: John Wiley.

Fazzi, L. (2015) 'Social work, exclusionary populism and xenophobia in Italy', *International Social Work*, 54(4): 595–605.

Forrest, R. and Yip, N.M. (2014) 'The future for reluctant intervention', *Housing Studies*, 29(4): 551–65.

Fung, K.K. (2012) 'Private rental housing', *Policy Bulletin*, 12: 9–15 (in Chinese).

Fung, K.K. (2014) 'Economic globalization, financial crisis, and the developmental states', *International Journal of Social Welfare*, 23(3): 321–32.

Fung, K.K. (2017) 'Neoliberalisation and community development practices in Hong Kong', *Community Development Journal*, 52(1), 55–75.

Fung, K.K. and Forrest, R. (2011) 'Securitization, the global financial crisis and residential capitalisms in an East Asian context', *Housing Studies*, 26(7–8): 1231–49.

Gerodimos, R. (2015) 'The ideology of far left populism in Greece', *Political Studies*, 63(3): 608–25.

Gonzalez-Vicente, R. and Carroll, T. (2017) 'Politics after national development', *Globalizations*, 14(6): 991–1013.

Gough, I. and Wood, G. (2004) *Insecurity and Welfare Regimes in Asia, Africa, and Latin America*, New York: Cambridge University Press.

Ho, W.C., Nor, L.T.Y. and Wu, J. (2014) 'Determinants of perceived integration among Chinese migrant mothers living in low-income communities of Hong Kong', *International Social Work*, 57(6): 661–75.

Holliday, I. (2000) 'Productivist welfare capitalism', *Political Studies*, 48(4): 706–25.

Hong Kong Government (various years) *Census and Statistics Reports*, Hong Kong: Hong Kong Government.

Hui, P.K. and Lau, K.C. (2015) ' "Living in truth" versus realpolitik', *Inter-Asia Cultural Studies*, 16(3): 348–66.

Hung, S.L. and Fung, K.K. (2015) 'Understanding social capital in migrant women from mainland China', *Journal of Social Service Research*, 42(1): 1–14.

Hung, S.L., Fung, K.K. and Lau, S.M. (2019) 'Grandparenting in Chinese skipped-generation families', *Journal of Family Studies* (RJFS), [online] https://doi.org/10.1080/13229400.2018.1526703

Ip, I.C. (2018) 'Political de-institutionalization and the rise of right-wing nativism 1', in T.L. Lui, W.K. Chiu and Ray Yip (eds), *Routledge Handbook of Contemporary Hong Kong*, Abingdon, Oxon and New York, NY: Routledge, pp 462–73.

Kaeding, M.P. (2017) 'The rise of "localism" in Hong Kong', *Journal of Democracy*, 28(1): 157–71.

Kazin, M. (1998) *The Populist Persuasion: An American History*, Ithaca, NY: Cornell University Press.

Kenny, S., Ife, J. and Westoby, P. (2018) *Call for Contribution to the Book: Community Development, Populism and Democratic Culture*, Bristol: Policy Press.

Kriesi, H., Grande, E., Lachat, R., Dolezal, M., Bornschier, S. and Frey, T. (2008) *West European Politics in the Age of Globalization*, Cambridge: Cambridge University Press.

Kriesi, H., Grande, E., Dolezal, M., Helbling, M., Höglinger, D., Hutter, S., and Wüest, B. (2012) *Political Conflict in Western Europe*, Cambridge: Cambridge University Press.

Kwon, H. (ed) (2005) *Transforming the Developmental Welfare State in East Asia*, New York: Palgrave Macmillan.

Laclau, E. (2005) *On Populist Reason*, London: Verso.

La Grange, A. and Petrorius, F. (2016) 'Redeveloping the global city', *Journal of Comparative Asian Development*, 15(2): 300–328.

Lau, K.Y. and Murie, A. (2017) 'Residualisation and resilience', *Housing Studies*, 32(3): 271–95.

Lee, E.W. (2005) 'The renegotiation of the social pact in Hong Kong', *Journal of Social Policy*, 34(2): 293–310.

Lee, S.Y. and Chou, K.L. (2016) 'Trends in elderly poverty in Hong Kong', *Social Indicators Research*, 129(2): 551–64.

Leung, K.M. and Yiu, C.Y. (2019) 'Rent determinants of sub-divided units in Hong Kong', *Journal of Housing and the Built Environment*, 34(1): 133–51.

Lindgren, C.J., Balino, T.J., Enoch, C., Gulde, A.M., Quintyn, M. and Teo, L. (1999) *Financial Sector Crisis and Restructuring*, Washington, DC International Monetary Fund.

Macaulay, M. (2019) 'A short introduction to populism', in M. Macaulay (ed), *Populist Discourse*, Cham: Palgrave Macmillan, pp 1–26.

Mair, P. (2013) *Ruling the Void*, London: Verso.

March, L. (2017) 'Left and right populism compared', *British Journal of Politics and International Relations*, 19(2): 282–303.

Marchart, O. (2012) 'Elements of protest', *Cultural studies*, 26(2–3): 223–41.

Motta, S.C. (2011) 'Populism's Achilles' heel', *Latin American Perspectives*, 38(1): 28–46.

Mouffe, C. (2018) *For a Left Populism*, London: Verso.

Mudde, C. (2004) 'The populist zeitgeist', *Government and Opposition*, 39(4): 541–63.

Mudde, C. and Kaltwasser, C.R. (2017) *Populism*, Oxford: Oxford University Press.

Nikku, B.R. and Azman, A. (2017) 'Populism in the Asia', *Social Dialogue*, 17(5), 9–11.

Noble, C. (2017) 'What is this new thing called "populism"?', *Social Dialogue*, 17(5): 6–8.

Nordgren, R.D. (2017) 'Age of turmoil', *Educational Leadership and Administration: Teaching and Program Development*, 28: 1–15.

Ortmann, S. (2015) 'The umbrella movement and Hong Kong's protracted democratization process', *Asian Affairs*, 46(1): 32–50.

Otjes, S. and Louwerse, T. (2015) 'Populists in parliament', *Political Studies*, 63(1): 60–79.

Ottmann, G. (2017) 'Nationalist populism and social work', *Social Dialogue*, 17(5): 33–5.

Oxfam, Hong Kong (2018) *Hong Kong Inequality Report*, [online] www.oxfam.org.hk/f/news_and_publication/16372/Oxfam_inequality%20report_Eng_FINAL.pdf

Pauwels, T. (2014) *Populism in Western Europe*, Abingdon: Routledge.

Peng, I. and Wong, J. (2008) 'Institutions and institutional purpose', *Politics & Society*, 36(1): 61–88.

Ramiro, L. and Gomez, R. (2017) 'Radical-left populism during the great recession', *Political Studies*, 65(1_suppl): 108–26.

Research Office (2018) *Housing-Statistical Highlights*, Hong Kong: Legislative Council Secretariat, Hong Kong SAR Government.

Rooduijn, M., De Lange, S.L. and Van der Brug, W. (2014) 'A populist Zeitgeist?', *Party Politics*, 20(4): 563–75.

Seligson, M.A. (2007) 'The rise of populism and the left in Latin America', *Journal of Democracy*, 18(3): 81–95.

So, A.Y. (2015) 'The making of Hong Kong nationalism', in J. Kingston (ed), *Asian Nationalisms Reconsidered*, New York: Routledge, pp 135–46.

Stanley, B. (2008) 'The thin ideology of populism', *Journal of Political Ideologies*, 13(1): 95–110.

Suiter, J. (2016) 'The rise of populism on the left and among independents', *Populist Political Communication in Europe*, 1: 127–36.

Taguieff, P.A. (2005) 'Populist movements in Europe', in L.B. Larsen, C. Ricupero and N. Schafhausen (eds), *The Populism Reader*, New York: Lukas & Sternberg, pp 47–62.

Tang, G. (2017) 'Media populism in post-handover Hong Kong', *Chinese Journal of Communication*, 10(4): 433–49.

Tang, G. and Yuen, R.H.Y. (2016) 'Hong Kong as the "neoliberal exception" of China', *Journal of Chinese Political Science*, 21(4): 469–84.

Tang, K.L. (2000) *Social Welfare Development in East Asia*, Basingstoke: Palgrave.

Tsui, V., Lee, A.S. and Chui, E. (2013) 'Social welfare in Hong Kong', in S. Furuto (ed), *Social Welfare in Asia and the Pacific*, New York: Columbia University, pp 67–86.

Turner, G. (2010) *Ordinary People and the Media*, London: SAGE.

Van Kessel, S. (2011) 'Explaining the electoral performance of populist parties', *Perspectives on European Politics and Society*, 12(1): 68–88.

Waller, R., Hodge, S., Holford, J., Milana, M. and Webb, S. (2017) 'Political populism and adult education', *International Journal of Lifelong Education*, 36(4): 383–6.

Westoby, P. (2017) 'Community development's response to "sham" right-wing nativist populism', *New Community*, 15(1): 19–23.

Westoby, P., Lathouras, A. and Shevellar, L. (2019) 'Radicalising community development within social work through popular education', *British Journal of Social Work*, 49(8): 2207–25.

Wodak, R. (2015) *The Politics of Fear*, London: Sage.

Wong, W.K., Ng, I.F. and Chou, K.L. (2017) 'Factors contributing to social support among female marriage migrants in Hong Kong', *International Social Work*, 60(2): 394–408.

Yuen, S. (2015) 'Hong Kong after the Umbrella Movement', *China Perspectives*, 2015(1): 49–53.

Ziai, A. (2004) 'The ambivalence of post-development', *Third World Quarterly*, 25(6): 1045–60.

Žižek, S. (2006) 'Against the populist temptation', *Critical Inquiry*, 32(3): 551–74.

THIRTEEN

Community development as counter-hegemony

Andie Reynolds

Introduction

Both politics and community development have changed in England since the 2007/8 financial crisis. Prior to the crisis, a decade-long renaissance of community development was supported by the New Labour government (1997–2010). Through its communitarian and third-way agenda, New Labour endorsed community development as a tool to foster social capital to build 'stronger' and more 'cohesive' communities (Kay, 2006). Its scope expanded, with considerable infrastructure investment in the public sector, and in service delivery contracts to the voluntary sector (Taylor, 2012). The financial crisis disrupted such growth, which, this chapter argues, has facilitated the decline of community development activity in the UK, particularly in England.

   This chapter analyses the relationship between the decline in status of community development, entrenching neoliberal hegemony, and the rise in populism. It does so using a post-structuralist discourse analysis methodology to analyse 74 texts which span national policy debate and the policy and practice within a case study local authority. The empirical evidence shows that, during the administration of the coalition government (2010–15), neoliberal and left-wing populist discourses competed to shape community development debate and practice in England. This chapter calls for community development to unite with left-wing populist strategies to generate and practise counter-hegemonic discourses. But the chapter also cautions that such discourses can reproduce unhelpful binaries which the community development field must attempt to reconcile.

Community development after the crisis

The 2007/8 global financial crisis has significantly shaped UK politics and social policy (Taylor-Gooby, 2011; Bailey and Ball, 2016). While the banking sector was responsible for the financial crisis (Barrell and Philips, 2008; Ivashina and Scharfsen, 2008), UK media debate blamed the New Labour government (1997–2010) for two 'failures': (i) to regulate the financial sector effectively, and (ii) to sustainably control the level of public sector spending in the years preceding the financial crisis (MacLeavy, 2011; Taylor-Gooby and Stoker, 2011). Academic debate challenged this, countering that UK public sector spending only increased in 2007/8 to bail out failing banks, provide investment capital and to cushion rising unemployment (Taylor-Gooby, 2011; Taylor-Gooby and Stoker, 2011). Yet a consensus remained that a substantive portion of the blame for the financial crisis was New Labour's governance of the public sector.

This consensus presented an opportunity for the main opposition parties – the Conservatives and the Liberal Democrats – to argue that New Labour was unable to deliver on promises of economic prosperity, and could not 'promote an alternative economic vision' (Taylor-Gooby and Stoker, 2011: 2) in time for the 2010 general election. An ideological battle for the centre ground resulted between all three parties (Cutts and Russell, 2015). The Conservative Party leader, David Cameron, urged the historically centre-right Conservative Party to transform and forge a centrist path (Blond, 2010). Cameron shared Philip Blond's progressive neoliberal conservative (PNLC) vision to replace the Conservative Party's individualistic neoliberalism with compassionate conservatism (Blond, 2010:2015). This promotes a libertarian theory of justice where 'people are entitled to the full fruits of their labour and to their assets, provided they have been obtained through fair exchange' (Burchardt, 2011: 10). The PNLC agenda also has roots in 19th century conservative communitarianism which 'emphasises "organic solidarity" in the form of voluntarism and "natural" inequalities, and strongly opposes equality' (Corbett and Walker, 2013: 456). Hence, the PNLC vision rejects a redistributive conceptualisation of equality and social justice.

The Conservative Party won the largest number of seats in the 2010 general election. But not enough to form a majority government. They quickly negotiated with the Liberal Democrats to form a coalition government, with Cameron becoming prime minister (Robinson, 2010). Prior to this, Cameron had delivered speeches about reducing big government to create a 'Big Society' (Cameron, 2009). This became a noteworthy policy driver for the coalition's programme of public sector reform and austerity (2010–15). Big Society aimed to reduce 'big government' by offering citizens, communities, the voluntary sector and the private sector more opportunities to run British public services without superfluous red tape (Alcock, 2010; Cabinet Office, 2010). This was influenced by Blond's (2010) predilection for social enterprises running public sector services; and calls for public sector professionals – including community development workers – and voluntary community groups to form such social enterprises. While the Liberal Democrats did not use the term 'Big Society', they did share with the Conservatives a commitment to devolution and localism (Taylor-Gooby and Stoker, 2011). Both terms appeared in New Labour's policy debate in the early 2000s as 'new localism'. New localism was an approach to public sector modernisation dedicated to building community partnerships, and a strategy 'aimed at devolving power and resources away from central control and towards front-line managers, local democratic structures and local consumers and communities' (Stoker, 2004: 117). Such repetitions reveal a striking convergence of ideological stipulations, and their policy implications, between all three political parties prior to the 2010 general election.

Once in office, the coalition government renamed the Office of the Third Sector as the Office for Civil Society (Ricketts, 2010). New Labour had applied the term 'third sector' soon after their 1997 election win to fuse organisations and groups not affiliated with the state or the market as one sector (Kendall, 2000). This name change was core to the coalition government's programme of public sector reform and austerity: to stress that the public sector not only 'crowds out' the voluntary sector and the private sector, but also civil society. In the coalition's programme, community groups and citizens were key civil society players that the term 'third sector' did not adequately convey (Alcock, 2010). This would increase 'efficiency' in service provision throughout civil society, with all three sectors 'encouraged' to work more collaboratively and holistically (Hastings et al, 2015). The Localism Act 2011 fortified this. It assisted civil society 'to take over public services, community assets and influence planning and development' through community asset transfers[1] (My Community, 2012: 1). Thus, public, voluntary and private sector professionals, and community groups, could legitimately 'bid' to take over council assets – including community, youth and children's centres – and galvanise social action to run them as social enterprises.

This all took place during the coalition government's adoption of austerity as their principal economic strategy. It proposed £81 billion in public sector cuts, with £53 million cut from government departments and local governments alone (Clayton et al, 2016). The Department for Communities and Local Government's budget was slashed by 51% over the five-year span, with local governments in England making one-third to one-half of its public sector workers redundant (Bailey et al, 2015). Local government cuts also slashed funding available to the voluntary sector, leading to unprecedented losses in community development infrastructure in both sectors (Lowndes and McCaughie, 2013; Clayton et al, 2016). Services most affected included support groups and refuges for women, children's services, youth services and libraries. Key voices in community development suggested that the coalition's programme constricted and altered the landscape of community development in England from 2010 to 2015, leaving community development's professional profile 'in decline' (Banks et al, 2013: 3).

This is the landscape that community development was negotiating through from 2010 to 2015. This chapter now turns to explore how this landscape facilitated the rise of populism in the UK, which also has implications for community development in England.

The shift to populism

Since the 2007/8 financial crisis, populist parties and movements have become a key feature of European political landscapes (Sanders et al, 2017). This can be explained as the convergence of a post-political consensus, a populist moment and post-democracy. Prior to the financial crisis, two conditions prevailed in Europe: the hegemony of neoliberal globalisation (Crouch, 1999; Harvey, 2005; Taylor-Gooby and Stoker, 2011); and a convergence onto the centre ground between parties on the political left and right (Powell, 2013; Mouffe, 2018). According to Crouch (1999: 102), this gradually eroded popular sovereignty, with citizens increasingly deprived of exercising their democratic rights and '"politics" once again becoming an affair of the elite classes'. This loss of popular sovereignty, distrust in 'elite' politicians and the financial crisis was a challenge to neoliberalism's hegemony and its sculpting of politics. Mouffe (2018: 1) calls this 'a populist moment', which has destabilised existing neoliberal institutions and reconstituted the political landscape across Europe.

Populism is a highly debated and contested concept (compare de la Torre, 2015; Müller, 2017; Sanders et al, 2017). Laclau's (2005) theory of populism rejects populism as an ideology, political regime or an arena outside of politics. Instead, it is a discursive strategy that can bypass existing political institutions to achieve power and governance for 'the people'. It does so by constructing a political frontier that divides society into two camps – 'the people' (we) and the evil elites (they). Like politics, populism's central axis of conflict produces left- and right-wing variations. These variations use the construct of the political frontier to divide society into these two opposing camps; but do so differently. For example, right-wing populism uses nationalism to stigmatise and scapegoat migrants (they); and appeals to the lower-middle classes (we) who are constructed as the losers of 'open door' immigration policies (Pelinka, 2013; de la Torre, 2015). It also seeks to 'liberate' the 'hard-working people' (we) from state bureaucrats and welfare 'scroungers' (they) (Pierson, 1994: 75). In contrast, left-wing populism defends equality and social justice by constructing a political frontier between 'the people' (we) as the oppressed, and 'the oligarchy' (they) as the oppressor (Iglesias, 2015; Mouffe, 2018). This tactic was most famously used by the left-wing populist movement, Occupy, and their 'We are the 99%' (we) slogan; used to expose the 1% 'global super rich' (they) (Ledwith, 2016: 165).

The UK Independence Party (UKIP) is illustrative of the rise in populism in the UK. UKIP is a right-wing populist party that constructs the lower-middle classes in Britain as losers (we) in the European Union's (EU) 'open door' policies that favour EU migrants (they). Its political objective was for the UK to exit the EU (Ford and Goodwin, 2014). From 2010 to 2015 it experienced a meteoric rise in profile, culminating in the 2014 European Parliament Election where UKIP won 27.5% of the UK vote and the largest number of seats (Hunt, 2014). In four years, the party had succeeded in swinging traditional voters from both the Conservative and Labour parties, and consistently outperformed the Liberal Democrats in polls and elections (Ford and Goodwin, 2014; Hunt, 2014). The party's membership more than doubled during this period, showcasing one of the most successful challenges to the main political parties in British history (Ford and Goodwin, 2014).

In 2013, Nigel Farage, the leader of UKIP, was asked to explain why 'the people' *en masse* were turning to, and voting for, UKIP:

> They are fed up to the back teeth with the cardboard cut-out careerists in Westminster. The spot-the-difference politicians. Desperate to fight the middle ground, but can't even find it ... the politicians who daren't say what they really mean. (Farage, 2013, cited in Ford and Goodwin, 2014: 4)

Such views demonstrate that right-wing populist parties do not solely 'Other' migrants who represent a threat to the people (de la Torre, 2015: 1), but also include the 'evil oligarchy' in the category of 'Others'. To combat the rise of such right-wing populist parties,

Mouffe (2018) calls for a left-populist strategy to defend equality and social justice. It also positions 'the people' (we) against 'the oligarchy' (they). Such a strategy was initiated in 2011, with anti-austerity protests erupting across Europe. This unevenly materialised in the UK. In Scotland and Wales, the main centre-left and nationalist parties – the Scottish National Party (SNP) and Plaid Cymru – soon adopted left-wing populist discourses rooted in a critique of austerity (Massetti, 2018). An anti-austerity and left-populist critique was auspiciously absent in English politics, with UKIP and the British National Party (BNP) reframing the August 2011 riots, in low-income suburbs and towns across England, as national discontent with the establishment, immigration and the EU (Ford and Goodwin, 2014; Massetti, 2018). This chapter highlights that an anti-austerity and left-populist strategy was largely absent from mainstream English politics from 2010 to 2015; which has implications for community development in England.

Irrespective of orientation, two criticisms are levied at populism. The first concerns how the role of the leader can slip into authoritarianism (de la Torre, 2015; Sanders et al, 2017; Mouffe, 2018). Populist representation involves 'merging and full identity between a representative and those that seek representation' (de la Torre, 2015: 9). Thus, a populist leader claims to be 'like' the people, but this often manifests as the leader believing they are the 'incarnation of the people' (de la Torre, 2015: 9). Additionally, 'the people' are often represented as lacking agency and critical consciousness; thus, they need the power and agency of populist leaders (de la Torre, 2015; Sanders et al, 2017). As recent events in Venezuela and Nicaragua highlight, this can result in populist leaders dismissing dissenting voices and expressing a reluctance to renounce power (compare Agren, 2018; Wade, 2018). Secondly, both left- and right-wing populism can 'display a rhetoric of exclusion which stigmatizes and scapegoats' (Sanders et al, 2017: 553). Although left-wing populism includes socially marginalised groups as 'we', to do so it must marginalise and stigmatise 'Others' as responsible for their marginalisation (Sanders et al, 2017). This calls into question how inclusionary left-wing populism is; and can have implications for community development discourses and practices influenced by such strategies.

Competing discourses

As previously discussed, populism is a discursive strategy that both left- and right-wing political parties can adopt to achieve power and governance for 'the people'. However, it is under-researched whether community development processes can adopt populist discourses for similar ends. Community development is rarely examined as a discursive strategy, and its relationship with populism is often overlooked.

My research is located in that lacuna and operationalises Hansen's (2006) post-structuralist discourse analysis methodology to reconceptualise community development as a discursive field of knowledge where competing discourses 'fight' for dominance and hegemonic articulation. Community development discourses are competing social and political projects that seek to establish a hegemonic articulation of community development, and shape the identities and social practices of agents working within such projects (Hansen, 2006). Using post-structuralist discourse analysis, my study analysed 74 texts that spanned national policy debate and the policy and practice within a case study local authority in England. These texts included interviews with 20 professionals, volunteers and local people involved in three community development projects in the case study local authority. All interviews were carried out between May and December 2013; and all participants are anonymised using pseudonyms.

The interview transcripts were analysed alongside 54 texts including: discourse by political and policy leaders; national and local policies; and academic debate. An objective of this research was not to generate discussions solely at a national, local authority or community level. An analyst using Hansen's (2006) methodology can determine which discourses materialise across *all* three levels. This is achieved by including texts from pre-set genres across different intertextual models. For Hansen (2006), the more intertextual models and genres an analyst uses, the stronger the foundation to assess the hegemony of a particular discourse; and for uncovering competing, but comparatively marginalised or silenced, discourses. This study analysed six genres of text across two intertextual models: three genres from official discourse (key political influences on policy; national policy documents; and case study local authority policy documents) and three from marginal political discourse (community development books; academic journal articles responding to official discourse; and interview transcripts with social actors in the case study local authority). All 74 texts were authored from 2010 to 2015 to cover the administration of the coalition government; discussed the practices of social actors involved in community development processes; and deliberated the coalition's programme of public sector reform and austerity. In doing so, it could be determined which community development discourses were present, and if any of these discourses were populist. Although this research cannot claim that all 325 local authorities in England will follow the case study local authority, it can establish whether the case study local authority is following national trends.

Volunteering, social enterprise and community organising emerged as state-endorsed practices to engineer the devolution of service provision responsibility to civil society, and its reconstruction. Such developments led to the silencing of community development as a unique and legitimate practice. In an austere climate with funding increasingly unavailable to community development, a common response for community development projects was to restructure their activities under these state-endorsed practices. This created a 'new' neoliberal discourse of community development solely endorsing entrepreneurial community-based practices capable of self-generating income and dedicated to the devolution of service provision responsibility. This is identified as the enterprise discourse.

By May 2015 all three community development projects involved in this study adopted a more prominent social enterprise structure, received less central and local government funding, and were more reliant on volunteers. Two of the projects (identified as Community Action and Foundations) also applied for central government funding to host community organisers[2] to generate more income. This suggests that the coalition government's neoliberal enterprise discourse successfully reshaped existing practices of community development within a case study local authority in England.

An alternative response was to practise marginal or silenced discourses. A discourse called here the social justice and democracy discourse (SJDD) materialised across three genres of text as a largely silenced, but counter-hegemonic, discourse shaped by left-wing populism. The following section presents this discourse, how it manifested and developed at a national and local level, and its implications for community development in England.

The social justice and democracy discourse

The counter-hegemonic SJDD offers a concise definition of community development as a radical and active democratic process that operates within civil society movements that are independent of the state and are committed to redistributive equality and social justice. Its dominant practices contest, debate and resist those promulgated by the hegemonic enterprise discourse. These oppositional practices appear in texts across the community development field, wider academic debate and a community development project, Autism Action, in the case study local authority.

First, the SJDD attacks the enterprise discourse's conceptualisations of equality and social justice. It claims the enterprise discourse – rooted in Blond and Cameron's progressive neoliberal conservative agenda – does not engage with either concept. Instead, it champions economic justice; arguing that entrepreneurial freedom – obtained through community asset transfers and owning public assets – is crucial for communities and local people to overcome economic deprivation. Such recommendations echo throughout national policy texts. For example, the Cabinet Office (2011:4) states that the coalition government's 'overwhelming imperative' and 'urgent moral purpose' is its 'desire to reform public services ... to make opportunity more equal.' The Cabinet Office (2012: 13) also claims: '[w]e will help everyone realise their potential irrespective of their background, and tackle persistent inequalities in access to training and jobs and in educational outcomes'. Both extracts understand equality as different groups in society accessing education, training and employment opportunities to overcome economic injustice and inequality. This confirms the PNLC agenda's presence in the hegemonic enterprise discourse, and its rejection of a more redistributive equality and social justice.

It is precisely a redistributive conceptualisation of equality and social justice the SJDD champions. The Community Development Exchange (2010, cited in Bunyan, 2012: 127) declares that 'equalities is [sic] not a luxury item', and advocates that the coalition government needs the values, principles and inclusive methods of community development to ensure equality – including equal opportunities and access to services – for all. The SJDD also attacks consecutive neoliberal governments and discourses for contributing to the 'dilution, distortion and appropriation of community development values and principles regarding social justice and equality' in England (Mills and Robson, 2010: 12). In doing so, it lambasts the coalition government's explicitly neoliberal objective 'of ending social justice as the basis of political community' (Powell, 2013: 15). This suggests the PNLC agenda is culpable for the dismissal of community development in national policy debate.

Similar to Mouffe's (2018) left-populist strategy, the SJDD seeks to re-establish the links between politics, equality and social justice. It uses community development 'underpinned by a framework of equality and social justice' (Mills and Robson, 2010: 12) to achieve this. A left-populist the people–wealthy elite binary emerges. The SJDD argues that 'the wealthy elite' have become 'even more powerful', with everyone else slipping 'further down the ever-narrowed pyramid' (Tam, 2011: 33). This discourse also accuses the coalition government's programme of public sector reform and austerity of eroding popular sovereignty, by making 'the people' financially responsible for a 'corrupt' and unscrupulous wealthy elite (Tam, 2011; Powell, 2013: 25). It does so through a left-populist lens that is anti-austerity and champions a more redistributive debate on rights, equality and social justice.

Next, the SJDD challenges the coalition government's central claim that it was New Labour's inefficiency, bureaucracy and unwelcome interference in the lives of citizens that 'broke' Britain. It counterargues that neoliberalism, and its resultant financial crisis, was responsible (Taylor-Gooby, 2011; Taylor-Gooby and Stoker, 2011). The SJDD also dismisses the coalition government's localism as 'a continuation and intensification of neoliberalism and its post-welfarist reconfiguration of "the social" as a series of individuals who operate within a framework of quasi-markets to provide services and expertise' (Davoudi and Madanipour, 2013: 559). As a result, the enterprise discourse's ratification of localism 'is part of a broader repertoire of practices through which the [Coalition] government has constructed the local as antagonistic to the state and invoked it to restructure the public sector' (Featherstone et al, 2012: 177–8). With the enterprise discourse and the coalition government's localism discredited, the SJDD is free to rearticulate what is a political alternative to neoliberalism.

The SJDD invokes left-wing populism to do this and looks to radical democratic and left-populist strategies, that is, *Occupy* and Spain's 15M,[3] to disrupt neoliberalism's fixation on the local to engage instead with global processes and networks (Powell, 2013). It re-articulates localism as progressive localism, defined as: 'community strategies that are outward-looking and that create positive affinities between places and social groups negotiating social processes' (Featherstone et al, 2012: 179). These strategies are left-wing populist, underpinned by social justice, equality and solidarity, and grounded in democratic projects that embrace difference, dissent and antagonism to bring to the fore oppressive forces within society so that they can be challenged (Laclau and Mouffe, 2001).

Empirically based theorists promulgating the SJDD carefully draw attention to how successive neoliberal governments and discourses have reshaped community development until it is, arguably, unrecognisable. For instance, Taylor (2012: 18) distinguishes between community movements and sectors; defining the former as: 'a counter narrative that told of the co-option by the state of community resources and energies, endangering the distinctiveness and independence of the community voice'. In contrast, a community sector is defined as: 'mainstream community work … embedded in a social work tradition, promoting non-contentious models ... based on a pluralist and consensus-orientated model of society' (Taylor, 2012: 18). Consequently, community development *must* be practised within community movements, not sectors, to retain its roots in radical and active democracy.

Such fault lines parallel the coalition government's narrowing of civil society to a sector where citizens and the statutory, voluntary and private sectors work collaboratively to deliver more 'effective' services. The SJDD broadens civil society to a communicative space where independent (of the state) social action and social relations occur (Alcock, 2010; Powell, 2013). Thus, the SJDD actively promotes civil society *movements* over a civil society sector and argues that the removal of 'movement', and addition of 'sector', from both community and civil society is a deliberate neoliberalisation of both spaces to disrupt the proliferation of counter-hegemonic movements and strategies (Powell, 2013). Accordingly, the SJDD 'fights' to rearticulate key concepts vulnerable to reshaping by neoliberal discourses, that is, localism, civil society, community and community development.

These findings from national debate replicate within the case study local authority. Like national policy, local policy understands equality as equal opportunities. For example, Council's (2010a: 4) local policy vision from 2010 to 2015 is 'to improve the wellbeing and equality of opportunity for everyone in [local authority district] so that all residents and businesses can fulfil their potential'. The enterprise discourse's focus on overcoming economic disparity through equality of opportunity is clear. Although an alternative narrative on equality exists. Council (2010b: 3) promotes 'equality for all people, and tackle[s] discrimination on the basis of race, age, disability, gender and gender identity, religion or belief'. Still, this narrative does not extend to social justice. Also reminiscent of national policy debate, discussions on social justice are silenced. These only materialise in Autism Action, which, the analysis will demonstrate, adopts a left-populist strategy.

It does so as equality and social justice underpin Autism Action. Its focus is the injustice experienced by autistic people, their families and carers in the case study local authority. Its co-founder, Maggie, discusses the incident that propelled her to start Autism Action:

'So ... I tried to get my son statemented. It took me five years to get the statement. And all the way through ... I was told that he would never be statemented ... and he would never go to [a special needs school]. Because [local authority council] were going to close it. So, I started helping the school to fight the closure. Because the council had ... sold land which didn't belong to them. [They] thought that no one would kick up a fuss. But, obviously, the staff and the parents at [the school] all started to do their own detective work and ... I think the council had to pay back quite a bit of money ... to the land developers ... because they promised them things that they obviously couldn't deliver. [The school] then became a Trust school.'

Paralleling academic debate, Autism Action uses the SJDD to directly challenge the enterprise discourse. It does this through a left-populist strategy that discredits local and central government as a bureaucratic and unscrupulous elite "who are only ... lining their own pockets" (Jeff). Autism Action mobilises 'the people' of the local authority to demand equality and social justice from local and national governments by using the campaigning and activism methods of community development. This confronts the enterprise discourse's articulation of campaigning and activism as volunteering, social action and state-funded community organising. Instead, Autism Action and the SJDD redefine campaigning and activism as using community development's confrontational and capacity-building methods – grounded in radical and active democracy – to 'empower' citizens through pressurising government into giving 'the people' the services and resources they need.

All Autism Action participants discuss the injustice experienced with professionals in their local authority: including doctors; teachers; social workers; and senior civil servants. For example, Dave, an unpaid carer, discloses how four successive general practitioners (GPs) refused to refer his client for an autism diagnosis. Maggie intervened and overturned the fourth GP's decision using confrontational methods to stress and exercise the legal rights of the client. These methods were successful, with the client soon diagnosed as autistic. For Autism Action, this example illustrates how the socially marginalised can be repeatedly blocked by 'incompetent' professionals employed with, or working on behalf of, the local authority. This creates a left-populist 'the people'–bureaucrat/oligarchy binary where ordinary people are denied their sovereignty and democratic rights by 'incompetent' agents of the state.

This binary critique extends to the voluntary sector. Paul admits: "I've got concerns about the voluntary sector becoming more engaged with statutory work ... we are moving towards voluntary sector organisations doing more statutory work but being less critical." Jeff agrees: "the best thing we can do is be independent from the council because we'd have to fear that the council were going to take money off us". Taking this money would make Autism Action "worthless" as "we'd have to give into the council all the time" (Jeff). This parallels academic analysis that successive UK governments have diluted the criticality of such organisations so that they cannot challenge the policies and practices of local and central government. As a result, the SJDD's left-populist strategy only legitimates radical democratic community development processes that are independent of the state; and committed to redistributive equality and social justice.

These debates have implications for social actors engaged in community development processes both nationally and across the case study local authority. Characteristic of left-populist strategies, the SJDD constructs the people (we)–oligarchy/bureaucrats (they) binary. Only 'empowering' and critically conscious leaders, like Maggie, who work independently of the state are endorsed as authentic community development practitioners. Similar practitioners who receive state funding are discredited as incompetent, unscrupulous and 'disempowering' agents of the state who deny 'the people' their sovereignty and democratic rights.

Similar issues arise with the SJDD's articulation of 'the people'. They are also binarised as angry, active, motivated and critically conscious; or apathetic, passive and lacking critical consciousness. Both nationally and locally, the latter can present as disempowered by bureaucrats and/or the oligarchy, thus requiring the intervention of community development practitioners and/or angry and critically conscious local people to obtain power and agency (Ledwith, 2011; Tam, 2011; Powell, 2013). This echoes criticism levied at left-wing populism where 'the people' require the agency of populist leaders to foster agency and critical consciousness. This chapter has argued that left-populist strategies are needed to reinvigorate community development, but it also underscores the importance of reconciling this drawback to effectively generate and practise counter-hegemonic discourses of community development.

Conclusion

This chapter offers new insights into the relationship between politics, populism and community development. It does so by examining the social, economic and political landscape of England since the 2007/8 financial crisis and during the administration of the coalition government. From 2010 to 2015 two political conditions prevailed in England: entrenching neoliberal hegemony and the rise of right-wing populism. Empirical evidence demonstrated that these conditions facilitated the decline in status, and reshaping, of community development – nationally and within a case study local authority – in England.

The evidence also presented a counter-hegemonic and left-populist discourse of community development with the potential to deconstruct neoliberal, austere and right-wing populist discourses. It endorses 'independent of the state' community development practices that employ rights-based campaigning and activist methods to challenge the professional 'incompetence' of central and local government, including their associated institutions and organisations. Characteristic of left-populist strategies, this discourse is underpinned by redistributive equality and social justice, and reproduces a 'the people' (we)–oligarchy/ bureaucrats (they) binary.

While this discourse presents an opportunity for the community development field to unite against the oligarchy and/or bureaucrats, its binaries can override community development's objective to 'empower' local people as power and agency can be bequeathed to community development practitioners and leaders. Echoing criticisms of left-wing populism (de la Torre, 2015), this could result in such leaders and practitioners dismissing dissenting voices and presenting a reluctance to renounce their leadership, power and agency.

To conclude, this chapter advocates that community development should connect to left-populist strategies emerging from spaces independent from the state and the civil society 'sector'. Such connections will reinvigorate community development and produce counter-hegemonic discourses that directly challenge neoliberal and conservative discourses and practices evident in some forms of community development in England. But the community development field should be sensitive to the problematic aspects of binary constructions within left-populist strategies, and work to reconcile them.[4]

Notes

[1] New Labour defined these as processes to allow local people to control and manage publicly owned assets (Cabinet Office, 2007). This was part of New Labour's short-lived interest in asset-based community development (Durose and Rees, 2012).

[2] The Community Organisers Programme was a £20 million state-funded programme to train 5000 community organisers (450 paid workers, 4,500 volunteers) over four years (2011–15) in low-income neighbourhoods in England (Grimshaw et al, 2018). The Foundations project was successful in this application.

[3] 15M is an anti-austerity movement that uses digital platforms and community organising strategies to coordinate protests and occupations of public squares, in addition to 'actions to stop evictions, self-management initiatives, bank boycotts,

popular legislation initiatives, protest outside politicians' homes … and new political parties' (Feenestra, 2018: 1205–6). It began in Spain on 15 May 2011.

⁴ This could include an appraisal of Marxist and Alinskyan community development practices also using binary constructions, such as Alinsky's have and have-nots and Marx's oppressor and oppressed, to establish strategies to resolve such drawbacks.

References

Agren, D. (2018) 'Criminalisation of health care in Nicaragua's political crisis', *The Lancet*, 392(10150): 807–8.

Alcock, P. (2010) 'Building the Big Society: a new policy environment for the third sector in England', *Voluntary Sector Review*, 1(3): 379–89.

Bailey, N., Bramley, G. and Hastings, A. (2015) 'Symposium introduction: local responses to "austerity"', *Local Government Studies*, 41(4): 571–81.

Bailey, P.L.J. and Ball, S.J. (2016) 'The coalition government, the general election and the policy ratchet in education: a reflection on the "ghosts" of policy past, present and yet to come', in H. Bochel and M. Powell (eds), *The Coalition Government and Social Policy: Restructuring the Welfare State*, Bristol: Policy Press, pp 127–52.

Banks, S., Butcher, H., Orton, A. and Robertson, J. (eds) (2013) *Managing Community Practice: Principles, Policies and Programmes* (2nd edn), Bristol: Policy Press.

Barrell, R. and Philips, P.E. (2008) 'The evolution of the financial crisis of 2007–8', *National Institute Economic Review*, 206(1): 5–14.

Blond, P. (2010) *Red Tory: How Left and Right Have Broken Britain and How We Can Fix It*, London. Faber and Faber.

Bunyan, P. (2012) 'Partnership, the Big Society and community organising: between romanticising, problematizing and politicizing community', *Community Development Journal*, 48(1): 119–33.

Burchardt, T. (2011) 'The UK welfare state going west', in N. Yeates, T. Haux, R. Jawad and M. Kilkey (eds), *In Defence of Welfare: The Impacts of the Spending Review*, Social Policy Association, pp 7–9, [online] www.social-policy.org.uk/downloads/idow.pdf

Cabinet Office (2007) *Making Assets Work: The Quirk Review of Community Management and Ownership of Public Assets*, Norwich: Office of Public Sector Information.

Cabinet Office (2010) *Building a Stronger Civil Society: A Strategy for Voluntary and Community Groups, Charities and Social Enterprises*, London: Office for Civil Society.

Cabinet Office (2011) *Open Public Services: White Paper*, London: The Parliamentary Bookshop.

Cabinet Office (2012) *Creating the Conditions for a More Integrated Society*, London: Office for Civil Society.

Cameron, D. (2009) 'Hugo Young Memorial Lecture', Transcript, 10 November, [online] http://conservative-speeches.sayit.mysociety.org/speech/601246" http://conservative-speeches.sayit.mysociety.org/speech/601246

Clayton, J., Donovan, C. and Merchant, J. (2016) 'Distancing and limited resourcefulness: third sector service provision under austerity localism in the north east of England', *Urban Studies*, 53(4): 723–40.

Corbett, S. and Walker, A. (2013) 'The big society: rediscovery of 'the social' or rhetorical fig-leaf for neoliberalism?', *Critical Social Policy*, 33(3): 451–72.

Council (2010a) *Vision 2030 Sustainable Community Strategy for [Local Authority]*, [Local Authority]: [Local Authority] Council.

Council (2010b) *The [Local Authority] Compact 2010–2013: Delivering Vision 2030*, [Local Authority]: [Local Authority] Council.

Crouch, C. (1999) *Social Change in Western Europe*, Oxford: Oxford University Press.

Cutts, D. and Russell, A. (2015) 'From coalition to catastrophe: the electoral meltdown of the Liberal Democrats', *Parliamentary Affairs*, 68(1): 70–87.

Davoudi, S. and Madanipour, A. (2013) 'Commentary: localism and neoliberal governmentality', *Town Planning Review*, 84(5): 551–63.

De la Torre, C. (2015) 'Introduction: power to the people? Populism, insurrections, democratization', in C. de la Torre (ed), *The Promise and Perils of Populism*, Lexington: University of Kentucky Press, pp 1–28.

Durose, C. and Rees, J. (2012) 'The rise and fall of neighbourhood in the New Labour era', *Policy & Politics*, 40(1): 38–54.

Featherstone, D., Ince, A., Mackinnon, D., Strauss, K. and Cumbers, A. (2012) 'Progressive localism and the construction of political alternatives', *Transactions of the Institute of British Geographers*, 37(2): 177–82.

Feenstra, R. A. (2018) 'Blurring the lines between civil society, volunteering and social movements: A reflection on redrawing boundaries inspired by the Spanish case', *VOLUNTAS*, 29(6), 1202–15.

Ford, R. and Goodwin, M. (2014) *Revolt on the Right: Explaining Support for the Radical Right in Britain,* London: Routledge.

Grimshaw, L., Mates, L. and Reynolds, A. (2018) 'The challenges and contradictions of state-funded community organizing', *Community Development Journal*, [online] https://academic.oup.com/cdj/advance-article-abstract/doi/10.1093/cdj/bsy040/5100752?redirectedFrom=f ulltext" https://academic.oup.com/cdj/advance-article-abstract/doi/10.1093/cdj/bsy040/5100752?redirectedFrom=fulltext

Hansen, L. (2006) *Security as Practice: Discourse Analysis and the Bosnian War*, London: Routledge.

Harvey, D. (2005) *A Brief History of Neoliberalism*, Oxford: Oxford University Press.

Hastings, A., Bailey, N., Gannon, M., Besemer, K. and Bramley, G. (2015) 'Coping with the cuts? The management of the worst financial settlement in living memory', *Local Government Studies*, 41(4): 601–21.

Hunt, A. (2014) 'UKIP: the story of the UK Independence Party's rise', *BBC News*, 21 November, [online] www.bbc.co.uk/news/uk-politics-21614073

Iglesias, P. (2015) *Politics in a Time of Crisis: Podemos and the Future of a Democratic Europe*, London: Verso.

Ivashina, V. and Scharfsen, D. (2008) 'Bank lending during the financial crisis of 2008', *Journal of Financial Economics,* 97(3): 319–38.

Kay, A. (2006) 'Social capital, urban regeneration and urban policy', *Community Development Journal*, 41(2): 160–73.

Kendall, J. (2000) *The Mainstreaming of the Third Sector into Public Policy in England in the Late 1990s: Whys and Wherefores*, Civil Society Working Paper 2, LSE Research Online, http://eprints.lse.ac.uk/29028/1/cswp2.pdf" http://eprints.lse.ac.uk/29028/1/cswp2.pdf

Laclau, E. (2005) *On Populist Reason*, London: Verso.

Laclau, E. and Mouffe, C. (2001) *Hegemony and Socialist Strategy: Towards a Radical Democratic Politics* (2nd edn), London: Verso.

Ledwith, M. (2011) *Community Development: A Critical Approach* (2nd edn), Bristol: Policy Press.

Ledwith, M. (2016) *Community Development in Action: Putting Freire into Practice*, Bristol: Policy Press.

Lowndes, V. and McCaughie, K. (2013) 'Weathering the perfect storm? Austerity and institutional resilience in local government', *Policy & Politics*, 41(4): 533–49.

MacLeavy, J. (2011) 'A "new politics" of austerity, workfare and gender? The UK Coalition Government's welfare reform proposals', *Cambridge Journal of Regions, Economy and Society,* 4(3): 355–67.

Massetti, E. (2018) 'Left-wing regionalist populism in the "Celtic" peripheries: *Plaid Cymru* and the Scottish National Party's anti-austerity challenge against the British elites', *Comparative European Politics*, 16(6): 937–53.

Mills, J. and Robson, S. (2010) 'Does community organising empower or oppress?', *CDX Magazine* (Winter): 12–14.

Mouffe, C. (2018) *For a Left Populism*, London: Verso.

Müller, J.-W. (2017) *What Is Populism?*, London: Penguin Books.

My Community (2012) *Community Right to Bid: Understanding the Community Right to Bid*, [online] https://mycommunity. org.uk/resources/understanding-the-communityright-to-bid/" https://mycommunity.org.uk/resources/understanding-the-communityright-to-bid/

Pelinka, A. (2013) 'Right-wing populism: concept and typology', in R. Wodak, M. KhosraviNik and B. Mral (eds), *Right-Wing Populism in Europe: Politics and Discourse*, London: Bloomsbury Academic, pp 3–22.

Pierson, P. (1994) *Dismantling the Welfare State? Regan, Thatcher and the Politics of Retrenchment*, Cambridge: Cambridge University Press.

Powell, F. (2013) *The Politics of Civil Society: Big Society and Small Government* (2nd edn), Bristol: Policy Press.

Ricketts, A. (2010) 'Office for Civil Society unveiled by the Cabinet Office', *Third Sector*, 18 May, [online] www.thirdsector.co.uk/office-civil-society-unveiledcabinet-office/policy-and-politics/article/1004125

Robinson, N. (2010) 'How the Coalition government was formed', *The Telegraph*, 29 July, [online] www.telegraph.co.uk/news/politics/7915918/How-the-Coalition-government-was-formed.html

Sanders, K., Molina Hurtado, M.J. and Zoragastua, J. (2017) 'Populism and exclusionary narratives: the "other" in Podemos' 2014 European Union election campaign', *European Journal of Communication*, 32(6): 552–67.

Stoker, G. (2004) 'New localism, progressive politics and democracy', *Political Quarterly*, 75(1): 117–29.

Tam, H. (2011) 'The big con: reframing the state/society debate', *Public Policy Research*, 18(1): 30–40.

Taylor, M. (2012) 'The changing fortunes of community', *Voluntary Sector Review*, 3(1): 15–34.

Taylor-Gooby, P. (2011) 'The UK welfare state going west', in N. Yeates, T. Haux, R. Jawad and M. Kilkey (eds), *In Defence of Welfare: The Impacts of the Spending Review*, Social Policy Association, pp 12–14, [online] www.social-policy.org.uk/downloads/idow.pdf

Taylor-Gooby, P. and Stoker, G. (2011) 'The coalition programme: a new vision for Britain or politics as usual?', *Political Quarterly*, 82(1): 4–15.

Wade, L. (2018) 'Universities "held hostage" in Nicaragua's political crisis', *Science*, 362(6421): 1338.

FOURTEEN

Religion and populism: the Aksi 212 movement in Indonesia

Ismet Fanany and Rebecca Fanany

Populism and inclusion

Populism, as a social and political construct that describes a particular relationship between the public and its leaders, has been observed to involve an understanding of society that positions ordinary people against the smaller group of elite individuals who hold power in the context in question. This relationship is seen as antagonistic, with the public being morally superior (Mudde and Kaltwasser, 2017). In this, it is important to note that populism does not align with a single political philosophy or position, and populist movements have emerged in a range of political contexts (Kaltwasser, 2013), as well as in various geographic locations and historical periods (Gidron and Bonikowski, 2013).

For this reason, it is possible to view populism as a vehicle for greater inclusion in the political and social context, a situation that is generally accepted as beneficial for well-being and giving individuals a stake in their community (Taket et al, 2009). It is this aspect of populism that has implications for action in various areas that include community development but also public health, education and politics itself, in which grassroots activities may figure prominently (Aslanidis, 2007). Filc (2010) notes the significance of inclusion and exclusion in populist politics and finds that inclusion and exclusion have three separate types: material, symbolic and political. In this conceptualisation, material inclusion and exclusion relate to policies that provide benefits or support to specific groups within the population, while symbolic inclusion and exclusion derive from political rhetoric that can be altered to create new social understandings. Finally, political inclusion and exclusion have to do with structures in the political environment, such as parties and organisations that can be structured to facilitate membership and participation. While it has been suggested that populism can be seen as a destabilising force in democracy because of the priority it gives to majority rule, for example (see Pappas, 2013), Kaltwasser and Mudde (2012) also note that populism *may* act as a corrective in a democratic system.

In Indonesia specifically, the period since the end of the New Order government of President Soeharto in 1998 and the subsequent period of *Reformasi* (Reform) has been characterised by dynamic discussion and celebration of democracy. Scholars and observers have tended to view the nation's political development favourably, particularly since the transition to democracy has been relatively free of violence and has resulted in press freedom that contrasts with the situation during the New Order (see, for example, Aspinall, 2015). Nonetheless, it has also been observed that Indonesia has shown a trend towards identity-based movements as well as challenges that may threaten democratic gains, not least as a result of regional autonomy, a programme of large scale decentralisation that took effect in 2001 (Davidson, 2018). In terms of populism specifically, the nation's current president, Joko Widodo, known familiarly as Jokowi, has been hailed as a populist leader, especially in the context of his recent electoral battle with Prabowo Subianto, a son-in-law of former President Soeharto, who is associated in this way with the New Order government (Mietzner, 2015).

A manifestation of populism as a force in Indonesian society emerged in the Aksi 212 (212 Action), a politico-religious movement that came to prominence as a reaction to a statement made by the then governor of Jakarta, Basuki Tjahaja Purnama (popularly known as Ahok), that many Muslims perceived as blasphemous. Ahok is Christian and was seen by many members of the public who embraced Aksi 212 as a threat to their values and religious sensibilities that would be inevitable if individuals of different backgrounds and religious faiths achieved positions of political leadership. The Aksi 212 movement, then, developed to warn Muslims of this perceived threat and advise them about the background and positions of various candidates. However, as the movement grew, it became increasingly clear that populism, in this context, does not represent an attempt to include the whole Muslim public (approximately 87% of Indonesia's population) and is, in fact, exclusionary, reflecting the specific views and interests of one part of the Muslim population against other groups that share the religion but have different theological and ideological views. Seen in the perspective of Filc's (2010) three-fold framework of inclusion and exclusion, this movement has elements of all three strands. Its supporters see it as offering material inclusion for Indonesian Muslims through creating pressure for policy that supports their interests. It provides for symbolic inclusion by creating public discourse about the position of Muslims in

Indonesian society who should, according to the view of supporters, be prioritised. And it offers political inclusion by positioning Muslim parties and candidates in advantaged positions, including the idea that the office of the president and other high-level positions must only be occupied by Muslims.

Aksi 212 (212 Action)

Aksi 212 emerged on 2 December 2016 (the date referred to in the name of the movement), when thousands of people rallied in support of an accusation of the then inactive governor of Jakarta, Ahok, having committed blasphemy based on a statement he made on 27 September 2016, in which he referred to a verse from the Quran. A video made by a member of the public who attended the event was circulated on Facebook and became viral, with a large number of viewers believing what Ahok had said violated a longstanding Indonesian law on citing issues that relate to ethnic groups, religion, race or intergroup relations. The video eventually came to the attention of Majelis Ulama Indonesia (The Council of Indonesian Ulamas or Islamic religious scholars), which issued a decree stating that Ahok's use of the Quranic verse constituted blasphemy. As a result of this, a number of groups, including the Front Pembela Islam (Islamic Defenders' Front), a group considered to be radical in Indonesia, made a formal charge against Ahok to the police. Those involved felt that this charge was not taken seriously by the authorities, so they called for two major demonstrations, first on 14 October 2016 and then on 4 November 2016. President Joko Widodo (Jokowi) was supposed to appear at the second of these demonstrations but failed to attend. The large number of participants became angry at this, again seeing it as an indication that their concerns were not being addressed, and the demonstration turned violent, with participants throwing rocks and bottles, and ended when the police used tear gas against the crowd. Finally, after an open hearing in which everyone was involved, including some members of Parliament, Ahok was summoned by the police, and was formally accused of blasphemy on 16 November, and the case began to be investigated by the police. The public then began to agitate for a quick resolution, with the implication that Ahok should be tried and found guilty. This led eventually to the 2 December 2017 demonstration in which the term Aksi 212 was invoked. This demonstration was far larger than any of the previous ones and is seen, along with another held on 5 May, as having contributed directly to the defeat of Ahok in the race for governor of Jakarta. Finally, after 21 separate sessions, the District Court in North Jakarta found

Ahok guilty of blasphemy and sentenced him to two years in prison. After an initial desire to appeal, Ahok changed his mind and sent his resignation as governor to Jokowi, an action interpreted by many Aksi 212 participants as an admission of guilt (Rahmadi, 2017).

Since then, Aksi 212 has grown and been maintained largely through social media and has attracted many new members. Its activities have centred on disseminating information about various political candidates and encouraging the public not to vote for non-Muslim politicians in elections at any level and, more recently, not to vote for Muslim candidates who do not, in their view, respect Islam and who are not receptive to the position of the movement on legislation and the behaviour of government officials. A second anniversary demonstration held on 2 December 2108 was attended by even more people than before (7.5 million by some estimates; see Indrawan, 2018), and the movement continues to play a major role in directing public opinion in Indonesian politics (Damanik, 2018).

As a populist movement, Aksi 212 appears to have become a vehicle for raising political awareness and supporting the empowerment of voters to make choices that will result in politicians sympathetic to their interests gaining elected office. The organisation has no formal membership and appears to be open to any interested citizen concerned about the political process. However, upon closer examination, Aksi 212 is actually aimed at dividing Indonesia's large Islamic community into those who are 'true and moral' Muslims, who support Islam (that is, who support the views of the movement), and those who do not. Such an approach is illustrative of the populist strategy of constructing wedge politics. Indeed, Aksi 212 is not, in fact, a non-political organisation supporting general political participation, but has become highly divisive, resulting in increasing fragmentation of the Muslim community and encouraging political behaviour contrary to Indonesia's legal and constitutional basis. This encouragement can be seen in the messages circulated among participants in the movement, who number in the millions, and it is expressed openly by these individuals when asked. The 2019 presidential election offered a new opportunity for followers of Aksi 212 to express such views, despite calls from a range of secular and religious organisations to accept the results of the election and refrain from demonstrating and other illegal activities. One individual, for example, expressed the following view in a long post in September 2019:

> Mereka bilang melakukan aksi itu haram, mereka bilang demo itu bukan solusi, mereka bilang kita harus bersabar

ketika dipimpin pemimpin yg mungkar ... Jangan lagi menghakimi mereka yg ikut aksi dg hukuman haram perbuatan sia2. Kalian sok berjiwa penyabar padahal pengecut!!! [They say action [against the election outcome] is forbidden, they say demonstration is not the answer, they say we have to be patient when we are governed by leaders who do not keep faith ... Stop condemning people who take action by saying what they do is forbidden and useless. You all are pretending to be patient but you're just cowards!!!]

Comments of this kind are characteristic of social media discussion of these issues and violate social conventions for discourse in traditional forums.

The assessment of the movement's role in the political and social environment is based on a comprehensive survey of Aksi 212 social media conducted by the authors of this chapter and ongoing interviews with 23 individuals over a two-year period since the inception of the movement. These people represent a range of ages and occupations and see themselves as ordinary citizens. Of the 23, five participated in the first Aksi 212 demonstration in 2016. In total, 12 have attended at least one additional gathering of the movement, including the anniversary demonstrations. All of them are active in social media groups that focus on the movement's activities, although they are not part of its formal leadership. One participant is the head of Majelis Ulama Indonesia at the provincial level and, as such, is a high-ranking government official directly involved in the politico-religious context.

Inside Aksi 212

As mentioned earlier, Aksi 212 exists largely across various social media platforms. There are numerous Facebook groups dedicated to the movement, on which those who maintain the page (often local leaders of the movement in various locations) as well as members of the public repost news articles and discuss the political contests of their local area and at the national level. YouTube offers more than a million videos that include footage of demonstrations and other events and also interviews and commentary about the movement and its achievements in the political environment. In addition, there is a large amount of traffic on Twitter that relates to the movement, with tweets and retweets numbering in the millions. However, most of the activity in the movement takes place in semi-private discussion groups on WhatsApp and other messaging platforms. Interested individuals must ask to join these groups, many of which were initially set up on the basis of other connections but evolved to include a focus on Aksi 212 and have gained new members through an expanding network of virtual acquaintances of participants (Priliantini and Damayanti, 2018). A Digitroops survey showed that Aksi 212 and the Ahok blasphemy case were the most significant topics of Indonesian social media activity across platforms in 2016 (La Batu, 2016).

The nature of the movement and its very strong basis in social media mean that individuals interested in its goals gain a great deal of information about the movement from other people whom they do not generally know. There is no reason to think that all the social media discussion about the issues of interest to the movement is factual or that participants have any special knowledge of it. Nonetheless, the participants in this study overwhelmingly felt that these media were reputable and grounded in knowledge and facts. An interesting example of this emerged in relation to the original blasphemy accusation against Ahok outlined earlier. All of the 23 participants learned about the incident from social media, despite the fact that it was also detailed in the regular news. All were aware that Ahok used the expression *membodohin orang* (make fools of the public), in conjunction with a religious verse, to comment on his opponents' tactics. When asked about this incident, all of the participants were certain that Ahok had committed blasphemy. The term they used was *menghina Islam* (demean Islam). Most of the participants explained that demeaning the Quran was the same as demeaning the whole religion, but five participants did not know in what way Ahok had been blasphemous, even though they knew he had been. All of them claim they accepted Ahok's apology despite being offended and demanding he be punished. This apology was discussed exhaustively in both social and mainstream media. All but two of the participants believed Ahok deserved the harshest punishment allowed by law, while the remaining two thought the general acceptance of his apology meant that he should not have been punished. The consistency of response among the participants is not surprising as their knowledge of this incident came entirely from discussion in social media and the views in that forum were uniform.

This is not unusual in Indonesia, which is a high-conformity society (see Minkov et al, 2017). People tend to be very concerned about being a part of the group and are highly sensitive about being different; '*semua orang tahu*' (everyone knows) is a common reason for accepting information or interpretation. When asked to further explain their views, it became clear the participants were reacting to the fact that Ahok is Christian and of Chinese ethnic background. When asked if a Muslim politician making the same comment would be blasphemous, most of them had to think about this before responding. All concluded that it would not be blasphemous. Several said that a Muslim who made that kind of comment would be "*bodoh*" (stupid), "*tidak mengerti ayat itu*" (did not understand the verse in question) or "*perlu diberi pelajaran*" (needed to be instructed [in religion]) but would not have done something wrong in a religious sense. Others insisted that any Muslims who supported Ahok were "*munafik*" (hypocrites in a religious sense).

The Ahok blasphemy case ignited a long-running debate that has continued to the present time. This discourse centres on whether non-Muslim political candidates should be accepted, especially in areas where the majority of the population is Muslim, and whether these individuals should be eligible for public office. It should be noted that Indonesia has six recognised religions: Islam, Protestantism, Catholicism, Hinduism, Buddhism and Confucianism, and the constitution guarantees freedom of religion and traditional (mostly nature-based animist) belief systems. The content of the debate relates to whether it is better to vote for a non-Muslim candidate who has proven honest, transparent, capable and not subject to corruption than a Muslim candidate who is dishonest, corrupt and unqualified. Some of the public who contribute to Aksi 212 social media dismiss this question, saying that there will always be a suitable Muslim candidate. A few have suggested that, in this hypothetical situation, it would be better to vote for the non-Muslim. However, they have been viciously attacked by those who read their comments and forced, at least in their posts, to change their opinion. The participants in this study all insist that it is never acceptable to vote for a non-Muslim candidate, regardless of that person's background and political record. Again, this shows the power of social conformity in Indonesia, as well as the kind of social pressure that the majority can exert to compel others to 'toe the line'.

Aksi 212 picked up steam during the 2019 elections that included Jokowi's run for a second term. Jokowi is Muslim but was accused by Aksi 212 of being a supporter of Ahok. By this point, the movement had expanded its position to include opposing Muslim candidates who are sympathetic to or willing to work with non-Muslim politicians. In 2019, there were many more candidates in elections at various levels who were not Muslim. The movement targeted all of them, especially in regions where the majority of the population is Muslim. In addition, Muslims who supported or did not denounce non-Muslim candidates were also deemed unacceptable, and the movement urged its members not to vote for these politicians. This is concerning, because the movement's interpretation of the interests of its members, whom it suggests represent the larger Muslim community in Indonesia, is increasingly eliminating individuals from that same community whose views differ from the movement's. In Indonesia, this kind of division contravenes the constitution, which makes no distinction between citizens of various religions or ethnic groups in eligibility for political office (see Kawamura, 2003). It also suggests that, as a populist movement, Aksi 212 is not really inclusive of the entire majority group it purports to serve.

Discussion

The brief examples reflect both the thinking of Aksi 212 members and the views of the movement's leaders. These views serve specific interests of those individuals and their associates. The existence of behind-the-scenes interests in Indonesia is well known, although it can be difficult to discern what exactly they are and what their aim might be. The possibility of this being the case has emerged in virtually every election or political change. At present, discussion in both the blogosphere and the regular media suggests that this might be the case with Aksi 212, but most observers feel that the movement has actual roots among the public and is a genuine populist effort to promote goals relevant to the average Indonesian (see, for example, Suleiman, 2016; Permatasari, 2018). These speculations generally suggest that it is "*pemain lama*" (old players) who are behind the movement. This refers to individuals who were prominent during the New Order period and who have subsequently fallen from power.

Rumours of this kind, as well as others involving foreign intervention in Indonesian politics through Aksi 212, suggest suspicions that this movement is not a spontaneous populist group that arose naturally, as the movement's leadership has indicated. In fact, the movement's political views and the way they are expressed in its social media reveal that its aims extend far beyond a desire to help the Muslim population make better political choices. For one thing, the movement is expanding across Indonesia, as the 2019 elections showed, and has begun to criticise and condemn politicians and laypeople who do not agree with its aims. This change might be seen to support the view that the movement is actually a front for specific political interests that wish to manipulate the political context. In this, it is apparent the movement is based more on what it is against than what it supports. In fact, it is not possible to discern a platform or set of ideas that Aksi 212 supports. Among its members, what the movement stands for is even less clear. However, everyone seems to know what the movement is against, and its opponents are becoming more numerous and include Muslim politicians. It is not unusual, however, for populist movements to rally against those seen to oppose them, and this has been observed in conservative politics in Europe and the United States among others (see, for example, Savage, 2013; Wodak et al, 2013).

Aksi 212 is unusual in that it has turned against those who were supposed to be the beneficiaries of its support, because they do not share a specific view of Islam and political participation. In other words, it has shifted from the idea of a common enemy, originally non-Muslim politicians seeking office in Muslim-majority regions, to a very prominent 'us versus them' mentality, including within the Muslim community, where 'us' is defined by adherence to and support for a very specific political conceptualisation centred on shared views and antagonism towards anyone of any faith who opposes that view. In this construct, the movement excludes much of the public it purports to support. At present, it is still growing and is increasingly divisive in both its orientation and impact. The potential danger of this type of movement in Indonesia has been noted by political observers as well as the authorities. However, the movement's very large following, as well as its appeal to ordinary voters, has meant that such warnings have not been given a great deal of attention (see, for example, Dinillah, 2018; Mualim, 2018).

The popularity of Aksi 212 can be attributed to a number of interrelated factors. The first of these is the uncertainty of the social and political context in Indonesia since the end of the New Order government, which, along with very major political change in the form of regional autonomy, has created a new environment which much of the public perceives as competitive and difficult to understand (see Holzappel and Ramstaedt, 2009). The second factor is the astounding popularity of social media in Indonesia, facilitated by smart technology, and the astute use of social media by Aksi 212. The unprecedented take-up of digital communication in the nation has been widely noted (Hussain, 2018). The nature of this kind of communication appears to fit very well with customary social practices of Indonesians, who seek to create large networks of friends and acquaintances because of the importance of such networks in identifying and securing opportunities and obtaining information. Finally, a changing social environment that has created a more prominent place for religion (specifically Islam) in the public context has meant that it is increasingly important for many Indonesians to be perceived as religious, moral and adherent to Islam.

This is expressed through visible actions that can be easily evaluated by observation but has not tended to generate an increase in religious feeling or faith; instead, support for specific views of religion is part of an image seen as desirable by a growing middle class (Hasan, 2009). This has created an environment in which a large number of domestic and foreign religious scholars, observers and commentators can flourish, including those associated with and in the leadership of Aksi 212. As has been noted (see *Republika*, 2016; Intan, 2017), religious knowledge among the Indonesian public is often unsophisticated, and, as a result, the messages of various religious figures are often accepted without critical analysis.

This situation has a number of implications for community development which represent a change in context that is likely to become increasingly significant. Local communities in Indonesia are more likely than not to be part of the nation's large Muslim population but tend to be seen as homogenous in the way in which they view issues that impinge upon religious practices and understanding, even by Indonesians. The emergence of Aksi 212 has shown that there are, in fact, significant differences of opinion within the Muslim community that are increasingly being translated into political action, exclusion and divisiveness. It is likely that some of this relates to a desire of certain individuals or groups to gain advantage over others, rather than genuine differences of opinion or belief. Community development initiatives, by their nature, require support from local community leaders. They must also identify such leaders and align with the interests that are most acceptable to the members of the community who might benefit from a community development project (see Botes and van Rensberg, 2000, for discussion of these issues). This is already difficult to do in Indonesia and is becoming much more difficult as the Muslim community fractures into segments based on shifting conceptualisations of what is 'non-Muslim'. The appearance of multiple in- and out-groups as well as the growing risk of being seen as against Islam for individuals and groups in areas affected by Aksi 212 (and potentially similar movements that may emerge in the future) is real and may affect public willingness to support and participate in broad-based community development initiatives. This is especially the case when community development funds originate outside the community and cannot be easily aligned with local political and social perspectives. In addition, religious issues are likely to be intractable, with compromise impossible. This means that potential participants must be especially aware of social and political advantage and the long-term need to be seen to be on the right side of local religious politics. Aksi 212, as a populist movement, claims to be speaking for all those deemed to be devoted Muslims and as such denies the commitment to pluralism that underpins community development. For this reason, it will be important to consider whether community leaders support majority views when they align with right-wing populist movements. If so, this will significantly undermine the potential of community development initiatives. Where this is not the case, more centrist leaders can best counter opposition by citing Indonesia's founding philosophy of Pancasila and laws that support pluralism, which are contradicted by much of the philosophy of movements like Aksi 212. Referring to Pancasila is perhaps one of the best strategies against right-wing populism, for even the leaders of Indonesia's most conservative Islamic organisations and movements continue to express support for it. The principles of Pancasila then, remain a powerful argument for moderation.

References

Aslanidis, P. (2007) 'Populism and social movements', in C.R. Kaltwasser, P. Taggert, P.O. Espejoand and P. Ostoguy (eds), *The Oxford Handbook of Populism*, Oxford: Oxford University Press, pp 305–25.

Aspinall, E. (2015) 'The surprising democratic behemoth: Indonesia in comparative Asian perspective', *Journal of Asian Studies*, 74(4): 880–902.

Botes, L. and van Rensberger, D. (2000) 'Community participation in development: nine plagues and twelve commandments', *Community Development Journal*, 35(1): 41–58.

Damanik, M.J. (2018) 'Novel Bamukmin: Gerakan 212 sukses karena medsos' [Novel Bakumunin says the 212 Movement is successful because of social media], *IDN Times*, 16 November, [online] www.idntimes.com/news/indonesia/margith-juita-damanik/novel-bamukmin-gerakan-212-sukses-karena-medsos

Davidson, J.S. (2018) *Indonesia: Twenty Years of Democracy*, Cambridge: Cambridge University Press.

Dinillah, M. (2018) 'Pengamat: Reuni 212 tidak hanya gerakan politik tapi Ideologi' [Observers state: the 212 reunion is not only a political movement but an ideological one], *Detik News*, 4 December, [online] https://news.detik.com/berita-jawa-barat/d-4330554/pengamat-reuni-212-tidak-hanya-gerakan-politik-tapi-ideologi

Filc, D. (2010) *The Political Right in Israel: Different Faces of Jewish Populism*, London: Routledge.

Gidron, N. and Bonikowski, B. (2013) *Varieties of Populism: Literature Review and Research Agenda, Working Paper 13-004*, Cambridge, MA: Weatherhead Center for International Affairs, Harvard University.

Hasan, N. (2009) 'The making of public Islam: piety, agency, and commodification on the landscape of the Indonesian public sphere', *Contemporary Islam*, 3: 229–50.

Holzappel, C.J.G. and Ramstaedt, M. (2009) *Regional Autonomy in Indonesia: Implementation and Challenges*, Singapore: ISEAS.

Hussain, O. (2018) 'An overview of Indonesia's internet market and what's to come', *eCommerceIQ*, 13 March, [online] https://ecommerceiq.asia/indonesia-internet-market-overview/

Indrawan, A.F. (2018) 'Panitia reuni 212: Peserta melebihi 7,5 juta' [The 212 reunion committee says: participants to exceed 7.5 million], *Detik*, 2 December, [online] https://news.detik.com/berita/d-3751896/panitia-reuni-212-peserta-melebihi-75-juta-orang

Intan, N. (2017) 'Pengajar pendidikan agama di Indonesia minim pengetahuan' [Religious educators in Indonesia have minimal knowledge], *Republika*, 14 December, [online] www.republika.co.id/berita/dunia-islam/islam-nusantara/17/12/14/p0wua5396-pengajar-pendidikan-agama-di-indonesia-minim-pengetahuan

Kaltwasser, C.R. (2013) 'The responses of populism to Dahl's democratic dilemmas', *Political Studies*, 62(3): 470–87.

Kaltwasser, C.R. and Mudde, C. (2012) *Populism in Europe and the Americas*, Cambridge: Cambridge University Press.

Kawamura, K. (2003) 'Politics of the 1945 constitution: democratization and its impact on political institutions in Indonesia', IDE Research Paper No 3, Chiba, Japan: IDE-Jetro, 1 September, [online] https://ir.ide.go.jp/?action=pages_view_main&active_action=repository_view_main_item_detail&item_id=33209&item_no=1&page_id=39&block_id=158

La Batu, S. (2016) 'Ahok's blasphemy case becomes most popular issue in 2016: survey', *The Jakarta Post*, 22 December, [online] www.thejakartapost.com/news/2016/12/22/ahoks-blasphemy-case-becomes-most-popular-issue-in-2016-survey.html

Mietzner, M. (2015) *Reinventing Asian Populism: Jokowi's Rise, Democracy and political Contestation in Indonesia*, Honolulu, HI: East West Center, University of Hawaii at Manoa.

Minkov, M., Dutt, P., Schachner, M., Morales, O., Sanchez, C., Jandosova, J., Khassdanbekov, Y. and Mudd, B. (2017) 'A revision of Hofstede's individualism–collectivisim dimension: a new national index from a 56-country study', *Cross Cultural & Strategic Management*, 24(3): 386–404.

Mualim, I. (2018) 'Bahaya! reuni 212 upaya menjadikan Indonesia seperti suriah?' [Danger! Is the 212 reunion and attempt to make Indonesia like Syria?], *Warta ekonomi*, 1 December, [online] www.wartaekonomi.co.id/read205771/bahaya-reuni-212-upaya-menjadikan-indonesia-seperti-suriah.html

Mudde, C. and Kaltwasser, C.R. (2017) *Populism: A Very Short Introduction*, Oxford: Oxford University Press.

Papas, T. (2013) 'Why Greece failed', *Journal of Democracy*, 24(2): 31–45.

Permatasari, N. (2018) 'Pentas politik di rencana reuni 212 mendatang, siapa dalangnya?' [The political stage in the planning for the 212 reunion, who is the puppeteer?], *Bali Express*, 20 November, [online] https://baliexpress.jawapos.com/read/2018/11/20/104270/pentas-politik-di-rencana-reuni-212-mendatang-siapa-dalangnya

Priliantini, A. and Damayanti (2018) 'Peran media sosial dalam membentuk solidaritas kelompok pada Aksi 411 dan 212' [The role of social media in creating group solidarity in the 411 and 212 Movements], *Jurnal Komunikasi, Media dan Informatika*, 7(1): 37–48.

Rahmadi, D. (2017) 'Kasus penistaan agama oleh Ahok hingga dibui 2 tahun' [Ahok given two years in prison in the religious blasphemy case], *Merdeka*, 30 December, [online] www.merdeka.com/peristiwa/kasus-penistaan-agama-oleh-ahok-hingga-dibui-2-tahun.html

Republika (2016) 'Masyarakat minim pengetahuan agama mudah diradikalisasi' [The public whose knowledge is religion is minimal is easily radicalised], *Republika*, 25 February, [online] www.republika.co.id/berita/dunia-islam/islam-nusantara/16/02/25/o32ysr366-masyarakat-minim-pengetahuan-agama-mudah-diradikalisasi

Savage, R. (2013) 'From McCarthyism to the Tea Party: interpreting anti-leftist forms of US populism in comparative perspective', *New Political Science*, 34(4): 564–84.

Suleiman, A. (2016) 'Aktor di balik aksi 212 adalah pemain lama' [The actors behind the 212 movement are old players], *Nusantara News*, 29 November, [online] https://nusantaranews.co/aktor-di-balik-aksi-212-adalah-pemain-lama/

Taket, A., Crisp, B.R., Nevill, A., Lamaro, G., Graham, M. and Barter-Godfrey, S. (eds) (2009) *Theorising Social Exclusion*, Abingdon: Routledge.

Wodak, R., KosraviNik, M. and Mral, B. (eds) (2013) *Right-Wing Populism in Europe: Politics and Discourse*, London: Bloomsbury.

Index

Index